SHAKESPEARE

AN ANTHOLOGY OF ENGLISH VERSE

AN ANTHOLOGY OF ENGLISH VERSE

BY

JOHN DRINKWATER

BOSTON AND NEW YORK
HOUGHTON MIFFLIN COMPANY
The Riverside Press Cambridge
1924

The Riverside Press
CAMBRIDGE · MASSACHUSETTS
PRINTED IN THE U.S.A.

To JEFF

ACKNOWLEDGMENTS

The Editor's thanks are due to the authors and publishers of the following poems:

Epitaph. By Lascelles Abercrombie. Unpublished.

Atlantis. By Gordon Bottomley. From an *Annual of New Poetry*, Messrs. Constable & Co. Ltd., London.

The Soldier. By Rupert Brooke. By permission of Mr. Edward Marsh, from *Collected Poems*, published by Messrs. Sidgwick & Jackson; and in the United States by Messrs. Dodd, Mead & Co.

Epilogue to Asolando, *Pippa's Song*, *The Lost Mistress*, *Prospice*, *A Light Woman*, *Shop*, *Evelyn Hope*. By Robert Browning. From *Poems*, published by Messrs. John Murray.

The Moon. By W. H. Davies. From *The Bird of Paradise*, published by Messrs. Methuen; also included in *Collected Poems of W. H. Davies*, published in the United States by Alfred A. Knopf.

Geraniums. By Wilfrid Wilson Gibson. From *Thoroughfares*, published by Messrs. Elkin Matthews; and in the United States by The Macmillan Company.

An Ancient to Ancients. By Thomas Hardy. From *Late Lyrics and Earlier*, published by Messrs. Macmillan & Co.; and in the United States by The Macmillan Company.

The Bride. By Ralph Hodgson. From *Poems*, published by Messrs. Macmillan & Co.; and in the United States by The Macmillan Company.

Sonnet — *Go Beauty*. By John Masefield. From *Lollingdon Downs*, published by Messrs. Heinemann; and in the United States by The Macmillan Company.

Dirge in Woods. By George Meredith. By permission of the Trustees, from *Poems*, published by Messrs. Constable & Co. Ltd., London; and in the United States by Messrs. Charles Scribner's Sons.

The Shepherdess. By Alice Meynell. By permission of Wilfred Meynell, from *Poems*, published by Messrs. Burns & Oates; and in the United States by Messrs. Dodd, Mead & Co.

Song from Jason. By William Morris. By permission of Mr. Sydney C. Cockerell, from *Life and Death of Jason*, published by Messrs. Longmans, Green & Co.

The Daisy. By Francis Thompson. By permission of Mr. Wilfred Meynell, from *Poems*, published by Messrs. Burns & Oates; and in the United States by Messrs. Dodd, Mead & Co.

Chorus from Atalanta in Calydon. By Algernon Swinburne. By permission of Messrs. Heinemann, from *Poems*, published by them.

Leavetaking. By William Watson. From *Poems*, published by Messrs. John Lane; and in the United States by Messrs. Dodd, Mead & Co.

The Song of Wandering Aengus. By W. B. Yeats. From *Poems*, published by Messrs. Fisher Unwin; and in the United States by The Macmillan Company.

CONTENTS

BOOK II

BOOK III

INTRODUCTION

'HE design of this Anthology is simple and unambi-
ous. Arranged chronologically in three sections, the
ook is intended primarily not for readers who al-
eady have an extensive acquaintance with the Eng-
sh poets and are familiar with the anthologies of
e past, but, rather, for those for whom it may be a
nvenience to find in one volume a small, but repre-
ntative, selection of English poetry from its begin-
ings until to-day. The choice of poems has been
uided by individual taste necessarily, and the in-
rmed critic, for whom the selection was not made,
ill doubtless note the omission of some poets alto-
ether. In no case can it be pretended that in a vol-
me of this scope the quality of a poet has been more
an suggested, but it may be hoped that a reader
ho is discovering that poetry is not the prerogative
f one or two favourite authors, or of a particular
me, but rather, and in our language particularly,
e common glory of genius through many centuries,
ill find familiarity with this volume no bad counsel
n the way.

The first section of the book consists of a small
athering from the immense treasure of English
ric. If I have in many cases included a poet's most
miliar work, it is, as I say, remembering that the
ook is to be read chiefly by people to whom poetry is
ot yet familiar at all. If it should fall into the hands
f others they will not complain of the occasion to re-
ew an old pleasure. Had the volume been intended
rimarily for scholarship my selection would have

been more adventurous, and as an earnest of this there is to be published at the same time as this book a small anthology of pieces gathered from almost unknown, or forgotten, poets of the seventeenth century, a period to which I have paid some particular attention, as other periods will doubtless be more fully served by others. Here and there in the present anthology I have inserted a song or so from one of these unrenowned, but for the present purpose they had necessarily in general to give way to more obvious claims. The second section shows the poets generally in a more reflective and elegiac mood, and in rather more elaborate flights than are to be found in the first. And in the third is what in the circumstances must be an almost arbitrary choice from the long poems in which English poetry is as rich as in lyric, though the way of public taste sometimes obscures the fact.

Epic and dramatic poetry have necessarily had to be omitted. Selections from *King Lear* or *Paradise Lost* are useless. A more serious difficulty has been the case of a poet like Chaucer. As a narrative poet he is perhaps the master of them all, and yet the objection to including one of his tales was that it was too long and also that even so it was but part of a whole. The logic of this reasoning may not be perfect, but compromise was inevitable in places, and this was one of them. Some poets of admirable quality, as, for example, Edward Young and Joseph Addison, are at their best only at considerable length, and their long pieces could find no place among others of wider merit. And poets like Pope, Crabbe, and Shakespeare himself can be but inadequately represented. Gold-

nith and Christopher Smart I should have included
ı the third section, but here again space forbade.
Since the aim is to give the reader nothing but the
ure joy of reading good poetry, the book has been
ıcumbered by no critical apparatus, a mere list of
ıe poets with their dates seeming to be enough.
In the matter of text, my first instinct was to use
ıodernised versions in all instances, and yet I can-
ot but think that a Shakespeare sonnet, for example,
ains definitely in beauty when read in the actual
ɔrm of its first appearance, and so, at the risk of put-
ng what I believe will be but a momentary difficulty
ı the way of some readers, I have decided to print
riginal texts always. Such texts have been taken
om what seem to me to be the best sources available,
ften from the original editions, sometimes from later
litings when these had authority.
A last problem has been the inclusion of living
riters. There are already in existence a number of
dmirable anthologies of contemporary work easily
ccessible to everybody. It is no part of this book
ɔ compete with these, but, on the other hand, one
ished to guard against the rather common supersti-
on that poetry was something that stopped at the
ıd of the last generation. So, as a mere indication
f what is being done to-day, I have included just
velve poems by writers later, say, than Meredith
ıd Swinburne. I need not say that there are another
velve, and yet another twelve, that are in every way
ıst as good and might have been chosen. And,
ıally, I hope that the book may bring quietness and
ɔy to many hours.

JOHN DRINKWATER.

LONDON, *October*, 1922.

AN ANTHOLOGY OF ENGLISH VERSE

. .
.

BOOK I

QUI BIEN AIME A TARD OUBLIE

Now welcom somer, with thy sonne softe,
That hast this wintres weders over-shake,
And driven awey the longe nightes blake!

Seynt Valentyn, that art ful hy onlofte; —
Thus singen smale foules for thy sake —
Now welcom somer, with thy sonne softe,
That hast this wintres weders over-shake.

Wel han they cause for to gladen ofte,
Sith ech of hem recovered hath his make;
Ful blisful may they singen whan they wake;
Now welcom somer, with thy sonne softe,
That hast this wintres weders over-shake,
And driven awey the longe nightes blake.

GEOFFREY CHAUCER.

CAPTIVITY

YOUR yën two wol slee me sodenly,
I may the beautè of hem not sustene,
So woundeth hit through-out my herte kene.

And but your word wol helen hastily
My hertes wounde, whyl that hit is grene,
Your yën two wol slee me sodenly,
I may the beautè of hem not sustene.

Upon my trouthe I sey yow feithfully,
That ye ben of my lyf and deeth the quene;
For with my deeth the trouthe shal be sene.
Your yën two wol slee me sodenly,
I may the beautè of hem not sustene,
So woundeth hit through-out my herte kene.

GEOFFREY CHAUCER.

MY LUTE AWAKE! PERFOURME THE LAST

MY Lute awake! perfourme the last
Labor that thou and I shall wast,
And end that I have now begon;
For when this song is song and past,
My lute be still, for I have done.

As to be herd where ere is none,
As lede to grave in marbill stone,
My song may perse her hert as sone;
Should we then sigh or sing or mone?
No! no! my lute, for I have done.

The Rokkes do not so cruelly
Repulse the waves continuelly
As she my suyte and affection;
So that I ame past remedy,
Whereby my lute and I have done.

Prowd of the spoyll that thou hast gott
Of simple hertes, thorough loves shot;
By whome, unkynd, thou hast theim wone.
Thinck not he hath his bow forgot,
All tho my lute and I have done.

Vengeaunce shall fall on thy disdain
That makest but game on ernest pain;
Thinck not alone under the sonne
Unquyt to cause thy lovers plain,
All tho my lute and I have done.

Perchaunce the lye wethered and old
The wynter nyght that are so cold,
Playning in vain unto the mone;
Thy wisshes then dare not be told;
Care then who lyst, for I have done.

And then may chaunce the to repent
The tyme that thou hast lost and spent
To cause thy lovers sigh and swone;
Then shalt thou knowe beaultie but lent,
And wisshe and want as I have done.

Now cesse, my lute: this is the last
Labor that thou and I shall wast,
And ended is that we begon;
Now is this song boeth song and past
My lute be still, for I have done.

SIR THOMAS WYATT.

THE MEANES TO ATTAIN HAPPY LIFE

MARTIALL, the thinges that do attayn
The happy life, be these, I finde.
The richesse left, not got with payn:
The frutefull ground: the quiet mynde:
The egall frend, no grudge, no strife:
No charge of rule, nor gouernance:
Without disease the healthfull lyfe;
The household of continuance:
The meane diet, no delicate fare:
True wisdom ioyned with simplenesse:
The night discharged of all care,
Where wine the wit may not oppresse:
The faithful wife, without debate:
Such slepes as may begyle the night:
Contented with thine owne estate,
Ne wish for death, ne feare his might.

HENRY HOWARD, Earl of Surrey.

HENCE, HAIRT

HENCE, hairt, with hir that most depairte,
  And hald thé with thy souerane;
For I had lever want ane harte
  Nor haif the hairt that dois me pane.
  Thairfoir go, with thy lufe remane,
 And lat me leif thus vnmolest;
   And se that thou cum nocht agane,
 Bot byd with hir thow luvis best.

Sen scho that I haif scheruit lang
  Is to depairt so suddanly,

Address thé now, for thow sall gang
  And beir thy lady cumpany.
  Fra scho be gon, hairtles am I;
For quhy? thow art with hir possest;
  Thairfoir, my hairt, go hence in hy,
And byd with hir thow luvis best.

Thocht this belappit body heir
  Be bound to scheruitude and thrall,
My fathfull hairt is fre inteir,
  And mynd to serf my lady at all.
  Wald God that I were perigall,
Vnder that redolent ross to rest;
  Yit at the leist, my hairt, thow sall
Abyd with hir thow luvis best.

Sen in your garth the lilly quhyte
  May nocht remane amang the laif,
Adew the flour of haill delyte,
  Adew the succour that ma me saif!
  Adew the fragrant balmé suaif,
And lamp of ladeis lustiest!
  My faythfull hairt scho sall it haif,
To byd with hir it luvis best.

Deploir, ye ladeis cleir of hew,
  Hir abscence, sen scho most depairte;
And specialy ye luvaris trew
  That woundit bene with luvis darte.
  For sum of yow sall want ane parte
Als weill as I; thairfoir at last
  Do go with myn, with mynd inwart,
And byd with hir thow luvis best.

ALEXANDER SCOTT.

SONNET XXXVI. FROM *AMORETTI*

TELL me when shall these wearie woes haue end,
or shall their ruthlesse torment neuer cease:
but al my dayes in pining languor spend,
without hope of aswagement or release.
Is there no meanes for me to purchase peace,
or make agreement with her thrilling eyes:
but that their cruelty doth still increace,
and dayly more augment my miseryes.
But when ye haue shewed all extremityes,
then thinke how little glory ye haue gayned:
by slaying him, whose lyfe though ye despyse,
mote haue your life in honour long maintayned.
But by his death which some perhaps will mone,
ye shall condemned be of many a one.

EDMUND SPENSER.

SONNET I. FROM *ASTROPHEL AND STELLA*

LOVING in trueth, and fayne my love in verse to show,
That the deere Shee, might take some pleasure of my paine:
Pleasure might cause her reade, reading might make her know,
Knowledge might pittie winne, and pittie grace obtaine.
I sought fit wordes, to paint the blackest face of woe,
Studying inventions fine, her wittes to entertaine,
Oft turning others leaves, to see if thence would flowe,
Some fresh and fruitfull showres upon my Sunne-burnt braine.

But wordes came halting out, wanting inventions stay,
Invention Natures childe, fledde Stepdames studies blowes:
And others feete, still seem'de but straungers in my way,
Thus great with Child to speake, and helplesse in my throwes,
Byting my tongue and penne, beating my selfe for spite:
Foole saide My muse to mee, looke in thy heart and write.

SIR PHILIP SIDNEY.

SONNET XXXI. FROM *ASTROPHEL AND STELLA*

WITH how sad steps ô Moone thou clim'st the skyes,
How silently, and with how meane a face,
What may it be, that even in heavenly place,
That busie Archer his sharpe Arrowes tryes?
Sure if that long with love acquainted eyes
Can judge of love, thou feelst a Lovers case,
I reade it in thy lookes thy languisht grace.
To mee that feele the like, my state discries.
Then even of fellowship ô Moone tell me,
Is constant love deemde there but want of wit?
Are beauties there, as proude as heere there be?
Doe they above, love to be lov'd, and yet
Those Lovers scorne, whom that love doth possesse?
Doe they call vertue there ungratefulnesse?

SIR PHILIP SIDNEY.

RING OUT YOUR BELLES

RING out your belles, let mourning shewes be spread,
For Love is dead:
All Love is dead, infected
With plague of deepe disdaine:
Worth as nought worth rejected,
And Faith faire scorne doth gaine.
From so ungratefull fancie,
From such a femall franzie,
From them that use men thus,
Good Lord deliver us.

Weepe neighbours, weepe, do you not heare it said,
That Love is dead:
His death-bed peacocks follie,
His winding sheete is shame,
His will false-seeming holie,
His sole exectour blame.
From so ungratefull fancie,
From such a femall franzie,
From them that use men thus,
Good Lord deliver us.

Let Dirge be sung, and Trentals rightly read,
For Love is dead:
Sir wrong his tombe ordaineth:
My mistresse Marble-heart,
Which Epitaph containeth,
Her eyes were once his dart.
From so ungratefull fancie,
From such a femall franzie,
From them that use men thus,
Good Lord deliver us.

Alas, I lie: rage hath this error bred,
Love is not dead.
Love is not dead, but sleepeth
In her unmatched mind:
Where she his counsell keepeth,
Till due desert she find.
Therefore from so vile fancie,
To call such wit a franzie,
Who love can temper thus,
Good Lord deliver us.

SIR PHILIP SIDNEY.

THE BURNING BABE

As I in hoarie Winters night stood shiuering in the snowe,
Surpris'd I was with sodaine heate, which made my hart to glowe,
And lifting vp a fearefull eye, to view what fire was neere,
A prettie Babe all burning bright did in the ayre appeare;
Who, scorched with excessiue heate, such floods of teares did shed,
As though his floods should quench his flames, which with his teares were bred:
Alas (quoth he), but newly borne, in fierie heates I frie,
Yet none approach to warme their harts, or feele my fire but I;
My faultlesse breast the furnace is, the fuell wounding thornes:
Loue is the fire, and sighes the smoake, the ashes shames and scornes;

The fewell Iustice layeth on, and Mercie blowes the coales,
The metall in this furnace wrought, are mens defiled soules:
For which, as now on fire I am to worke them to their good,
So will I melt into a bath, to wash them in my blood.
With this he vanisht out of sight, and swiftly shrunk away,
And straight I called vnto minde, that it was Christmasse day.

ROBERT SOUTHWELL.

TIMES GOE BY TURNES

THE lopped tree in time may grow againe,
Most naked plants renew both fruite and flower:
The sorriest wight may find release of paine,
The dryest soyle sucke in some moystning shower.
Times goe by turnes, and chaunces change by course,
From foule to faire: from better hap to worse.

The sea of Fortune doth not euer flow,
She drawes her fauours to the lowest ebbe;
Her tides haue equall times to come and goe,
Her Loome doth weaue the fine and coarsest webbe.
No ioy so great, but runneth to an end:
No hap so hard, but may in fine amend.

Not alwaies fall of leafe, nor euer spring,
No endlesse night, nor yet eternall day:
The saddest Birds a season find to sing,

The roughest storme a calme may soone allay.
Thus with succeeding turnes God tempereth all:
That man may hope to rise, yet feare to fal.

A chaunce may winne that by mischaunce was
lost,
That net that holds no great, takes little fish;
In some things all, in all things none are crost,
Fewe all they neede: but none haue all they wish,
Vnmeddled ioyes heere to no man befall:
Who least, hath some, who most, hath neuer all.

ROBERT SOUTHWELL.

SONNET: WERE I AS BASE AS IS THE LOWLY PLAINE

WERE I as base as is the lowly plaine,
And you (my loue) as high as heau'n aboue,
Yet should the thoughts of me your humble swaine,
Ascend to heauen, in honour of my loue,
Were I as high as heau'n aboue the plaine,
And you (my loue) as humble and as low
As are the deepest bottoms of the Mayne,
Whereso'ere you were, with you my loue should go,
Were you the earth (deere loue) and I the skies,
My loue should shine on you like to the Sun,
And looke vpon you with ten thousand eyes,
Till heau'n wax't blind, and till the world were dun.
Whereso'ere I am, below, or else aboue you,
Whereso'ere you are, my heart shall truly loue
you.

JOSHUA SYLVESTER.

SONNET: SINCE THER'S NO HELPE

SINCE ther's no helpe, Come let vs kisse and part,
Nay, I haue done: You get no more of Me,
And I am glad, yea glad withall my heart,
That thus so cleanly, I my selfe can free,
Shake hands for euer, Cancell all our Vowes,
And when We meet at any time againe,
Be it not seene in either of our Browes,
That We one iot of former Loue reteyne;
Now at the last gaspe, of Loues latest Breath,
When his Pulse fayling, Passion speechlesse lies,
When Faith is kneeling by his bed of Death,
And Innocence is closing vp his Eyes,
Now if thou would'st, when all haue giuen him ouer,
From Death to Life, thou might'st him yet recouer.

MICHAEL DRAYTON.

THE MILKMAID'S SONG

COME liue with mee and be my loue,
And we will all the pleasures proue,
That vallies, groues, hills, and fieldes,
Woods, and steepie mountaine yeeldes.

Where we will sit vpon the Rocks,
And see the Sheepheards feede theyr flocks,
By shallow Riuers, to whose falls,
Melodious byrds sings Madrigals.

And I will make thee beds of Roses,
And then a thousand fragrant poesies,

A cap of flowers, and a kirtle
Embroydred all with leaues of Mirtle.

A gowne made of the finest wooll,
Which from our pretty Lambes we pull,
Fayre lined slippers for the cold:
With buckles of the purest gold.

A belt of straw, and Iuie buds,
With Corall clasps and Amber studs,
And if these pleasures may thee moue,
Come liue with mee, and be my loue.

The Sheepheards Swaines shall daance and sing,
For thy delight each May-morning,
If these delights thy minde may moue;
Then liue with mee, and be my loue.

CHRISTOPHER MARLOWE.

SONNET XVII

WHO will beleeue my verse in time to come
If it were fild with your most high deserts?
Though yet heauen knowes it is but as a tombe
Which hides your life, and shewes not halfe your
  parts:
If I could write the beauty of your eyes,
And in fresh numbers number all your graces,
The age to come would say this Poet lies,
Such heauenly touches nere toucht earthly faces.
So should my papers (yellowed with their age)
Be scorn'd, like old men of lesse truth then tongue,
And your true rights be termd a Poets rage,

And stretched miter of an Antique song.
But were some childe of yours aliue that time,
You should liue twise, in it and in my rime.

WILLIAM SHAKESPEARE.

SONNET XXIX

WHEN in disgrace with Fortune and mens eyes,
I all alone beweepe my out-cast state,
And trouble deafe heauen with my bootlesse cries,
And looke vpon my selfe and curse my fate,
Wishing me like to one more rich in hope,
Featur'd like him, like him with friends possest,
Desiring this mans art, and that mans skope,
With what I most inioy contented least,
Yet in these thoughts my selfe almost despising,
Haplye I thinke on thee, and then my state,
(Like to the Larke at breake of daye arising)
From sullen earth sings himns at Heauens gate,
For thy sweet loue remembred such welth, brings,
And then I skorne to change my state with Kings.

WILLIAM SHAKESPEARE.

SONNET XXX

WHEN to the Sessions of sweet silent thought,
I sommon vp remembrance of things past,
I sigh the lacke of many a thing I sought,
And with old woes new waile my deare times waste:
Then can I drowne an eye (vn-vs'd to flow)
For precious friends hid in deaths dateless night,
And weepe a fresh loues long since canceld woe,
And mone th'expence of many a vannisht sight.

Then can I greeue at greeuances fore-gon,
And heauily from woe to woe tell ore
The sad account of fore-bemoned mone,
Which I new pay as if not payd before.
But if the while I thinke on thee (deere friend)
All losses are restord, and sorrowes end.

WILLIAM SHAKESPEARE.

SONNET XXXIII

FVLL many a glorious morning haue I seene,
Flatter the mountaine tops with soueraine eie,
Kissing with golden face the meddowes greene,
Guilding pale streames with heauenly alcumy:
Anon permit the basest cloudes to ride,
With ougly rack on his celestiall face,
And from the for-lorne world his visage hide
Stealing vnseene to west with this disgrace:
Euen so my Sunne one early morne did shine,
With all triumphant splendor on my brow,
But out alack, he was but one houre mine,
The region cloude hath mask'd him from me now.
Yet him for this, my loue no whit disdaineth,
Suns of the world may staine, when heauens sun staineth.

WILLIAM SHAKESPEARE.

SONNET LV

NOT marble, nor the guilded monuments,
Of Princes shall out-liue this powrefull rime,
But you shall shine more bright in these contents
Then vnswept stone, besmeer'd with sluttish time.

When wastefull warre shall Statues ouer-turne,
And broiles roote out the worke of masonry,
Nor Mars his sword, nor warres quick fire shall
burne
The liuing record of your memory.
Gainst death, and all-obliuious enmity
Shall you pace forth, your praise shall stil finde
roome,
Euen in the eyes of all posterity
That weare this world out to the ending doome.
So til the iudgement that your selfe arise,
You liue in this, and dwell in louers eies.

WILLIAM SHAKESPEARE.

SONNET LXV

SINCE brasse, nor stone, nor earth nor boundlesse
sea,
But sad mortallity ore-swaies their power,
How with this rage shall beautie hold a plea,
Whose action is no stronger then a flower?
O how shall summers hunny breath hold out,
Against the wrackfull siedge of battring dayes.
When rocks impregnable are not so stoute,
Nor gates of steele so strong but time decayes?
O fearefull meditation, where alack,
Shall times best Iewell from times chest lie hid?
Or what strong hand can hold his swift foote back,
Or who his spoile of beautie can forbid?
O none, vnless this miracle haue might,
That in black inck my loue may still shine bright.

WILLIAM SHAKESPEARE.

SONNET LXXIII

THAT time of yeeare thou maist in me behold,
When yellow leaues, or none, or few doe hange
Vpon those boughes which shake against the could,
Bare ruin'd quiers, where late the sweet birds sang.
In me thou seest the twi-light of such day,
As after Sun-set fadeth in the West,
Which by and by blacke night doth take away,
Deaths second selfe that seals vp all in rest.
In me thou seest the glowing of such fire,
That on the ashes of his youth doth lye,
As the death bed, whereon it must expire,
Consum'd with that which it was nurrisht by.
This thou perceu'st, which makes thy loue more strong,
To loue that well, which thou must leaue ere long.

WILLIAM SHAKESPEARE.

SONNET LXXVI

WHY is my verse so barren of new pride?
So far from variation or quicke change?
Why with the time do I not glance aside
To new found methods, and to compounds strange?
Why write I still all one, euer the same,
And keepe inuention in a noted weed,
That euery word doth almost tel my name,
Shewing their birth, and where they did proceed?
O know sweet loue I alwaies write of you,
And you and loue are still my argument:
So all my best is dressing old words new,

Spending againe what is already spent:
For as the Sun is daily new and old,
So is my loue still telling what is told.

William Shakespeare.

COME VNTO THESE YELLOW SANDS, FROM *THE TEMPEST*

Come vnto these yellow sands,
and then take hands:
Curtsied when you haue, and kist
the wilde waves whist:
Foote it featly heere, and there, and sweete Sprights
beare the burthen.
Harke, harke, bowgh, wawgh: the watch-Dogges
barke, bowgh-wawgh,
Harke, harke, I heare, the straine of strutting
Chanticlere cry cockadidle-dowe.

William Shakespeare.

FEARE NO MORE THE HEATE O' TH' SUN, FROM *CYMBELINE*

Feare no more the heate o' th' Sun,
Nor the furious Winters rages,
Thou thy worldly task hast don,
Home art gon, and tane thy wages.
Golden Lads and Girles all must,
As Chimney-Sweepers come to dust.

Feare no more the frowne o' th' Great,
Thou art past the Tirants stroake,
Care no more to cloath and eat,

To thee the Reede is as the Oake:
The Scepter, Learning, Physicke must
All follow this and come to dust.

Feare no more the Lightning flash,
Nor th' all-dreaded Thunder stone;
Feare not Slander, Censure rash.
Thou hast finish'd Ioy and mone.
All Louers young, all Louers must,
Consigne to thee and come to dust.

No Exorcisor harme thee,
Nor no witch-craft charme thee.
Ghost vnlaid forbeare thee.
Nothing ill come neere thee.
Quiet consumation haue,
And renowned be thy graue.

WILLIAM SHAKESPEARE.

WHEN ICICLES HANG BY THE WALL, FROM *LOVE'S LABOUR'S LOST*

WHEN Icicles hang by the wall,
And Dicke the Shepheard blowes his naile;
And Tom beares Logges into the hall,
And Milke comes frozen home in paile:
When blood is nipt, and waies be fowle,
Then nightly sings the staring Owle
Tu-whit to-who.
A merrie note,
While greasie Ione doth keele the pot.

When all aloud the winde doth blow,
And coffing drownes the Parsons saw:

And birds sit brooding in the snow,
And Marrians nose lookes red and raw:
When roasted Crabs hisse in the bowle,
Then nightly sings the staring Owle,
Tu-whit to-who.
  A merrie note,
  While greasie Ione doth keele the pot.

WILLIAM SHAKESPEARE.

O MISTRESS MINE WHERE ARE YOU ROAMING? FROM *TWELFTH NIGHT*

O MISTRESS mine where are you roaming?
O stay and heare, your true loues coming,
That can sing both high and low.
Trip no further prettie sweeting.
Journeys end in louers meeting,
Eury wise mans sonne doth know.

What is loue, tis not heereafter,
Present mirth, hath present laughter:
What's to come, is still vnsure.
In delay there lies no plentie:
Then come kisse me sweet and twentie:
Youths a stuffe will not endure.

WILLIAM SHAKESPEARE.

FOLLOW YOUR SAINT

FOLLOW your saint, follow with accents sweet,
Haste you, sad notes, fall at her flying feete,
There, wrapt in cloud of sorrowe, pitie moue,
And tell the rauisher of my soule I perish for her loue:

Ha' you mark't but the fall o' the Snow
  Before the soyle hath smutch'd it?
Ha' you felt the wooll of Bever?
      Or Swans Downe ever?
Or have smelt o' the bud o' the Brier?
      Or the Nard in the fire?
Or have you tasted the bag of the Bee?
O so white! O so soft! O so sweet is she!

BEN JONSON.

TO CELIA, FROM *THE FORREST*

DRINKE to me, onely with thine eyes,
  And I will pledge with mine;
Or leave a kisse but in the cup,
  And Ile not looke for wine.

The thirst, that from the soule doth rise,
  Doth aske a drinke diuine:
But might I of Jove's Nectar sup,
  I would not change for thine.

I sent thee, late, a rosie wreath,
  Not so much honoring thee,
As giuing it a hope, that there
  It could not withered bee.

But thou thereon did'st onely breath,
  And sent'st it backe to me:
Since when it growes, and smells, I sweare,
  Not of it selfe but thee.

BEN JONSON.

A DIRGE, FROM *THE WHITE DIVEL*

CALL for the Robin-Red-Brest and the Wren,
Since ore shadie groues they houer,
And with leaues and flowres do couer
The friendlesse bodies of unburied men.
Call unto his funerall Dole
The Ante, the field-mouse, and the mole
To reare him hillockes, that shall keep him warme,
And (when gay tombes are rob'd) sustaine no harme,
But keepe the wolfe far thence: that's foe to men,
For with his nailes hee'l dig them up agen.

JOHN WEBSTER.

GLIDE SOFT YE SILUER FLOODS, FROM *BRITANNIA'S PASTORALS*

GLIDE soft ye siluer Floods,
And eury Spring:
Within the shady Woods,
Let no Bird sing!
Nor from the Groue a Turtle Doue,
Be seene to couple with her loue,
But silence on each Dale and Mountaine dwell
Whilst Willy bids his friend and ioy Farewell.

But (of great Thetis' trayne)
Ye Mermaides faire,
That on the shores doe plaine
Your Sea-greene haire,
As yee in tramels knit your locks
Weepe yee; and so inforce the rocks

In heauy murmures through the broade shores tell,
How Willy bad his friend and ioy Farewell.

Cease, cease, yee murdring winds
To moue a waue;
But if with troubled minds
You seeke his graue;
Know 'tis as various as your selues,
Now in the deepe, then on the shelues,
His coffin tossd by fish and surges fell,
Whilst Willy weepes and bids all ioy Farewell.

Had he Arion like
Been iudg'd to drowne,
Hee on his Lute could strike
So rare a sown';
A thousand Dolphins would haue come
And ioyntly strive to bring him home.
But he on Ship-board dyde, by sicknesse fell,
Since when his Willy bad all ioy Farewell.

Great Neptune heare a Swaine!
His Coffin take,
And with a golden chaine
(For pitie) make
It fast unto a rocke neere land!
Where eu'ry calmy morne Ile stand
And ere one sheepe out of my fold I tell
Sad Willy's Pipe shall bid his friend Farewell.

WILLIAM BROWNE.

PRAYER TO BEN JONSON

When I a Verse shall make,
Know I have praid thee,
For old Religions sake,
Saint Ben to aide me.

Make the way smooth for me,
When I, thy Herrick,
Honouring thee, on my knee
Offer my Lyrick.

Candles Ile give to thee,
And a new Altar;
And thou Saint Ben, shalt be
Writ in my Psalter.

Robert Herrick.

UPON JULIA'S CLOTHES

When as in silks my Julia goes,
Then, then (methinks) how sweetly flowes
The liquefaction of her clothes.

Next, when I cast mine eyes and see
That brave Vibration each way free;
O how that glittering taketh me!

Robert Herrick.

TO MEADOWS

Ye have been fresh and green,
  Ye have been fill'd with flowers:

And ye the Walks have been
  Where Maids have spent their houres.

Ye have beheld, how they
  With Wicker Arks did come
To kisse, and beare away
  The richer Couslips home.

Y'ave heard them sweetly sing,
  And seen them in a Round:
Each Virgin, like a Spring,
  With Hony-succles crown'd.

But now, we see, none here,
  Whose silv'rie feet did tread,
And with dishevel'd Haire,
  Adorn'd this smoother Mead.

Like Unthrifts, having spent,
  Your stock and needy grown,
Y'are left here to lament
  Your poore estates, alone.

ROBERT HERRICK.

DAVID'S EPITAPH ON JONATHAN

HERE lyes the fairest Flowre, that stood
In Isr'el's Garden; now, in Blood;
Which, Death to make her Girland gay,
Hath cropt, against her Triumph Day:
Here, here lies Hee, whose Actions pen'd
The perfect Copie of a Frend,

Whose milk-white Vellam did incurre
No least suspition of a Blurre:
Here lyes th'example of a Brother,
Not to bee follow'd by another;
The faire-indented Counter-part
Of David's Joy, of David's Heart:
Rest then; For ever, rest alone;
Thy Ashes can be touch'd by none,
Till Death hath pickt out such another:
Here lyes a Flow'r, a Friend, a Brother.

FRANCIS QUARLES.

SONNET: TELL ME NO MORE HOW FAIR SHE IS

TELL me no more how fair she is,
 I have no minde to hear
The story of that distant bliss
 I never shall come near:
By sad experience I have found
That her perfection is my wound.

And tell me not how fond I am
 To tempt a daring Fate,
From whence no triumph ever came,
 But to repent too late;
There is some hope ere long I may
In silence dote myself away.

I ask not pity (Love) from thee,
 Nor will thy justice blame,
So that thou wilt not envy mee
 The glory of my flame:

Which crowns my heart when ere it dyes,
In that it falls her sacrifice.

HENRY KING.

THE ELIXER

TEACH me, my God and King,
In all things thee to see,
And what I do in anything,
To do it as for thee:

Not rudely, as a beast,
To runne into an action;
But still to make thee prepossest,
And give it his perfection.

A man that looks on glasse,
On it may stay his eye;
Or if he pleaseth, through it passe,
And then the heav'n espie.

All may of thee partake:
Nothing can be so mean,
Which with his tincture (for thy sake)
Will not grow bright and clean.

A servant with this clause
Makes drudgerie divine:
Who sweeps a room, as for thy laws,
Makes that and th'action fine.

This is the famous stone
That turneth all to gold:

For that which God doth touch and own
    Cannot for lesse be told.

GEORGE HERBERT.

ASK ME NO MORE

ASKE me no more where Jove bestowes,
When June is past the fading rose:
For in your beauties orient deepe,
These flowers as in their causes, sleepe.

Aske me no more whether do stray,
The golden Atomes of the day:
For in pure love Heaven did prepare,
Those powders to inrich your haire.

Aske me no more whether doth hast,
The Nightingale when May is past:
For in your sweet divining throat,
She winters and keepes warme her note.

Aske me no more where those starres light,
That downewards fall in dead of night:
For in your eyes they sit and there
Fixed become as in their sphere.

Aske me no more if East and West,
The Phenix builds her spicy nest:
For unto you at last shee flies,
And in your fragrant bosome dyes.

THOMAS CAREW.

THE GLORIES OF OUR BLOOD AND STATE, FROM *THE CONTENTION OF AJAX AND ULYSSES*

The glories of our blood and state
  Are shadows, not substantial things,
There is no armour against fate,
  Death lays his icy hand on Kings,
    Scepter and Crown,
    Must tumble down,
And in the dust be equal made,
With the poor crooked sithe and spade.

Some men with swords may reap the field,
  And plant fresh laurels where they kill,
But their strong nerves at last must yield,
  They tame but one another still;
    Early or late,
    They stoop to fate,
And must give up their murmuring breath,
When they pale Captives creep to death.

The Garlands wither on your brow,
  Then boast no more your mighty deeds,
Upon Deaths purple Altar now,
  See where the Victor-victim bleeds,
    Your heads must come,
    To the cold Tomb,
Onely the actions of the just
Smell sweet, and blossom in the dust.

JAMES SHIRLEY.

TO CYNTHIA

WHEN I behold the heaven of thy face,
And see how every beauty, every grace
        Move, and are there
        As in their Sphere,
What need have I (my Cynthia) to conferre
With any Chalde, or Astrologer:
Since in the Scheme of thy faire face I see
All the Aspects of my nativity.

For if at any time thou should'st cast downe
From thy serenest brow an angry frowne,
        Or should'st reflect
        That dire aspect
Of opposition, or of enmity,
That looke would sure be fatall unto me,
Unlesse faire Venus kinde succeeding ray,
Did much of the malignity allay.

Or if I should be so unfortunate
To see a looke, though of imperfect hate,
        I am most sure
        That quadrature
Would cast me in a quartan love-sicke fever,
Of which I should recover late, if ever,
Or into a consumption, so should I
Perish at last, although not suddenly.

But when I see those starry Twins of thine,
Behold me with a Sextile, or a Trine,
        And that they move
        In perfect love

With amorous beams, they plainly do discover,
My horoscope markt me to be a lover:
And that I onely should not have the honor
To be borne under Venus, but upon her.

Sir Francis Kynaston.

UPON THE THOUGHT OF AGE AND DEATH

The breath of time shall blast the flowry Spring,
Which so perfumes thy cheeke, and with it bring
So darke a mist, as shall eclipse the light
Of thy faire eyes, in an eternall night.
Some melancholly chamber of the earth,
(For that like Time devoures whom it gave breath)
Thy beauties shall entombe, while all who ere
Lov'd nobly, offer up their sorrowes there.
But I whose griefe no formall limits bound,
Beholding the darke caverne of that ground,
Will there immure myselfe. And thus I shall
Thy mourner be, and my owne funerall.
Else by the weeping magicke of my verse,
Thou hadst reviv'd to triumph o're thy hearse.

William Habington.

GO, LOVELY ROSE

Go, lovely Rose,
Tell her that wastes her time and me,
That now she knows,
When I resemble her to thee
How sweet and fair she seems to be.

Tell her that's young,
And shuns to have her graces spy'd,
That hadst thou sprung
In deserts where no men abide,
Thou must have uncommended dy'd.

Small is the worth
Of beauty from the light retir'd;
Bid her come forth,
Suffer her self to be desir'd,
And not blush so to be admir'd.

Then die that she,
The common fate of all things rare
May read in thee
How small a part of time they share
That are so wondrous sweet and fair.

EDMUND WALLER.

SONNET: HOW SOON HATH TIME

How soon hath Time the suttle theef of youth,
Stoln on his wing my three and twentieth yeer!
My hasting dayes flie on with full career,
But my late spring no bud or blossom shew'th.
Perhaps my semblance might deceive the truth,
That I to manhood am arriv'd so near,
And inward ripenes doth much less appear,
That som more timely-happy spirits indu'th.
Yet be it less or more, or soon or slow,
It shall be still in strictest measure eev'n,
To that same lot, however mean, or high,

Toward which Time leads me, and the will of Heav'n;
 All is, if I have grace to use it so,
 As ever in my great task Masters eye.

JOHN MILTON.

SONNET: WHEN I CONSIDER HOW MY LIGHT IS SPENT

WHEN I consider how my light is spent,
 E're half my days, in this dark world and wide,
 And that one Talent which is death to hide,
 Lodg'd with me useless, though my Soul more bent
To serve therewith my Maker, and present
 My true account, least he returning chide,
 Doth God exact day-labour, light deny'd,
 I fondly ask; But patience to prevent
That murmur, soon replies, God doth not need
 Either man's work or his own gifts, who best
 Bear his milde yoak, they serve him best, his State
Is Kingly. Thousands at his bidding speed
 And post o're Land and Ocean without rest:
 They also serve who only stand and waite.

JOHN MILTON.

SONNET: AVENGE O LORD THY SLAUGHTER'D SAINTS

AVENGE O Lord thy slaughter'd Saints, whose bones
 Lie scatter'd on the Alpine mountains cold,
 Ev'n them who kept thy truth so rare of old
 When all our Fathers worship't Stocks and Stones,
Forget not: In thy book record their groanes
 Who were thy Sheep and in their antient Fold

Slayn by the bloody Piedmontese that roll'd
Mother with Infant down the Rocks. Their moans
The Vales redoubl'd to the Hills, and they
To Heav'n. Their martyr'd blood and ashes sow
O're all th' Italian fields where still doth sway
The triple Tyrant: that from these may grow
A hunder'd-fold, who having learnt thy way,
Early may fly the Babylonian wo.

JOHN MILTON.

A CONSTANT LOVER

OUT upon it, I have lov'd
Three whole days together;
And am like to love three more,
If it prove fair weather.

Time shall moult away his wings
Ere he shall discover
In the whole wide world agen
Such a constant Lover.

But the spite on't is, no praise
Is due at all to me:
Love with me had made no staies,
Had it any been but she.

Had it any been but she
And that very Face,
There had been at least ere this
A dozen dozen in her place.

SIR JOHN SUCKLING.

WHY SO PALE AND WAN FOND LOVER?

Why so pale and wan fond Lover?
prethee why so pale?
Will, when looking wel can't move her
looking ill prevail?
prethee why so pale?

Why so dull and mute young sinner?
prethee why so mute?
Will, when speaking well can't win her,
saying nothing doe't?
prethee why so mute?

Quit, quit for shame, this will not move,
this cannot take her;
If of her self she will not love,
nothing can make her:
the divel take her.

Sir John Suckling.

AN EPITAPH FOR A GODLY MAN'S TOMB

Here lies a piece of Christ, a Star in Dust;
A Vein of Gold, a China Dish that must
Be us'd in Heav'n, when God shall Feast the Just,

Robert Wilde.

MY DEAR AND ONLY LOVE

My dear and only love I pray
That little World of thee,

Be govern'd by no other sway,
  Than purest monarchie.
For if Confusion have a part,
  Which vertuous souls abhore,
I'le cull a *synod* in my heart,
  I'le never love thee more.

As Alexander I will reign,
  And I will reign alone;
My thoughts did ever yet disdain
  A Rival on my throne.
He either fears his fate too much,
  Or his deserts are small,
That dares not put it to the touch,
  To gain or lose it all.

But I will reign and govern still,
  And alwayes give the Law,
And have each Subject at my will,
  And all to stand in aw:
But 'gainst my Batteries if I find
  Thou kick or vex me sore,
As that thou set me up a blind,
  I'le never love thee more.

And in the Empire of thy heart
  Where I should solely be
If others do pretend a part,
  Or dares to vie with me:
Or Committees if thou erect,
  And go on such a score:
I'le laugh and sing at thy neglect,
  And never love thee more.

But if thou wilt prove faithful then,
And constant is thy word,
I'le make thee glorious by my Pen,
And famous by my sword.
I'le serve thee in such noble sort
Was never heard before,
I'le crown and deck thee all with bays,
And love thee more and more.

JAMES GRAHAM, Marquis of Montrose.

DIVES ASKING A DROP

Luke 16

A DROP, one drop, how sweetly one fair drop
Would tremble on my Pearl-tipt fingers top?
My Wealth is gone, O go it where it will,
Spare this one Jewel; I'll be Dives still.

RICHARD CRASHAW.

TRIOLETS

"I will sing unto the Lord." Psalm xiii. vers. 6

I

WORLDLY designes, feares, hopes, farewell!
Farewell all earthly joyes and cares!
On nobler thoughts my soule shall dwell,
Worldly designes, feares, hopes, farewell!
Att quiett in my peacefull cell,
I'le thincke on God, free from your snares;
Worldly designes, feares, hopes, farewell!
Farewell all earthly joys and cares.

II

I'le seeke my God's law to fulfill
Riches and power I'le sett att nought;
Lett others striue for them that will,
I'le seeke my God's law to fulfil:
Lest sinfull pleasures my soule kill,
(By folleye's uayne delights first caught),
I'le seeke my God's law to fulfill,
Riches and power I'le sett att nought.

III

Yes (my deare Lord!) I'ue found itt soe;
Noe joyes but thine are purely sweet;
Other delights come mixt with woe,
Yes (my deare Lord!) I'ue found itt soe.
Pleasure att courts is but in show,
With true content in cells wee meete;
Yes (my deare Lord!) I'ue found it soe,
No joyes but thine are purely sweet.

PATRICK CAREY.

STAY! O STAY! YE WINGED HOWERS, FROM *AT THE FLORISTS FEAST IN NORWICH*

THE SONG

STAY! O stay! ye winged howers,
  The windes that ransack East, and West,
Have breathd perfumes upon our flowers,
  More fragrant then the Phœnix nest:
    Then stay! O stay sweet howers! that yee,
    May witnesse that, which time nere see.

Stay a while, thou featherd Syth-man,
And attend the Queen of flowers,
Show thy self for once a blyth man,
Come dispence with a few howers:
Else we our selves will stay a while,
And make our pastime, Time beguile.

This day is deignd to Floras use,
If yee will revell too, to night
Weel presse the Grape, to lend ye juyce,
Shall make a deluge of delight:
And when yee cant hold up your heads,
Our Garden shall afford ye beds.

MATHEW STEVENSON.

TO THE SOUL

DULL soul aspire,
Thou art not earth, mount higher:
Heav'n gave the spark, to it return the fire.

Let sin ne'er quench
Thy high flam'd spirit hence
The earth the heat, to heaven the flame dispence.

Rejoyce, rejoyce,
Turn, turn each part a voice:
While to the heart-strings tun'd ye all rejoyce.

The house is swept
Which sin so long foul kept:
The peny's found for which the loser wept.

And purg'd with tears,
Gods Image re-appears.
The peny truly shews whose stamp it bears.

The sheep long lost,
Sins wilderness oft crost,
Is found, regain'd, return'd; spare, spare no cost.

'Tis heav'ns own suit,
Hark how it woo's you to't:
When Angels needs must speak, shall man be mute?

JOHN COLLOP.

THE WEDDING GARMENT

FAITH is the wedding garment, lind within,
With love, without foul spots, or staines of sin.
Humility is the most decent lace,
And patient hope, which doth this garment grace.
Without this royal robe no guest is fit
To sup, or at the Lords own table sit.

ROWLAND WATKYNS.

TO ALTHEA, FROM PRISON

I

WHEN Love with unconfined wings
Hovers within my Gates;
And my divine Althea brings
To whisper at the Grates:
When I lye tangled in her haire,
And fetterd to her eye;

The Gods that wanton in the Aire,
  Know no such Liberty.

II

When flowing Cups run swiftly round
  With no allaying Thames,
Our carelesse heads with Roses bound,
  Our hearts with Loyal Flames;
When thirsty griefe in Wine we steepe,
  When Healths and draughts go free,
Fishes that tipple in the Deepe,
  Know no such Libertie.

III

When (like committed Linnets) I
  With shriller throat shall sing
The sweetnes, Mercy, Majesty,
  And glories of my King;
When I shall voyce aloud, how Good
  He is, how Great should be;
Inlarged Winds that curle the Flood,
  Know no such Liberty.

IV

Stone Walls doe not a Prison make,
  Nor I'ron bars a Cage;
Mindes innocent and quiet take
  That for an Hermitage;
If I have freedom in my Love,
  And in my soule am free;
Angels alone that soar above,
  Enjoy such Liberty.

RICHARD LOVELACE.

TO LUCASTA GOING TO THE WARS

I

Tell me not (Sweet) I am unkinde,
That from the Nunnery
Of thy chaste breast, and quiet minde,
To War and Armes I flie.

II

True; a new Mistresse now I chase,
The first Foe in the Field;
And with a stronger Faith imbrace
A Sword, a Horse, a Shield.

III

Yet this Inconstancy is such,
As you too shall adore;
I could not love thee (Deare) so much,
Loved I not Honour more.

Richard Lovelace.

AND SHE WASHED HIS FEET WITH HER TEARES

The proud Ægyptian Queen, her Roman Guest,
(T'express her Love in Hight of State, and Pleasure)
With Pearl dissolv'd in Gold, did feast,
Both Food, and Treasure.

And now (dear Lord!) thy Lover, on the fair
And silver Tables of thy Feet, behold!
Pearl in her Tears, and in her Hair,
Offers thee Gold.

Edward Sherburne.

A SONG TO AMORET

If I were dead, and in my place,
  Some fresher youth design'd,
To warme thee with new fires, and grace
  Those Armes I left behind;

Were he as faithfull as the Sunne,
  That's wedded to the Sphere;
His bloud as chaste, and temp'rate runne,
  As Aprils mildest teare;

Or were he rich, and with his heapes,
  And spacious share of Earth,
Could make divine affection cheape,
  And court his golden birth:

For all these Arts I'de not believe,
  (No though he should be thine)
The mighty Amorist could give
  So rich a heart as mine.

Fortune and beauty thou mightst finde,
  And greater men then I:
But my true resolved minde,
  They never shall come nigh.

For I not for an hour did love,
  Or for a day desire,
But with my soule had from above,
  This endles holy fire.

Henry Vaughan.

PEACE

My Soul, there is a Countrie
  Far beyond the stars,
Where stands a winged Centrie
  All skilfull in the wars,
There above noise, and danger
  Sweet peace sits crown'd with smiles,
And one born in a Manger
  Commands the Beauteous files,
He is thy gracious friend,
  And (O my Soul awake!)
Did in pure love descend
  To die here for thy sake,
If thou canst get but thither,
  There growes the flowre of peace,
The Rose that cannot wither,
  Thy fortresse, and thy ease;
Leave then thy foolish ranges;
  For none can thee secure,
But one, who never changes,
  Thy God, thy life, thy Cure.

HENRY VAUGHAN.

THE CALL

Romira, stay,
And run not thus like a young Roe away,
No enemie
Pursues thee (foolish girle) tis onely I,
I'le keep off harms,
If thou'l be pleas'd to garrison mine arms;
What dost thou fear

I'le turn a Traiteur? may these Roses here
To palenesse shred,
And Lilies stand disguised in new Red,
If that I lay
A snare, wherein thou wouldst not gladly stay;
See see the Sunne
Does slowly to his azure Lodging run,
Come sit but here
And presently hee'l quit our Hemisphere,
So still among
Lovers, time is too short or else too long;
Here will we spin
Legends for them that have Love Martyrs been,
Here on this plain
Wee'l talk Narcissus to a flour again;
Come here and chose
On which of these proud plats thou would repose,
Here maiest thou shame
The rusty Violets, with the crimson flame
Of either cheek,
And Primroses white as thy fingers seek,
Nay, thou maiest prove
That mans most Noble Passion is to Love.

JOHN HALL.

HOME TRAVELL

WHAT need I travell, since I may
More choiser wonders here survay?
What need I Tire for purple seek
When I may find it in a cheek?
Or sack the Eastern shores, there lies
More precious Diamonds in her eyes?

What need I dig Peru for Oare
When every hair of her yields more?
Or toile for Gummes in India
Since she can breath more rich then they?
Or ransack Africk, there will be
On either hand more Ivory?
But look within, all Vertues that
Each nation would appropriate,
And with the glory of them rest,
Are in this map at large exprest;
That who would travell here might know
The little world in Folio.

JOHN HALL.

DEATH

I

How weak a Star doth rule Mankind,
  Which owes its ruine to the same
Causes which Nature had design'd
  To cherish and preserve the frame!

2

As Commonwealths may be secure,
  And no remote Invasion dread;
Yet may a sadder fall endure
  From Traitors in their bosom bred:

3

So while we feel no violence,
  And on our active Health do trust,
A secret hand doth snatch us hence,
  And tumbles us into the dust.

4

Yet carelesly we run our race,
As if we could Death's summons wave;
And think not on the narrow space
Between a Table and a Grave.

5

But since we cannot Death reprieve,
Our Souls and Fame we ought to mind,
For they our Bodies will survive;
That goes beyond, this stays behind.

6

If I be sure my Soul is safe,
And that my Actions will provide
My Tomb a nobler Epitaph,
Then that I onely liv'd and dy'd.

7

So that in various accidents
I Conscience may and Honour keep;
I with that ease and innocence
Shall die, as Infants go to sleep.

KATHERINE PHILIPS (*Orinda*).

SONG TO A FAIR YOUNG LADY GOING OUT OF THE TOWN IN THE SPRING

ASK not the Cause, why sullen Spring
So long delays her flow'rs to bear;
Why warbling Birds forget to sing,
And Winter Storms invert the Year?

Chloris is gone; and Fate provides
To make it Spring, where she resides.

Chloris is gone, the Cruel Fair;
  She cast not back a pitying Eye:
But left her Lover in Despair,
  To sigh, to languish, and to die:
Ah, how can those fair Eyes endure
To give the wounds they will not cure!

Great God of Love, why hast thou made
  A Face that can all Hearts command,
That all Religions can invade,
  And change the Laws of ev'ry Land?
Where thou hadst plac'd such Pow'r before,
Thou shou'dst have made her Mercy more.

When Chloris to the Temple comes,
  Adoring Crowds before her Fall;
She can restore the Dead from Tombs,
  And every Life but mine recall.
I only am by Love design'd
To be the Victim for Mankind.

JOHN DRYDEN.

THE DEFIANCE

BE not too proud imperious Dame,
  Your charms are transitory things,
May melt, while you at Heaven aim,
  Like Icarus's waxen wings;
And you a part in his misfortunes bear,
Drown'd in a briny Ocean of despair.

You think your beauties are above
  The Poet's Brain, the Painter's Hand,
As if upon the throne of Love
  You only should the world command:
Yet know though you presume your title true,
There are pretenders that will rival you.

There's an experienc't Rebel, Time,
  And in his Squadrons Poverty;
There's Age that bring's along with him
  A terrible Artillery:
And if against all these thou keep'st thy Crown,
Th' Usurper Death will make thee lay it down.

THOMAS FLATMAN.

ON OLD ROME

HERE was old Rome that stretch'd her Empire far,
In Peace was fear'd, triumphant was in War:
Here 'twas, for now its place is only found,
All that was Rome lyes buried under Ground.

These Ruines hid in Weeds, on which Man treads,
Were Structures which to Heav'n rais'd their proud
  Heads:
Rome that subdu'd the World, to Time now yields,
With Rubbish swells the Plains, and strews the
  Fields.

Think not to see what so Renown'd has been,
Nothing of Rome, in Rome is to be seen;
Vulcan and Mars, those wasting Gods, have come,
And ta'en Romes Greatness utterly from Rome.

They spoil'd with Malice, e're they would depart,
What e'er was rare of Nature or of Art:
Its greatest Trophies they destroy'd and burn'd;
She that o'erturn'd the World, to Dust is turn'd.

Well might she fall, 'gainst whom such Foes conspire,
Old Time, Revengeful Man, and Sword and Fire:
Now all we see of the Great Empress Rome,
Are but the Sacred Reliques of her Tomb.

PHILIP AYRES.

LOVE STILL HAS SOMETHING OF THE SEA

LOVE still has something of the Sea,
  From whence his Mother rose;
No time his Slaves from Doubt can free,
  Nor give their Thoughts repose:

They are becalm'd in clearest Days,
  And in rough Weather tost;
They wither under cold Delays
  Or are in Tempests lost.

One while they seem to touch the Port,
  Then straight into the Main,
Some angry Wind in cruel sport
  The Vessel drives again.

At first Disdain and Pride they fear,
  Which if they chance to 'scape,
Rivals and Falshood soon appear
  In a more dreadful shape.

By such Degrees to Joy they come,
And are so long withstood,
So slowly they receive the Sum,
It hardly does them good.

'Tis cruel to prolong a Pain;
And to defer a Joy;
Believe me, gentle Celemene
Offends the winged Boy.

An hundred thousand Oaths your Fears
Perhaps would not remove;
And if I gaz'd a thousand Years
I could no deeper love.

SIR CHARLES SEDLEY.

ABSENT FROM THEE I LANGUISH STILL

ABSENT from thee I languish still,
Then ask me not, when I return?
The straying Fool 'twill plainly kill,
To wish all Day, all Night to Mourn.

Dear; from thine Arms then let me flie,
That my Fantastick mind may prove,
The Torments it deserves to try,
That tears my fixd Heart from my Love.

When wearied with a world of Woe,
To thy safe Bosom I retire
Where Love and Peace and Truth does flow,
May I contented there expire.

Lest once more wandring from that Heav'n
  I fall on some base heart unblest;
Faithless to thee, False, unforgiv'n,
  And lose my Everlasting rest.

JOHN WILMOT, Earl of Rochester.

NANNETTE

I

HASTE my Nannette, my lovely maid,
Haste to the bower, thy swain has made.

II

For thee alone I made the bower,
And strew'd the couch with many a flower.

III

None but my Sheep shall near us come,
Venus be prais'd, my sheep are dumb.

IV

Great God of love, take thou my crook,
To keep the wolf from Nannette's flock.

V

Guard thou the sheep, to her so dear,
My own, alas! are less my care.

VI

But of the wolf, if thou'rt afraid,
Come not to us to call for aid.

VII

For with her swain my love shall stay,
Tho' the wolf strole, and the sheep stray.

MATTHEW PRIOR.

TO A CHILD OF QUALITY

LORDS, knights, and squires, the num'rous band,
That wear the fair miss Mary's fetters,
Were summon'd by her high command,
To show their passions by their letters.

My pen among the rest I took,
Lest those bright eyes that cannot read
Shou'd dart their kindling fires, and look,
The power they have to be obey'd.

Nor quality, nor reputation,
Forbid me yet my flame to tell,
Dear five years old befriends my passion,
And I may write till she can spell.

For while she makes her silk-worms beds,
With all the tender things I swear,
Whilst all the house my passion reads,
In papers round her baby's hair.

She may receive and own my flame,
For tho' the strictest prudes shou'd know it,
She'll pass for a most virtuous dame,
And I for an unhappy poet.

Then too alas! when she shall tear
  The lines some younger rival sends,
She'll give me leave to write I fear,
  And we shall still continue friends.

For, as our diff'rent ages move,
  'Tis so ordain'd, wou'd Fate but mend it,
That I shall be past making love
  When she begins to comprehend it.

MATTHEW PRIOR.

THUS STEAL THE SILENT HOURS AWAY, FROM *INSCRIPTIONS ON DIALS*

THUS steal the silent hours away,
The sun thus hastes to reach the sea,
And men to mingle with their clay.
Thus light and shade divide the year,
Thus, till the last great day appear,
And shut the starry theater.

ISAAC WATTS.

SONNET: I DIE WITH TOO TRANSPORTING JOY

(From the French)

I DIE with too transporting Joy,
  If she I love rewards my Fire;
If She's inexorably Coy,
  With too much Passion I expire.

No Way the Fates afford to shun
  The cruel Torment I endure;

Since I am doom'd to be undone
By the Disease, or by the Cure.

JOHN HUGHES.

PRESENTING TO A LADY A WHITE ROSE AND A RED, ON THE TENTH OF JUNE

IF this pale Rose offend your Sight,
It in your Bosom wear;
'Twill blush to find itself less white,
And turn Lancastrian there.

But, Celia, should the Red be chose,
With gay Vermilion bright;
'Twou'd sicken at each Blush that glows,
And in Despair turn White.

Let Politicians idly prate,
Their Babels build in vain;
As uncontrolable as Fate,
Imperial Love shall reign.

Each haughty Faction shall obey,
And Whigs, and Tories join,
Submit to your Despotick Sway,
Confess your Right Divine.

Yet this (my gracious Monarch) own,
They're Tyrants that oppress;
'Tis Mercy must support your Throne,
And 'tis like Heav'n to Bless.

WILLIAM SOMERVILE.

OLIVIA

I

OLIVIA'S lewd, but looks devout,
And Scripture-Proofs she throws about,
When first you try to win her;
But pull your Fob of Guineas out;
Fee Jenny first, and never doubt
To find the Saint a Sinner.

II

Baxter by Day is her Delight:
No Chocolate must come in Sight
Before two Morning Chapters:
But lest the Spleen should spoil her quite,
She takes a civil Friend at Night
To raise her holy Raptures.

III

Thus oft' we see a Glow-Worm gay,
At large her fiery Tail display,
Encourag'd by the dark:
And yet the sullen Thing all Day
Snug in the lonely Thicket lay,
And hid the native Spark.

ELIJAH FENTON.

RULE BRITANNIA! FROM *ALFRED, AN OPERA*

WHEN Britain first, at heaven's command,
Arose from out the azure main;

This was the charter of the land,
  And guardian-Angels sung this strain:
    Rule, Britannia, rule the waves;
    Britons never will be slaves.

The nations, not so blest as thee,
  Must, in their turns, to tyrants fall:
While thou shalt flourish great and free,
  The dread and envy of them all.
    Rule, Britannia, rule the waves;
    Britons never will be slaves.

Still more majestic shalt thou rise,
  More dreadful, from each foreign stroke:
As the loud blast that tears the skies,
  Serves but to root thy native oak.
    Rule, Britannia, rule the waves;
    Britons never will be slaves.

Thee haughty tyrants ne'er shall tame:
  All their attempts to bend thee down,
Will but arouse thy generous flame;
  But work their woe, and thy renown.
    Rule, Britannia, rule the waves;
    Britons never will be slaves.

To thee belongs the rural reign;
  Thy cities shall with commerce shine:
All thine shall be the subject main,
  And every shore it circles thine.
    Rule, Britannia, rule the waves;
    Britons never will be slaves.

The Muses, still with freedom found,
Shall to thy happy coast repair:
Blest isle! with matchless beauty crown'd,
And manly hearts to guard the fair.
Rule, Britannia, rule the waves;
Britons never will be slaves.

JAMES THOMSON.

O'ER DESERT PLAINS, AND RUSHY MEERS

O'ER desert plains, and rushy meers,
And wither'd heaths I rove;
Where tree, nor spire, nor cot appears,
I pass to meet my love.

But tho' my path were damask'd o'er
With beauties e'er so fine;
My busy thoughts would fly before,
To fix alone — on thine.

No fir-crown'd hills cou'd give delight,
No palace please mine eye:
No pyramid's aerial height,
Where mouldering monarchs lie.

Unmov'd, should Eastern kings advance,
Could I the pageant see:
Splendour might catch one scornful glance,
Not steal one thought from thee.

WILLIAM SHENSTONE.

LIGHT SHINING OUT OF DARKNESS

God moves in a mysterious way,
His wonders to perform;
He plants his footsteps in the sea,
And rides upon the storm.

Deep in unfathomable mines
Of never failing skill
He treasures up his bright designs,
And works his sovereign will.

Ye fearful saints fresh courage take,
The clouds ye so much dread
Are big with mercy, and shall break
In blessings on your head.

Judge not the Lord by feeble sense,
But trust him for his grace;
Behind a frowning providence,
He hides a smiling face.

His purposes will ripen fast,
Unfolding ev'ry hour;
The bud may have a bitter taste,
But sweet will be the flow'r.

Blind unbelief is sure to err,
And scan his work in vain;
God is his own interpreter,
And he will make it plain.

William Cowper.

THE POOR, FROM *THE BOROUGH*

SHOW not to the Poor thy pride,
Let their home a cottage be;
Nor the feeble body hide
In a palace fit for thee;
Let him not about him see
Lofty ceilings, ample halls,
Or a gate his boundary be,
Where nor friend or kinsman calls.

Let him not one walk behold,
That only one which he must tread,
Nor a chamber large and cold,
Where the ag'd and sick are led;
Better far his humble shed,
Humble sheds of neighbours by,
And the old and tattered bed,
Where he sleeps and hopes to die.

GEORGE CRABBE.

AND DID THOSE FEET IN ANCIENT TIME FROM *MILTON*

AND did those feet in ancient time
Walk upon England's mountains green?
And was the holy Lamb of God
On England's pleasant pastures seen?

And did the Countenance Divine
Shine forth upon our clouded hills?
And was Jerusalem builded here
Among these dark Satanic Mills?

Bring me my bow of burning gold!
  Bring me my arrows of desire!
Bring me my spear! O clouds, unfold!
  Bring me my chariot of fire!

I will not cease from mental fight,
  Nor shall my sword sleep in my hand,
Till we have built Jerusalem
  In England's green and pleasant land.

WILLIAM BLAKE.

THE TIGER

TIGER! Tiger! burning bright
In the forests of the night,
What immortal hand or eye
Could frame thy fearful symmetry?

In what distant deeps or skies
Burnt the fire of thine eyes?
On what wings dare he aspire?
What the hand dare seize the fire?

And what shoulder, and what art
Could twist the sinews of thy heart?
And when thy heart began to beat,
What dread hand? and what dread feet?

What the hammer? what the chain?
In what furnace was thy brain?
What the anvil? what dread grasp
Dare its deadly terrors clasp?

When the stars threw down their spears,
And water'd heaven with their tears,
Did he smile his work to see?
Did he who made the lamb make thee?

Tiger! Tiger! burning bright
In the forests of the night,
What immortal hand or eye
Dare frame thy fearful symmetry?

WILLIAM BLAKE.

A RED, RED ROSE

O, MY luve is like a red, red rose,
That's newly sprung in June.
O, my luve is like the melodie,
That's sweetly play'd in tune.

As fair thou art, my bonie lass,
So deep in luve am I,
And I will luve thee still, my dear,
Till a' the seas gang dry.

Till a' the seas gang dry, my dear,
And the rocks melt wi' the sun!
And I will luve thee still, my dear,
While the sands o' life shall run.

And fare thee weel, my only luve,
And fare thee weel a while!
And I will come again, my luve,
Tho' it were ten thousand mile!

ROBERT BURNS.

JOHN ANDERSON MY JO

John Anderson my jo, John,
  When we were first acquent,
Your locks were like the raven,
  Your bonie brow was brent;
But now your brow is beld, John,
  Your locks are like the snaw,
But blessings on your frosty pow,
  John Anderson my jo!

John Anderson my jo, John,
  We clamb the hill thegither,
And monie a cantie day, John,
  We've had wi' ane anither;
Now we maun totter down, John,
  And hand in hand we'll go,
And sleep thegither at the foot,
  John Anderson my jo!

Robert Burns.

HIGHLAND MARY

Ye banks and braes and streams around
  The castle o' Montgomery,
Green be your woods, and fair your flowers,
  Your waters never drumlie!
There Summer first unfald her robes,
  And there the langest tarry!
For there I took the last fareweel
  O' my sweet Highland Mary!

How sweetly bloom'd the gay, green birk,
  How rich the hawthorn's blossom,
As underneath their fragrant shade
  I clasp'd her to my bosom!
The golden hours on angel wings
  Flew o'er me and my dearie:
For dear to me as light and life
  Was my sweet Highland Mary.

Wi' monie a vow and lock'd embrace
  Our parting was fu' tender;
And, pledging aft to meet again,
  We tore oursels asunder.
But O, fell Death's untimely frost,
  That nipt my flower sae early!
Now green's the sod and cauld's the clay,
  That wraps my Highland Mary!

O pale, pale now, those rosy lips
  I aft hae kiss'd sae fondly;
And clos'd for ay the sparkling glance
  That dwelt on me sae kindly;
And mouldering now in silent dust
  That heart that lo'ed me dearly!
But still within my bosom's core
  Shall live my Highland Mary.

ROBERT BURNS.

THE GREEN LINNET

BENEATH these fruit-tree boughs that shed
Their snow-white blossoms on my head,

With brightest sunshine round me spread
  Of spring's unclouded weather,
In this sequestered nook how sweet
To sit upon my orchard-seat!
And birds and flowers once more to greet,
  My last year's friends together.

One have I marked, the happiest guest
In all this covert of the blest:
Hail to Thee, far above the rest
  In joy of voice and pinion!
Thou, Linnet! in thy green array,
Presiding Spirit here to-day,
Dost lead the revels of the May;
  And this is thy dominion.

While birds, and butterflies, and flowers,
Make all one band of paramours,
Thou, ranging up and down the bowers,
  Art sole in thy employment:
A Life, a Presence like the Air,
Scattering thy gladness without care,
Too blest with any one to pair;
  Thyself thy own enjoyment.

Amid yon tuft of hazel trees,
That twinkle to the gusty breeze,
Behold him perched in ecstasies,
  Yet seeming still to hover;
There! where the flutter of his wings
Upon his back and body flings
Shadows and sunny glimmerings,
  That cover him all over.

My dazzled sight he oft deceives,
A Brother of the dancing leaves;
Then flits, and from the cottage eaves
  Pours forth his song in gushes;
As if by that exulting strain
He mocked and treated with disdain
The voiceless Form he chose to feign,
  While fluttering in the bushes.

WILLIAM WORDSWORTH.

THE SOLITARY REAPER

BEHOLD her, single in the field,
Yon solitary Highland Lass!
Reaping and singing by herself;
Stop here, or gently pass!
Alone she cuts and binds the grain,
And sings a melancholy strain;
O listen! for the Vale profound
Is overflowing with the sound.

No Nightingale did ever chaunt
More welcome notes to weary bands
Of travellers in some shady haunt,
Among Arabian sands:
A voice so thrilling ne'er was heard
In spring-time from the Cuckoo-bird,
Breaking the silence of the seas
Among the farthest Hebrides.

Will no one tell me what she sings? —
Perhaps the plaintive numbers flow

For old, unhappy, far-off things,
And battles long ago:
Or is it some more humble lay,
Familiar matter of to-day?
Some natural sorrow, loss, or pain,
That has been, and may be again?

Whate'er the theme, the Maiden sang
As if her song could have no ending;
I saw her singing at her work,
And o'er the sickle bending; —
I listened, motionless and still;
And, as I mounted up the hill,
The music in my heart I bore,
Long after it was heard no more.

William Wordsworth.

SONNET: COMPOSED UPON WESTMINSTER BRIDGE

Earth has not anything to show more fair:
Dull would he be of soul who could pass by
A sight so touching in its majesty:
This City now doth, like a garment, wear
The beauty of the morning; silent, bare,
Ships, towers, domes, theatres, and temples lie
Open unto the fields, and to the sky;
All bright and glittering in the smokeless air.
Never did sun more beautifully steep
In his first splendour, valley, rock, or hill;
Ne'er saw I, never felt, a calm so deep!
The river glideth at his own sweet will:

Dear God! the very houses seem asleep;
And all that mighty heart is lying still!

WILLIAM WORDSWORTH.

I WANDERED LONELY AS A CLOUD

I WANDERED lonely as a cloud
That floats on high o'er vales and hills,
When all at once I saw a crowd,
A host, of golden daffodils;
Beside the lake, beneath the trees,
Fluttering and dancing in the breeze.

Continuous as the stars that shine
And twinkle on the milky way,
They stretched in never-ending line
Along the margin of a bay:
Ten thousand saw I at a glance,
Tossing their heads in sprightly dance.

The waves beside them danced; but they
Out-did the sparkling waves in glee:
A poet could not but be gay,
In such a jocund company:
I gazed — and gazed — but little thought
What wealth the show to me had brought:

For oft, when on my couch I lie
In vacant or in pensive mood,
They flash upon that inward eye
Which is the bliss of solitude;
And then my heart with pleasure fills,
And dances with the daffodils.

WILLIAM WORDSWORTH.

THE KNIGHT'S TOMB

WHERE is the grave of Sir Arthur O'Kellyn?
Where may the grave of that good man be? —
By the side of a spring, on the breast of Helvellyn
Under the twigs of a young birch tree!
The oak that in summer was sweet to hear,
And rustled its leaves in the fall of the year,
And whistled and roared in the winter alone,
Is gone, — and the birch in its stead is grown. —
The Knight's bones are dust,
And his good sword rust; —
His soul is with the saints, I trust.

SAMUEL TAYLOR COLERIDGE.

ON HIS SEVENTY-FIFTH BIRTHDAY

I STROVE with none, for none was worth my strife,
  Nature I loved, and next to Nature, Art;
I warmed both hands before the fire of life,
  It sinks, and I am ready to depart.

WALTER SAVAGE LANDOR.

DEATH STANDS ABOVE ME

DEATH stands above me, whispering low
  I know not what into my ear:
Of his strange language all I know
  Is, there is not a word of fear.

WALTER SAVAGE LANDOR.

ROSE AYLMER

Ah what avails the sceptred race,
  Ah what the form divine!
What every virtue, every grace!
  Rose Aylmer, all were thine.
Rose Aylmer, whom these wakeful eyes
  May weep, but never see,
A night of memories and of sighs
  I consecrate to thee.

WALTER SAVAGE LANDOR.

EPIGRAM: STAND CLOSE AROUND, YE STYGIAN SET

Stand close around, ye Stygian set,
  With Dirce in one boat conveyed!
Or Charon, seeing, may forget
  That he is old and she a shade.

WALTER SAVAGE LANDOR.

SHE WALKS IN BEAUTY, LIKE THE NIGHT

I

She walks in Beauty, like the night
  Of cloudless climes and starry skies;
And all that's best of dark and bright
  Meets in her aspect and her eyes:
Thus mellowed to that tender light
  Which Heaven to gaudy day denies.

II

One shade the more, one ray the less,
  Had half impaired the nameless grace
Which waves in every raven tress,
  Or softly lightens o'er her face;
Where thoughts serenely sweet express,
  How pure, how dear their dwelling-place.

III

And on that cheek, and o'er that brow,
  So soft, so calm, yet eloquent,
The smiles that win, the tints that glow,
  But tell of days in goodness spent,
A mind at peace with all below,
  A heart whose love is innocent!

LORD BYRON.

LOVE'S PHILOSOPHY

I

THE fountains mingle with the river
  And the rivers with the Ocean,
The winds of Heaven mix for ever
  With a sweet emotion;
Nothing in the world is single;
  All things by a law divine
In one spirit meet and mingle.
  Why not I with thine? —

II

See the mountains kiss high Heaven
  And the waves clasp one another;

No sister-flower would be forgiven
  If it disdained its brother;
And the sunlight clasps the earth
  And the moonbeams kiss the sea:
What is all this sweet work worth
  If thou kiss not me?

PERCY BYSSHE SHELLEY.

AUTUMN: A DIRGE

I

THE warm sun is failing, the bleak wind is wailing,
The bare boughs are sighing, the pale flowers are dying,
    And the Year
On the earth her death-bed, in a shroud of leaves dead,
    Is lying.
  Come, Months, come away,
  From November to May,
  In your saddest array;
  Follow the bier
  Of the dead cold Year,
And like dim shadows watch by her sepulchre.

II

The chill rain is falling, the nipped worm is crawling,
The rivers are swelling, the thunder is knelling
    For the Year;
The blithe swallows are flown, and the lizards each gone
    To his dwelling;

Come, Months, come away;
Put on white, black, and gray;
Let your light sisters play —
Ye, follow the bier
Of the dead cold Year,
And make her grave green with tear on tear.

PERCY BYSSHE SHELLEY.

SONNET: WHY DID I LAUGH TO-NIGHT?

VHY did I laugh to-night? No voice will tell:
No God, no Demon of severe response,
)eigns to reply from Heaven or from Hell.
Then to my human heart I turn at once.
Ieart! Thou and I are here, sad and alone;
Say, wherefore did I laugh? O mortal pain!
) Darkness! Darkness! ever must I moan,
To question Heaven and Hell and Heart in vain.
Vhy did I laugh? I know this Being's lease,
My fancy to its utmost blisses spreads;
'et would I on this very midnight cease,
And the world's gaudy ensigns see in shreds;
'erse, Fame, and Beauty are intense indeed,
But Death intenser — Death is Life's high meed.

JOHN KEATS.

ON FIRST LOOKING INTO CHAPMAN'S HOMER

MUCH have I travell'd in the realms of gold,
And many goodly states and kingdoms seen;
Round many western islands have I been

Which bards in fealty to Apollo hold.
Oft of one wide expanse had I been told
That deep-brow'd Homer ruled as his demesne;
Yet did I never breathe its pure serene
Till I heard Chapman speak out loud and bold:
Then felt I like some watcher of the skies
When a new planet swims into his ken;
Or like stout Cortez when with eagle eyes
He stared at the Pacific — and all his men
Look'd at each other with a wild surmise —
Silent, upon a peak in Darien.

JOHN KEATS.

TO AUTUMN

SEASON of mists and mellow fruitfulness,
Close bosom-friend of the maturing sun;
Conspiring with him how to load and bless
With fruit the vines that round the thatch-eaves run,
To bend with apples the moss'd cottage-trees,
And fill all fruit with ripeness to the core;
To swell the gourd, and plump the hazel shells
With a sweet kernel; to set budding more,
And still more, later flowers for the bees,
Until they think warm days will never cease,
For Summer has o'er-brimm'd their clammy cells.

Who hath not seen thee oft amid thy store?
Sometimes whoever seeks abroad may find
Thee sitting careless on a granary floor,
Thy hair soft-lifted by the winnowing wind;

Or on a half-reap'd furrow sound asleep,
Drowsed with the fume of poppies, while thy hook
Spares the next swath and all its twined flowers:
And sometimes like a gleaner thou dost keep
Steady thy laden head across a brook;
Or by a cyder-press, with patient look,
Thou watchest the last oozings hours by hours.

Where are the songs of Spring? Ay, where are they?
Think not of them, thou hast thy music too,—
While barred clouds bloom the soft-dying day,
And touch the stubble-plains with rosy hue;
Then in a wailful choir the small gnats mourn
Among the river sallows, borne aloft
Or sinking as the light wind lives or dies;
And full-grown lambs loud bleat from hilly bourn;
Hedge-crickets sing; and now with treble soft
The red-breast whistles from a garden-croft,
And gathering swallows twitter in the skies.

JOHN KEATS.

THE DIRGE

I

"SING from the chamber to the grave!"
Thus did the dead man say:
"A sound of melody I crave
Upon my burial-day.

II

"Bring forth some tuneful instrument,
And let your voices rise:

My spirit listened, as it went,
  To music of the skies.

III

"Sing sweetly while you travel on,
  And keep the funeral slow:—
The angels sing where I am gone,
  And you should sing below.

IV

"Sing from the threshold to the porch!
  Until you hear the bell:
And sing you loudly in the church,
  The Psalms I love so well.

V

"Then bear me gently to my grave,
  And as you pass along,
Remember 'twas my wish to have
  A pleasant funeral song.

VI

"So earth to earth, and dust to dust!
  And though my flesh decay,
My soul shall sing among the just,
  Until the judgment day."

ROBERT STEPHEN HAWKER.

Author's Note.—The first of these verses haunted th
memory and the lips of a good and blameless young farme
who died in my parish some years ago. It was, as I conceiv
a fragment of some forgotten dirge, of which he could remen
ber no more. But it was his strong desire that "the words
should be "put upon his headstone," and he wished me als

to write "some other words, to make it complete." I fulfilled his entreaty, and the stranger who visits my churchyard will find this dirge carven in stone, "in sweet remembrance of the just," and to the praise of the dead, Richard Cann.

THE SONG OF THE WESTERN MEN

A GOOD sword and a trusty hand!
  A merry heart and true!
King James's men shall understand
  What Cornish lads can do.

And have they fixed the where and when?
  And shall Trelawny die?
Here's twenty thousand Cornish men
  Will know the reason why!

Out spake their captain brave and bold,
  A merry wight was he:
"If London Tower were Michael's hold,
  We'll set Trelawny free!

"We'll cross the Tamar, land to land,
  The Severn is no stay,
With 'one and all,' and hand in hand,
  And who shall bid us nay?

"And when we come to London Wall,
  A pleasant sight to view,
Come forth! come forth, ye cowards all,
  Here's men as good as you!

"Trelawny he's in keep and hold,
  Trelawny he may die;—

But here's twenty thousand Cornish bold,
Will know the reason why!"

ROBERT STEPHEN HAWKER.

IN LOVE, IF LOVE BE LOVE, FROM *MERLIN AND VIVIEN*

IN Love, if Love be Love, if Love be ours,
Faith and unfaith can ne'er be equal powers:
Unfaith in aught is want of faith in all.

It is the little rift within the lute,
That by and by will make the music mute,
And ever widening slowly silence all.

The little rift within the lover's lute
Or little pitted speck in garner'd fruit,
That rotting inward slowly moulders all.

It is not worth the keeping: let it go:
But shall it? answer, darling, answer, no.
And trust me not at all or all in all.

LORD TENNYSON.

EPILOGUE TO ASOLANDO

AT the midnight in the silence of the sleep-time,
When you set your fancies free,
Will they pass to where — by death, fools think, imprisoned —
Low he lies who once so loved you, whom you loved so,
— Pity me?

Oh to love so, be so loved, yet so mistaken!
What had I on earth to do
With the slothful, with the mawkish, the unmanly?
Like the aimless, helpless, hopeless, did I drivel
— Being — who?

One who never turned his back but marched breast forward,
Never doubted clouds would break,
Never dreamed, though right were worsted, wrong would triumph,
Held we fall to rise, are baffled to fight better,
Sleep to wake.

No, at noonday in the bustle of man's work-time
Greet the unseen with a cheer!
Bid him forward, breast and back as either should be,
"Strive and thrive!" cry "Speed, — fight on, fare ever
There as here!"

ROBERT BROWNING.

THE YEAR'S AT THE SPRING, FROM *PIPPA PASSES*

THE year's at the spring
And day's at the morn;
Morning's at seven;
The hill-side's dew-pearl'd;
The lark's on the wing;
The snail's on the thorn:
God's in his heaven —
All's right with the world!

ROBERT BROWNING.

THE LOST MISTRESS

I

All's over, then: does truth sound bitter
  As one at first believes?
Hark, 'tis the sparrows' good-night twitter
  About your cottage eaves!

II

And the leaf-buds on the vine are woolly,
  I noticed that, to-day;
One day more bursts them open fully
  — You know the red turns grey.

III

To-morrow we meet the same then, dearest?
  May I take your hand in mine?
Mere friends are we, — well, friends the merest
  Keep much that I'll resign:

IV

For each glance of the eye so bright and black,
  Though I keep with heart's endeavour, —
Your voice, when you wish the snowdrops back,
  Though it stay in my soul for ever! —

V

Yet I will but say what mere friends say,
  Or only a thought stronger;
I will hold your hand but as long as all may,
  Or so very little longer!

Robert Browning.

PROSPICE

FEAR death? — to feel the fog in my throat,
The mist in my face,
When the snows begin, and the blasts denote
I am nearing the place,
The power of the night, the press of the storm,
The post of the foe;
Where he stands, the Arch Fear in a visible form,
Yet the strong man must go:
For the journey is done and the summit attained
And the barriers fall,
Though a battle's to fight ere the guerdon be gained,
The reward of it all.
I was ever a fighter, so — one fight more,
The best and the last!
I would hate that death bandaged my eyes, and forbore,
And bade me creep past.
No! let me taste the whole of it, fare like my peers
The heroes of old,
Bear the brunt, in a minute pay glad life's arrears
Of pain, darkness and cold.
For sudden the worst turns the best to the brave,
The black minute's at end,
And the elements' rage, the fiend-voices that rave,
Shall dwindle, shall blend,
Shall change, shall become first a peace out of pain,
Then a light, then thy breast,
O thou soul of my soul! I shall clasp thee again,
And with God be the rest!

ROBERT BROWNING.

DEATH

DEATH! that struck when I was most confiding
In my certain faith of joy to be —
Strike again, Time's withered branch dividing
From the fresh root of Eternity!

Leaves upon Time's branch were growing brightly,
Full of sap, and full of silver dew;
Birds beneath its shelter gathered nightly;
Daily round its flowers the wild bees flew.

Sorrow passed, and plucked the golden blossom;
Guilt stripped off the foliage in its pride;
But, within its parent's kindly bosom,
Flowed for ever Life's restoring tide.

Little mourned I for the parted gladness,
For the vacant nest and silent song —
Hope was there, and laughed me out of sadness;
Whispering, "Winter will not linger long!"

And, behold! with tenfold increase blessing,
Spring adorned the beauty-burdened spray;
Wind and rain and fervent heat, caressing,
Lavished glory on that second May!

. . . .

Cruel Death! The young leaves droop and languish;
Evening's gentle air may still restore —
No! the morning's sunshine mocks my anguish —
Time, for me, must never blossom more!

Strike it down, that other boughs may flourish
  Where that perished sapling used to be;
Thus, at least, its mouldering corpse will nourish
  That from which it sprung — Eternity.

EMILY BRONTË.

SAY NOT, THE STRUGGLE NOUGHT AVAILETH

SAY not, the struggle nought availeth,
  The labour and the wounds are vain,
The enemy faints not, nor faileth,
  And as things have been, they remain.

If hopes were dupes, fears may be liars;
  It may be, in yon smoke concealed,
Your comrades chase e'en now the fliers,
  And, but for you, possess the field.

For while the tired waves, vainly breaking,
  Seem here no painful inch to gain,
Far back, through creeks and inlets making,
  Comes silent, flooding in, the main.

And not by eastern windows only,
  When daylight comes, comes in the light;
In front, the sun climbs slow, how slowly,
  But westward, look, the land is bright.

ARTHUR HUGH CLOUGH.

DOVER BEACH

THE sea is calm to-night,
The tide is full, the moon lies fair

Upon the Straits; — on the French coast, the light
Gleams, and is gone; the cliffs of England stand,
Glimmering and vast, out in the tranquil bay.
Come to the window, sweet is the night air!
Only, from the long line of spray
Where the ebb meets the moon-blanch'd sand,
Listen! you hear the grating roar
Of pebbles which the waves suck back, and fling,
At their return, up the high strand,
Begin, and cease, and then again begin,
With tremulous cadence slow, and bring
The eternal note of sadness in.

Sophocles long ago
Heard it on the Ægæan, and it brought
Into his mind the turbid ebb and flow
Of human misery; we
Find also in the sound a thought,
Hearing it by this distant northern sea.
The sea of faith
Was once, too, at the full, and round earth's shore
Lay like the folds of a bright girdle furl'd;
But now I only hear
Its melancholy, long, withdrawing roar,
Retreating to the breath
Of the night-wind down the vast edges drear
And naked shingles of the world.

Ah, love, let us be true
To one another! for the world, which seems
To lie before us like a land of dreams,
So various, so beautiful, so new,
Hath really neither joy, nor love, nor light,

Nor certitude, nor peace, nor help for pain;
And we are here as on a darkling plain
Swept with confused alarms of struggle and flight,
Where ignorant armies clash by night.

MATTHEW ARNOLD.

SHAKESPEARE

OTHERS abide our question. Thou art free.
We ask and ask: Thou smilest and art still,
Out-topping knowledge. For the loftiest hill
That to the stars uncrowns his majesty,
Planting his steadfast footsteps in the sea,
Making the Heaven of Heavens his dwelling-place,
Spares but the cloudy border of his base
To the foil'd searching of mortality;
And thou, who didst the stars and sunbeams know,
Self-school'd, self-scann'd, self-honour'd, self-secure,
Didst walk on Earth unguess'd at. Better so!
All pains the immortal spirit must endure,
All weakness that impairs, all griefs that bow,
Find their sole voice in that victorious brow.

MATTHEW ARNOLD.

A SWEET SONG SUNG NOT YET TO ANY MAN, FROM *THE LIFE AND DEATH OF JASON*

I KNOW a little garden close
Set thick with lily and red rose,
Where I would wander if I might
From dewy dawn to dewy night,
And have one with me wandering.

And though within it no birds sing,
And though no pillared house is there,
And though the apple boughs are bare
Of fruit and blossom, would to God
Her feet upon the green grass trod,
And I beheld them as before.
There comes a murmur from the shore,
And in the place two fair streams are,
Drawn from the purple hills afar,
Drawn down unto the restless sea;
The hills whose flowers ne'er fed the bee,
The shore no ship has ever seen,
Still beaten by the billows green,
Whose murmur comes unceasingly
Unto the place for which I cry.
For which I cry both day and night,
For which I let slip all delight,
That maketh me both deaf and blind
Careless to win, unskilled to find,
And quick to lose what all men seek.
Yet tottering as I am, and weak,
Still have I left a little breath
To seek within the jaws of death
An entrance to that happy place,
To seek the unforgotten face
Once seen, once kissed, once reft from me
Anigh the murmuring of the sea.

William Morris.

DIRGE IN WOODS

A WIND sways the pines,
And below
Not a breath of wild air;
Still as the mosses that glow
On the flooring and over the lines
Of the roots here and there.
The pine-tree drops its dead;
They are quiet, as under the sea.
Overhead, overhead
Rushes life in a race,
As the clouds the clouds chase;
And we go,
And we drop like the fruits of the tree,
Even we,
Even so.

GEORGE MEREDITH.

THE SOLDIER

IF I should die, think only this of me:
That there's some corner of a foreign field
That is for ever England. There shall be
In that rich earth a richer dust concealed;
A dust whom England bore, shaped, made aware,
Gave, once, her flowers to love, her ways to roam,
A body of England's, breathing English air,
Washed by the rivers, blest by suns of home.

And think, this heart, all evil shed away,
A pulse in the eternal mind, no less

Gives somewhere back the thoughts by England
given;
Her sights and sounds; dreams happy as her day;
And laughter, learnt of friends; and gentleness,
In hearts at peace, under an English heaven.

RUPERT BROOKE.

THE SHEPHERDESS

SHE walks — the lady of my delight —
A shepherdess of sheep.
Her flocks are thoughts. She keeps them white
She guards them from the steep.
She feeds them on the fragrant height,
And folds them in for sleep.

She roams maternal hills and bright,
Dark valleys safe and deep.
Into that tender breast at night
The chastest stars may peep.
She walks — the lady of my delight —
A shepherdess of sheep.

She holds her little thoughts in sight,
Though gay they run and leap.
She is so circumspect and right;
She has her soul to keep.
She walks — the lady of my delight —
A shepherdess of sheep.

ALICE MEYNELL.

LEAVETAKING

Pass, thou wild light,
Wild light on peaks that so
Grieve to let go
The day.
Lovely thy tarrying, lovely too is night:
Pass thou away.

Pass, thou wild heart,
Wild heart of youth that still
Hast half a will
To stay.
I grow too old a comrade, let us part.
Pass thou away.

Sir William Watson.

THE SONG OF WANDERING AENGUS

I went out to the hazel wood,
Because a fire was in my head,
And cut and peeled a hazel wand,
And hooked a berry to a thread;
And when white moths were on the wing,
And moth-like stars were flickering out,
I dropped the berry in a stream
And caught a little silver trout.

When I had laid it on the floor
I went to blow the fire a-flame,
But something rustled on the floor,
And someone called me by my name:

It had become a glimmering girl
With apple blossom in her hair
Who called me by my name and ran
And faded through the brightening air.

Though I am old with wandering
Through hollow lands and hilly lands,
I will find out where she has gone,
And kiss her lips and take her hands;
And walk among long dappled grass,
And pluck till time and times are done
The silver apples of the moon,
The golden apples of the sun.

WILLIAM BUTLER YEATS.

THE MOON

THY beauty haunts me heart and soul,
  Oh thou fair Moon, so close and bright;
Thy beauty makes me like the child
  That cries aloud to own thy light:
The little child that lifts each arm
To press thee to her bosom warm.

Though there are birds that sing this night
  With thy white beams across their throats,
Let my deep silence speak for me
  More than for them their sweetest notes:
Who worships thee till music fails,
Is greater than thy nightingales.

W. H. DAVIES.

SONNET: GO, SPEND YOUR PENNY, BEAUTY

Go, spend your penny, Beauty, when you will,
In the grave's darkness let the stamp be lost.
The water still will bubble from the hill,
And April quick the meadows with her ghost;
Over the grass the daffodils will shiver,
The primroses with their pale beauty abound,
The blackbird be a lover and make quiver
With his glad singing the great soul of the ground;
So that if the body rot, it will not matter;
Up in the earth the great game will go on,
The coming of spring and running of the water,
And the young things glad of the womb's darkness
  gone.
And the joy we felt will be a part of the glory
In the Lover's kiss that makes the old couple's story.

JOHN MASEFIELD.

ATLANTIS

WHAT poets sang in Atlantis? Who can tell
The epics of Atlantis or their names?
The sea hath its own murmurs, and sounds not
The secrets of its silences beneath,
And knows not any cadences enfolded
When the last bubbles of Atlantis broke
Among the quieting of its heaving floor.

O, years and tides and leagues and all their billows
Can alter not man's knowledge of men's hearts —
While trees and rocks and clouds include our being

We know the epics of Atlantis still:
A hero gave himself to lesser men,
Who first misunderstood and murdered him,
And then misunderstood and worshipped him;
A woman was lovely and men fought for her,
Towns burnt for her, and men put men in bondage,
But she put lengthier bondage on them all;
A wanderer toiled among all the isles
That fleck this turning star of shifting sea,
Or lonely purgatories of the mind,
In longing for his home or his lost love.

Poetry is founded on the hearts of men:
Though in Nirvana or the Heavenly courts
The principle of beauty shall persist,
Its body of poetry, as the body of man,
Is but a terrene form, a terrene use,
That swifter being will not loiter with;
And, when mankind is dead and the world cold,
Poetry's immortality will pass.

GORDON BOTTOMLEY.

GERANIUMS

STUCK in a bottle on the window-sill,
In the cold gaslight burning gaily red
Against the luminous blue of London night,
These flowers are mine; while somewhere out
of sight
In some black-throated alley's stench and heat,
Oblivious of the racket of the street,
A poor old weary woman lies in bed.

Broken with lust and drink, blear-eyed and ill,
Her battered bonnet nodding on her head,
From a dark arch she clutched my sleeve and said:
"I've sold no bunch to-day, nor touched a bite....
Son, buy six-penn'orth; and 'twill mean a bed."

So blazing gaily red
Against the luminous deeps
Of starless London night,
They burn for my delight:
While somewhere, snug in bed,
A worn old woman sleeps.

And yet to-morrow will these blooms be dead
With all their lively beauty; and to-morrow
May end the light lusts and the heavy sorrow
Of that old body with the nodding head.
The last oath muttered, the last pint drained deep,
She'll sink, as Cleopatra sank, to sleep;
Nor need to barter blossoms for a bed.

WILFRID WILSON GIBSON.

EPITAPH

Written for the Liverpool University Roll of Honour

THESE, who desired to live, went out to death:
Dark underground their golden youth is lying.
We live: and there is brightness in our breath
They could not know — the splendour of their
dying.

LASCELLES ABERCROMBIE.

BOOK II

LAMENT FOR THE MAKARIS

Quhen he wes seik

I THAT in heill[1] wes and glaidnes
Am trublit now with gret seiknes
And feblit with infirmitie;
Timor Mortis conturbat me.

Our plesance heir is all vane glory,
This fals warld is bot transitory,
The flesche is brukle, the Feynd is sle;
Timor Mortis conturbat me.

The stait of man dois change and vary,
Now sound, now seik, now blyth, now sary,
Now dans and mirry, now like to dee;
Timor Mortis conturbat me.

No stait in erd heir standis sickir;[2]
As with the wynd wavis the wickir
So wavis this warldis vanite;
Timor Mortis conturbat me.

Onto the ded gois all estatis,
Princis, prelotis, and potestatis,
Baith riche and pur of all degre;
Timor Mortis conturbat me.

[1] Health. [2] Sure.

He takis the kynchtis in-to feild,
Anarmit vnder helme and scheild;
Wictour he is at all melle;
    Timor Mortis conturbat me.

That strang vnmercifull tyrand
Takis on the moderis breist sowkand
The bab full of benignite;
    Timor Mortis conturbat me.

He takis the campion in the stour,[1]
The capitane closit in the tour,
The lady in bour full of bewte;
    Timor Mortis conturbat me.

He spairis no lord for his piscence,[2]
Na clerk for his intelligence;
His awfull strak may no man fle;
    Timor Mortis conturbat me.

Art magicianis, and astrologgis,
Rethoris, logicians, and theologgis,
Thame helpis no conclusionis sle;
    Timor Mortis conturbat me.

In medecyne the most practicianis,
Lechis, surrigianis, and phisicianis,
Thame-self fra ded may not supple;[3]
    Timor Mortis conturbat me.

I see that makaris[4] amang the laif
Playis heir ther padyanis,[5] syne gois to graif;

[1] Fight. [2] Power. [3] Save. [4] Poets. [5] Pageants.

Sparit is nocht ther faculte;
  Timor Mortis conturbat me.

He hes done petuously devour
The noble Chaucer, of makaris flouir,
The monk of Bery and Grower all thre
  Timor Mortis conturbat me.

The gude Syr Hew of Eglintoun,
Ettrik, Heryot, et Wyntoun
He hes tane out of this cuntre;
  Timor Mortis conturbat me.

That scorpioun fell hes done infek
Maister Iohne Clerk and James Afflek
Fra balat making and trigidë;
  Timor Mortis conturbat me.

Holland and Barbour he has berevit;
Allace, that he nought with ws lewit
Schir Mungo Lokert of the Le!
  Timor Mortis conturbat me.

Clerk of Tranent eik he has tane,
That maid the anteris of Gawane;
Schir Gilbert Hay endit has he;
  Timor Mortis conturbat me.

He has Blind Hary et Sandy Traill
Slaine with his schot of mortall haill,
Quhilk Patrik Johnistoun myght nought fle;
  Timor Mortis conturbat me.

He hes reft Merseir his endite,
That did in luf so lifly write,
So schort, so quyk, of sentence hie;
Timor Mortis conturbat me.

He hes tane Roull of Aberdene,
And gentill Roull of Corstorphin;
Two bettir fallowis did no man se;
Timor Mortis conturbat me.

In Dunfermelyne he has done rovne
With gude Maister Robert Henrisoun;
Schir Iohne the Ros enbrast hes he;
Timor Mortis conturbat me.

And he has now tane, last of aw,
Gud gentill Stobo and Quintyne Schaw,
Of quham all wichtis hes pete;
Timor Mortis conturbat me.

Gud Maister Walter Kennedy
In poynt of dede lyis veraly;
Gret reuth it wer that so suld be;
Timor Mortis conturbat me.

Sen he has all my brether tane
He will naught lat me lif alane;
On forse I man his nyxt pray be;
Timor Mortis conturbat me.

Sen for the deid remeid is non,
Best is that we for deid dispone,

Eftir our deid that lif may we;
Timor Mortis conturbat me.

WILLIAM DUNBAR.

MY MYNDE TO ME A KYNGDOME IS

My mynde to me a kyngdome is;
Such preasente joyes therein I fynd,
That it excells all other blisse
That earth affords or growes by kynde:
Thoughe muche I wante which moste would have
Yet still my mynde forbiddes to crave.

No princely pompe, no wealthy store,
No force to winne the victorye,
No wilye wit to salve a sore,
No shape to feede a loving eye;
To none of these I yielde as thrall:
For why? My mynde doth serve for all.

I see how plenty (surfeits) ofte,
And hasty clymers soon do fall;
I see that those which are alofte,
Mishapp doth threaten moste of all;
They get with toyle, they keepe with feare;
Such cares my mynde could never beare.

Content to live, this is my staye,
I seeke no more than maye suffyse;
I presse to beare no haughty swaye;
Look what I lack, my mynde supplies:
Lo, thus I triumph like a kynge,
Content with that my mynde doth bringe.

Some have too muche, yet still do crave;
  I little have, and seek no more.
They are but poore, though muche they have,
  And I am ryche with lyttle store;
They poore, I ryche; they begge, I gyve;
They lacke, I leave; they pyne, I lyve.

I laughe not at another's losse,
  I grudge not at another's gayne;
No worldly waues my mynde can toss:
  My state at one dothe still remayne:
I fear no foe, I fawn no friende;
I loathe not lyfe, nor dread my ende.

Some weighe their pleasure by theyre luste,
  Theyre wisdom by theyre rage of wyll;
Theyre treasure is theyre only truste,
  A clokèd crafte theyre store of skylle.
But all the pleasure that I fynde
Is to mayntayne a quiet mynde.

My wealthe is healthe and perfect ease;
  My conscience cleere my choice defence;
I neither seeke by brybes to please
  Nor by deceyte to breede offence;
Thus do I lyve, thus will I dye;
Would all did so well as I.

SIR EDWARD DYER.

SONG: WHO FINDS A WOMAN GOOD AND WISE

I

Who finds a Woman good and wise,
A gemme more worth then Pearls hath got:
Her Husbands heart on her relies:
To liue by spoyle he needeth not.
His comfort all his life is she.
No wrong she willingly will doe:
For Woole and Flax her searches be:
And cheerefull hands she puts there to.

II

The Merchant-ship resembling right,
Her food she from a farre doth set.
E're day she wakes, that giue she might
Her maids their taske, her houshold meat.
A field she viewes and that she buyes;
Her hand doth plant a vine yard there,
Her loynes with courage up she tyes;
Her Armes with vigor strengthened are.

III

If in her worke she profit feele,
By night her Candle goes not out;
She puts her finger to the wheele,
Her hand the spindle twirls about.
To such as poore and needy are,
Her hand (yea, both hands) reacheth she:
The winter none of hers doth feare,
For, double cloath'd her houshold be.

IV

She Mantles maketh, wrought by hand:
And silke and purple clothing gets:
Among the Rulers of the Land
(Knowne in the Gate) her husband sits.
For Sale, fine Linnen weaueth she,
And girdles to the Marchant sends:
Renowne and strength her clothings be,
And ioy her later time, attends.

V

She speakes discreetly when she talkes;
The law of Grace her tongue hath learn'd:
She heeds the way her houshold walkes,
And feedeth not on bread un-earn'd.
Her children rise, and blest her call:
Her Husband thus applaudeth her;
Oh! thou hast farre surpast them all,
Though many Daughters thriving are.

VI

Deceitfull Fauour quickly weares,
And Beauty suddenly decayes:
But, if the Lord she truly feares
That woman well deserueth praise.
The fruit her handy-worke obtaines,
Without repining grant her that:
And yeeld her what her labour gaines,
To doe her honour in the Gate.

GEORGE WITHER.

A THANKSGIVING TO GOD FOR HIS HOUSE

LORD, thou hast given me a cell
Wherein to dwell;
A little house, whose humble Roof
Is weather-proof;
Under the sparres of which I lie
Both soft, and drie;
Where Thou my chamber for to ward
Hast set a Guard
Of harmlesse thoughts, to watch and keep
Me, while I sleep.
Low is my porch, as is my Fate,
Both void of state;
And yet the threshold of my doore
Is worn by th' poore,
Who thither come, and freely get
Good words, or meat:
Like as my Parlour, so my Hall
And Kitchin's small:
A little Butterie, and therein
A little Byn,
Which keeps my little loafe of Bread
Unchipt, unflead:
Some brittle sticks of Thorne or Briar
Make me a fire,
Close by whose living coale I sit,
And glow like it.
Lord, I confesse too, when I dine,
The Pulse is Thine,
And all those other Bits, that bee
There plac'd by Thee;

The Worts, the Purslain, and the Messe
Of Water-cresse,
Which of Thy kindnesse Thou hast sent;
And my content
Makes those, and my beloved Beet,
To be more sweet.
'Tis thou that crown'st my glittering Hearth
With guiltlesse mirth;
And giv'st me Wassaile Bowles to drink,
Spic'd to the brink.
Lord, 'tis thy plenty-dropping hand,
That soiles my land;
And giv'st me, for my Bushel sowne,
Twice ten for one.
Thou mak'st my teeming Hen to lay
Her egg each day:
Besides my healthful Ewes to beare
Me twins each yeare:
The while the conduits of my Kine
Run Creame, (for Wine.)
All these, and better Thou dost send
Me, to this end,
That I should render, for my part,
A thankfull heart;
Which, fir'd with incense, I resigne,
As wholly Thine;
But the acceptance, that must be,
My Christ, by Thee.

ROBERT HERRICK.

THE EXEQUY

Accept, thou Shrine of my dead Saint,
Instead of Dirges this complaint;
And for sweet flowres to crown thy hearse,
Receive a strew of weeping verse
From thy griev'd friend, whom thou might'st see
Quite melted into tears for thee.

Dear loss! since thy untimely fate,
My task hath been to meditate
On thee, on thee: thou art the book,
The library, whereon I look
Though almost blind. For thee (lov'd clay)
I languish out not live the day,
Using no other exercise
But what I practise with mine eyes:
By which wet glasses, I find out
How lazily time creeps about
To one that mourns: this, onely this
My exercise and bus'ness is:
So I compute the weary houres
With sighs dissolved into showres.

Nor wonder if my time go thus
Backward and most preposterous;
Thou hast benighted me, thy set
This Eve of blackness did beget,
Who was't my day, (though overcast
Before thou had'st thy Noon-tide past)
And I remember must in tears,
Thou scarce had'st seen so many years

As Day tells houres. By thy cleer Sun
My love and fortune first did run;
But thou wilt never more appear
Folded within my Hemisphear,
Since both thy light and motion
Like a fled Star is fall'n and gon,
And twixt me and my soules dear wish
The earth now interposed is,
Which such a strange eclipse doth make
As ne're was read in Almanake.

I could allow thee for a time
To darken me and my sad Clime,
Were it a month, a year, or ten,
I would thy exile live till then;
And all that space my mirth adjourn,
So thou wouldst promise to return;
And putting off thy ashy shrowd
At length disperse this sorrows cloud.

But woe is me! the longest date
Too narrow is to calculate
These empty hopes: never shall I
Be so much blest as to descry
A glimpse of thee, till that day come
Which shall the earth to cinders doome,
And a fierce Feaver must calcine
The body of this world like thine,
(My Little World!) That fit of fire
Once off, our bodies shall aspire
To our soules bliss: then we shall rise,
And view our selves with cleerer eyes

In that calm Region, where no night
Can hide us from each others sight.

Mean time, thou hast her earth: much good
May my harm do thee. Since it stood
With Heavens will I might not call
Her longer mine, I give thee all
My short-liv'd right and interest
In her, whom living I lov'd best:
With a most free and bounteous grief,
I give thee what I could not keep.
Be kind to her, and prethee look
Thou write into thy Dooms-day book
Each parcell of this Rarity
Which in thy Casket shrin'd doth ly:
See that thou make thy reck'ning streight,
And yield her back again by weight;
For thou must audit on thy trust
Each graine and atome of this dust,
As thou wilt answer *Him* that lent,
Not gave thee my dear Monument.

So close the ground, and 'bout her shade
Black curtains draw, my *Bride* is laid.

Sleep on, my *Love* in thy cold bed
Never to be disquieted!
My last good night! Thou wilt not wake
Till I thy fate shall overtake:
Till age, or grief, or sickness must
Marry my body to that dust
It so much loves; and fill the room
My heart keeps empty in thy Tomb.

Stay for me there; I will not faile
To meet thee in that hallow Vale.
And think not much of my delay;
I am already on the way,
And follow thee with all the speed
Desire can make, or sorrows breed.
Every minute is a short degree,
And ev'ry houre a step towards thee.
At night when I betake to rest,
Next morn I rise neerer my West
Of life, almost by eight houres saile,
Then when sleep breath'd his drowsie gale.

Thus from the Sun my Bottom stears,
And my dayes Compass downward bears:
Nor labour I to stemme the tide
Through which to *Thee* I swiftly glide.

'Tis true, with shame and grief I yield,
Thou like the Vann first took'st the field,
And gotten hast the victory
In thus adventuring to dy
Before me, whose more years might crave
A just precedence in the grave.
But heark! My Pulse, like a soft Drum
Beats my approch, tells *Thee* I come;
And slow howere my marches be,
I shall at last sit down by *Thee*.

The thought of this bids me go on,
And wait my dissolution
With hope and comfort. *Dear* (forgive
The crime), I am content to live

Divided, with but half a heart,
Till we shall meet and never part.

HENRY KING.

LYCIDAS

YET once more, O ye laurels, and once more,
Ye Myrtles brown, with Ivy never-sear,
I com to pluck your Berries harsh and crude,
And with forc'd fingers rude,
Shatter your leaves before the mellowing year.
Bitter constraint, and sad occasion dear,
Compels me to disturb your season due:
For Lycidas is dead, dead ere his prime,
Young Lycidas, and hath not left his peer:
Who would not sing for Lycidas? he knew
Himself to sing, and build the lofty rhyme.
He must not flote upon his watry bear
Unwept, and welter to the parching wind,
Without the meed of som melodious tear.
Begin then, Sisters of the sacred well,
That from beneath the sea of Jove doth spring,
Begin, and somwhat loudly sweep the string.
Hence with denial vain, and coy excuse,
So may som gentle Muse
With lucky words favour my destin'd Urn,
And as he passes turn,
And bid fair peace be to my sable shrowd.
For we were nurst upon the self-same hill,
Fed the same flock, by fountain, shade, and rill.
Together both, ere the high Lawns appear'd
Under the opening eye-lids of the morn,
We drove a-field, and both together heard

What time the Gray-fly winds her sultry horn,
Batt'ning our flocks with the fresh dews of night,
Oft till the Star that rose, at Ev'ning, bright
Toward Heav'ns descent had slop'd his westering wheel.
Mean while the Rural ditties were not mute,
Temper'd to th' Oaten Flute;
Rough Satyrs danc'd, and Fauns with clov'n heel,
From the glad sound would not be absent long,
And old Damœtas lov'd to hear our song.
But O the heavy change, now thou art gon,
Now thou art gon, and never must return!
Thee Shepherd, thee the Woods, and desert Caves
With wild Thyme and the gadding Vine o'regrown,
And all their echoes mourn.
The Willows, and the Hazle Copses green,
Shall now no more be seen,
Fanning their joyous Leaves to thy soft layes.
As killing as the Canker to the Rose,
Or Taint-worm to the weanling Herds that graze,
Or Frost to Flowers, that their gay wardrop wear,
When first the White thorn blows;
Such, Lycidas, thy loss to Shepherds ear.
Where were ye Nymphs when the remorseless deep
Clos'd o're the head of your lov'd Lycidas?
For neither were ye playing on the steep,
Where your old Bards, the famous Druids ly,
Nor on the shaggy top of Mona high,
Nor yet where Deva spreads her wisard stream:
Ay me, I fondly dream!
Had ye bin there — for what could that have don?
What could the Muse her self that Orpheus bore,

The Muse her self, for her inchanting son
Whom Universal nature did lament,
When by the rout that made the hideous roar,
His goary visage down the stream was sent,
Down the swift Hebrus to the Lesbian shore.
  Alas! what boots it with uncessant care
To tend the homely slighted Shepherds trade,
And strictly meditate the thankles Muse,
Were it not better don as others use,
To sport with Amaryllis in the shade,
Or with the tangles of Neæra's hair?
Fame is the spur that the clear spirit doth raise
(That last infirmity of Noble mind)
To scorn delights, and live laborious dayes;
But the fair Guerdon when we hope to find,
And think to burst out into sudden blaze,
Comes the blind Fury with th' abhorred shears,
And slits the thin spun life. But not the praise,
Phœbus repli'd, and touch'd my trembling ears;
Fame is no plant that grows on mortal soil,
Nor in the glistering foil
Set off to th' world, nor in broad rumour lies,
But lives and spreds aloft by those pure eyes,
And perfet witnes of all judging Jove;
As he pronounces lastly on each deed,
Of so much fame in Heav'n expect thy meed.
  O Fountain Arethuse, and thou honour'd floud,
Smooth-sliding Mincius, crown'd with vocall reeds,
That strain I heard was of a higher mood:
But now my Oate proceeds,
And listens to the Herald of the Sea
That came in Neptune's plea,
He ask'd the Waves, and ask'd the Fellon winds,

What hard mishap hath doom'd this gentle swain?
And question'd every gust of rugged wings
That blows from off each beaked Promontory,
They knew not of his story,
And sage Hippotades their answer brings,
That not a blast was from his dungeon stray'd,
The Ayr was calm, and on the level brine
Sleek Panope with all her sisters play'd.
It was that fatall and perfidious Bark
Built in th' eclipse, and rigg'd with curses dark,
That sunk so low that sacred head of thine.
  Next Camus, reverend Sire, went footing slow,
His Mantle hairy, and his Bonnet sedge,
Inwrought with figures dim, and on the edge
Like to that sanguine flower inscrib'd with woe.
Ah; who hath reft (quoth he) my dearest pledge?
Last came, and last did go,
The Pilot of the Galilean lake,
Two massy Keyes he bore of metals twain,
(The Golden opes, the Iron shuts amain)
He shook his Mitr'd locks, and stern bespake,
How well could I have spar'd for thee, young swain,
Enow of such as for their bellies sake,
Creep and intrude, and climb into the fold?
Of other care they little reck'ning make,
Then how to scramble at the shearers feast,
And shove away the worthy bidden guest.
Blind mouthes! that scarce themselves know how to hold
A Sheep-hook, or have learn'd ought els the least
That to the faithfull Herdmans art belongs!
What recks it them? What need they? They are sped;

And when they list, their lean and flashy songs
Grate on their scrannel Pipes of wretched straw,
The hungry Sheep look up, and are not fed,
But swoln with wind, and the rank mist they draw,
Rot inwardly, and foul contagion spread:
Besides what the grim Woolf with privy paw
Daily devours apace, and nothing sed,
But that two-handed engine at the door,
Stands ready to smite once, and smite no more.
  Return, Alpheus, the dread voice is past,
That shrunk thy streams; Return Sicilian Muse,
And call the Vales, and bid them hither cast
Their Bels, and Flourets of a thousand hues.
Ye valleys low, where the milde whispers use,
Of shades and wanton winds, and gushing brooks
On whose fresh lap the swart Star sparely looks,
Throw hither all your quaint enameld eyes,
That on the green terf suck the honied showres,
And purple all the ground with vernal flowres.
Bring the rathe Primrose that forsaken dies.
The tufted Crow-toe, and pale Gessamine,
The white Pink, and the Pansie freakt with jeat,
The glowing Violet,
The Musk-rose, and the well attir'd Woodbine.
With Cowslips wan that hang the pensive hed,
And every flower that sad embroidery wears:
Bid Amaranthus all his beauty shed,
And Daffadillies fill their cups with tears,
To strew the Laureat Herse where Lycid lies.
For so to interpose a little ease,
Let our frail thoughts dally with false surmise.
Ay me! Whilst thee the shores, and sounding Seas
Wash far away, where ere thy bones are hurld,

Whether beyond the stormy Hebrides,
Where thou perhaps under the whelming tide
Visit'st the bottom of the monstrous world;
Or whether thou to our moist vows deny'd,
Sleep'st by the fable of Bellerus old,
Where the great vision of the guarded Mount
Looks toward Namancos and Bayona's hold;
Look homeward Angel now, and melt with ruth.
And, O ye Dolphins, waft the haples youth.
  Weep no more, woful Shepherds weep no more,
For Lycidas your sorrow is not dead,
Sunk though he be beneath the watry floar,
So sinks the day-star in the Ocean bed,
And yet anon repairs his drooping head,
And tricks his beams, and with new spangled Ore,
Flames in the forehead of the morning sky:
So Lycidas sunk low, but mounted high,
Through the dear might of him that walk'd the waves
Where other groves, and other streams along,
With Nectar pure his oozy Lock's he laves,
And hears the unexpressive nuptiall Song,
In the blest Kingdoms meek of joy and love.
There entertain him all the Saints above,
In solemn troops, and sweet Societies
That sing, and singing in their glory move,
And wipe the tears for ever from his eyes.
Now Lycidas the Shepherds weep no more;
Hence forth thou art the Genius of the shore,
In thy large recompense, and shalt be good
To all that wander in that perilous flood.
  Thus sang the uncouth Swain to th' Okes and rills,

While the still morn went out with Sandals gray,
He touch'd the tender stops of various Quills,
With eager thought warbling his Dorick lay:
And now the Sun had stretch'd out all the hills,
And now was dropt into the Western bay;
At last he rose, and twitch'd his Mantle blew:
To morrow to fresh Woods, and Pastures new.

JOHN MILTON.

WISHES

To his (supposed) Mistress

WHOE'RE she be,
That not impossible she
That shall Command my Heart and me;

Where're she lye,
Lock't up from mortal Eye,
In the shady Leaves of Destiny;

Till that ripe Birth
Of studied Fate stand forth,
And teach her fair steps to our Earth;

Till that Divine
Idea take a shrine
Of Chrystal flesh, through which to shine:

Meet you her my wishes,
Bespeak her to my blisses,
And be ye calld my absent kisses.

I wish her Beauty,
That ows not all its Duty
To gaudy Tire, or glistring shoo-ty,

Something more than
Taffeta or Tissew can,
Or rampant Feather, or rich Fan.

More then the spoil
Of shop, or silkworms Toil,
Or a bought Blush, or a set smile.

A Face that's best
By its own Beauty drest,
And can alone command the rest.

A Face made up
Out of no other shop,
Than what Natures white hand sets ope.

A Cheek where Youth,
And Blood, with Pen of Truth
Write, what the Reader sweetly ru'th.

A Cheek, where grows
More then a Morning Rose:
Which to no Box his Being owes.

Lips, where all day
A Lovers Kiss may play,
Yet carry nothing thence away.

Looks that oppress
Their richest Tires, but dresse
And cloath their simplest Nakedness.

Eyes, that displaces
The Neighbour Diamond, and out-faces
That Sun-shine by their own sweet Graces.

Tresses, that wear
Jewels, but to declare
How much themselves more precious are.

Whose native Ray,
Can tame the wanton Day
Of Gems, that in their bright shades play.

Each Ruby there
Or Pearl that dare appear,
Be its own blush, be its own Tear.

A well-tam'd Heart,
For whose more Noble smart
Love may be long choosing a Dart.

Eyes, that bestow
Full Quivers on Loves Bow;
Yet pay less Arrows then they owe.

Smiles, that can warm
The Blood, yet teach a Charm,
That Chastity shall take no harm.

Blushes, that bin
The burnish of no sin,
Nor Flames of ought too hot within.

Joys, that confess
Virtue their Mistresse,
And have no other Head to dress.

Fears, fond and slight
As the coy Brides, when Night
First does the longing Lover right.

Tears, quickly fled,
And vain, as those are shed
For a dying Maidenhead.

Days, that need borrow,
No part of their good Morrow,
From a fore spent night of sorrow.

Days, that in spight
Of Darkness, by the Light
Of a clear mind are Day all Night.

Nights, sweet as they,
Made short by Lovers play,
Yet long by th' absence of the Day.

Life, that dares send,
A challenge to his end,
And when it comes say *Welcome, Friend.*

Sydneian showers
Of sweet discourse, whose pow'rs
Can Crown old Winters head with Flow'rs.

Soft silken Hours,
Open Sunnes; shady Bow'rs,
'Bove all; Nothing within that low'rs.

Whate'r Delight
Can make Days forehead bright,
Or give Down to the Wings of Night.

In her whole frame,
Have Nature all the Name,
Art and Ornament the shame.

Her flattery,
Picture and Poesie,
Her Counsel her own Vertue be.

I wish, her store
Of worth, may leave her poor
Of wishes; and I wish — no more.

Now if Time knows
That her whose radiant Brows,
Weave them a Garland of my vows;

Her whose just Bayes,
My future hopes can raise,
A Trophy to her present praise;

Her that dares be,
What these Lines wish to see:
I seek no further, it is she.

'Tis she, and here
Lo I uncloath and clear
My wishes cloudy Character.

May she enjoy it,
Whose Merit dare apply it,
But Modestly dares still deny it.

Such Worth as this is,
Shall fix my flying wishes,
And determine them to kisses.

Let her full Glory,
My Fancies, fly before ye,
Be ye my fictions; but her story.

RICHARD CRASHAW.

ON THE ASSUMPTION

HARK! she is call'd, the parting houre is come.
Take thy farewell, poore world! Heav'n must goe
home.
A peece of Heav'nly Earth, purer and brighter
Than the chast stars, whose choice lamps come tc
light her,
While through the Christall orbes, clearer than they,
She climbs; and makes a farre more milky way;
She's call'd. Harke how the deare immortall Dove
Sighes to his silver mate. *Rise up my Love,*

Rise up my faire, my spotlesse one,
The winter's past, the Rain is gone:
The spring is come, the Flowers appeare,
No sweets but thou are wanting here.
Come away my love,
Come away my dove
Cast off delay:
The Court of Heav'n is come,
To waite upon thee home;
Come, come away.
— The Flowers appeare,
Or quickly would, were thou once here.
The spring is come; or if it stay,
'Tis to keepe time with thy delay.
The raine is gone, Except as much as wee,
Detain in needfull Teares, to weep the want of
thee.
— The winters past,
Or if he make lesse haste,
His answer is, why she does so,
If summer come not, how can winter go?
Come away, come away,
The shrill winds chide, the waters weep thy stay,
The fountaines murmure; and each loftiest Tree,
Bowes lowest his leavy top, to looke for thee.
Come away my love,
Come away my dove, *etc.*
She's call'd again; And will she goe?
When Heav'n bids come, who can say No?
Heav'n calls her, and she must away,
Heav'n will not, and she cannot stay.
Goe then, goe (*glorious*) on the golden wings
Of the bright youth of Heav'n that sings

Under so great a burden, *Goe*,
Since thy dread *Son* will have it so,
And while thou goest, our Song and wee,
Will as wee may reach after thee.
    Haile, holy Queen, of humble Hearts!
    We in thy praise wil have our parts.
And though thy dearest lookes must now be ligh
To none but the blest heavens, whose bright
Beholders lost in sweet delight,
Feed for ever their faire sight
With those divinest eyes, which wee
And our darke world no more shall see;
Though our poore joyes are parted so,
Yet shall our lips never let goe
Thy gracious name, but to the last
Our loving song shall hold it fast.
    Thy precious Name shall bee
    Thy self to us, and wee
    With holy care will keep it by us.
        Wee to the last
        Will hold it fast;
    And no Assumption shall deny us.
        All the sweetest showers
        Of our fairest flowers,
    Will wee strow upon it;
        Though our sweets cannot make
        It sweeter, they can take
    Themselves new sweetnesse from it.
        Maria, Men and Angels sing,
        Maria, Mother of our King.
Live, *Rosie Princesse*, *live*, and may the bright
Crowne of a most incomparable light
Embrace thy radiant browes: O may the best

Of everlasting joyes bath thy white brest.
Live our chaste love. The holy mirth
Of heav'n, the Humble pride of Earth.
Live, crowne of women, Queen of men;
Live Mistrisse of our Song; And when
Our weake desires have done their best,
Sweet Angels come, and sing the Rest.

RICHARD CRASHAW.

ON THE DEATH OF MR. CRASHAW

OET and Saint! to thee alone are given
he two most sacred Names of Earth and Heav'n.
he hard and rarest Union which can be
ext that of Godhead with Humanitie.
ong did the Muses banisht Slaves abide,
nd built vain Pyramids to mortal pride;
ike Moses Thou (though Spells and Charms withstand)
ast brought them nobly home back to their Holy Land.
Ah wretched We, Poets of Earth! but Thou
'ert Living the same Poet which thou'rt Now.
'hilst Angels sing to thee their ayres divine,
nd joy in an applause so great as thine.
qual society with them to hold,
hou needst not make new Songs, but say the Old.
nd they (kind Spirits!) shall all rejoyce to see
ow little less then They, Exalted Man may be.
till the old Heathen Gods in Numbers dwell,
he Heav'enliest thing on Earth still keeps up Hell.
or have we yet quite purg'd the Christian Land;
till Idols here, like Calves at Bethel stand.

And though Pans Death long since all Oracles broke
Yet still in Rhyme the Fiend Apollo spoke:
Nay, with the worst of Heathen dotage We
(Vain men!) the Monster Woman deifie;
Find Stars, and tye our Fates there in a Face
And Paradise in them by whom we lost it, place.
What different faults corrupt our Muses thus?
Wanton as Girles, as old Wives, Fabulous!
Thy spotless Muse, like Mary, did contain
The boundless Godhead; she did well disdain
That her eternal Verse employ'd should be
On a less subject than Eternitie;
And for a sacred Mistress scorn'd to take,
By her whom God himself scorn'd not his Spouse to
make.
It (in a kind) her Miracle did do;
A fruitful Mother was, and Virgin too.
How well (blest Swan) did Fate contrive thy
death;
And make thee render up thy tuneful breath
In thy great Mistress Arms? thou most divine
And richest Offe'ring of Loretto's Shrine!
Where like some holy Sacrifice t'expire,
A Fever burns thee, and Love lights the Fire.
Angels (they say) brought the fam'ed Chappel there
And bore the sacred Load in Triumph through the
air.
'Tis surer much they brought thee there, and They
And Thou, their charge, went singing all the way.
Pardon, my Mother Church, if I consent
That Angels led him when from thee he went,
For even in Error sure no Danger is
When joyn'd with so much Piety as His.

Ah, mighty God, with shame I speak't, and grief,
Ah, that our greatest Faults were in Belief!
And our weak Reason were ev'en weaker yet,
Rather than thus our Wills too strong for it.
His Faith perhaps in some nice Tenets might
Be wrong; his Life, I'm sure, was in the right.
And I my self a Catholick will be,
So far at least, great Saint, to Pray to thee.
Hail, Bard Triumphant! and some care bestow
On us, the Poet's Militant Below!
Oppos'ed by our old En'emy, adverse Chance,
Attacqu'ed by Envy, and by Ignorance,
Enchain'ed by Beauty, tortur'ed by Desires,
Expos'ed by Tyrant-Love to savage Beasts and Fires.
Thou from low earth in nobler Flames didst rise,
And like Elijah, mount alive the Skies.
Elisha-like (but with a wish much less,
More fit thy Greatness, and my Littleness)
Lo here I beg (I whom thou once didst prove
So Humble to Esteem, so Good to Love)
Not that thy Spirit might on me Doubled be,
I ask but half thy mighty Spirit for Me.
And when my Muse soars with so strong a Wing,
'Twill learn of things Divine, and first of Thee to
sing.

ABRAHAM COWLEY.

TO HIS COY MISTRESS

HAD we but World enough, and Time,
This coyness Lady were no crime.
We would sit down, and think which way
To walk, and pass our long Loves Day.

Thou by the Indian Ganges side
Should'st Rubies find: I by the Tide
Of Humber would complain. I would
Love you ten years before the Flood:
And you should if you please refuse
Till the Conversion of the Jews.
My vegetable Love should grow
Vaster then Empires, and more slow.
An hundred years should go to praise
Thine Eyes, and on thy Forehead Gaze.
Two hundred to adore each Breast:
But thirty thousand to the rest.
An Age at least to every part,
And the last Age should show your Heart.
For Lady you deserve this State;
Nor would I love at lower rate.
  But at my back I alwaies hear
Times winged Charriot hurrying near:
And yonder all before us lye
Desarts of vast Eternity.
Thy Beauty shall no more be found;
Nor, in thy marble Vault, shall sound
My ecchoing Song: then Worms shall try
That long preserv'd Virginity:
And your quaint Honour turn to dust;
And into ashes all my Lust.
The Grave's a fine and private place,
But none I think do there embrace.
  Now therefore, while the youthful hew
Sits on thy skin like morning glew,
And while thy willing Soul transpires
At every pore with instant Fires,
Now let us sport us while we may;

And now, like am'rous birds of prey,
Rather at once our Time devour,
Than languish in his slow-chapt pow'r.
Let us roll all our Strength and all
Our sweetness, up into one Ball:
And tear our pleasures with rough strife,
Thorough the Iron gates of Life.
Thus, though we cannot make our Sun
Stand still, yet we will make him run.

ANDREW MARVELL.

THE GARDEN

How vainly men themselves amaze
To win the Palm, the Oke, or Bayes,
And their uncessant Labours see
Crown'd from some single Herb or Tree,
Whose short and narrow verged Shad
Does prudently their Toyles upbraid;
While all the Flow'rs and all Trees do close
To weave the Garlands of repose.

Fair quiet, have I found thee here
And Innocence thy Sister dear!
Mistaken long, I sought you then
In busie Companies of Men.
Your sacred Plants, if here below,
Only among the Plants will grow:
Society is all but rude,
To this delicious Solitude.

No white nor red was ever seen
So am'rous as this lovely green.

Fond Lovers, cruel as their Flame,
Cut in these Trees their Mistress name:
Little, Alas, they know, or heed
How far these Beauties Hers exceed!
Fair Trees! wheres'eer your barkes I wound,
No Name shall but your own be found.

When we have run our Passions heat,
Love hither makes his best retreat.
The Gods, that mortal Beauty chase,
Still in a Tree did end their race.
Apollo hunted Daphne so,
Only that She might Laurel grow.
And Pan did after Syrinx speed,
Not as a Nymph, but for a Reed.

What wond'rous Life is this I lead!
Ripe Apples drop about my head;
The Luscious Clusters of the Vine
Upon my Mouth do crush their Wine;
The Nectaren and curious Peach,
Into my hands themselves do reach;
Stumbling on Melons, as I pass,
Ensnar'd with Flow'rs, I fall on Grass.

Mean while the Mind, from pleasure less;
Withdraws into its happiness,
The Mind, that Ocean where each kind
Does streight its own resemblance find;
Yet it creates, transcending these,
Far other Worlds, and other Seas;
Annihilating all that's made
To a green Thought in a green Shade.

Here at the Fountains sliding foot,
Or at some Fruit-tree's mossy root,
Casting the Bodies Vest aside,
My Soul into the boughs does glide;
There like a Bird it sits and sings,
Then whets, and combs its silver Wings:
And, till prepar'd for longer flight,
Waves in its Plumes the various Light.

Such was that happy Garden-state
While Man there walk'd without a Mate:
After a Place so pure and sweet,
What other Help could yet be meet!
But 'twas beyond a Mortal's share
To wander solitary there:
Two Paradises 'twere in one,
To live in Paradise alone.

How well the skilful Gardner drew
Of flow'rs and herbes this Dial new;
Where from above the milder Sun
Does through a fragrant Zodiac run;
And, as it works th' industrious Bee
Computes its time as well as we.
How could such sweet and wholesome Hours
Be reckon'd, but with herbs and flow'rs!

ANDREW MARVELL.

REGENERATION

I

A Ward, and still in bonds, one day
I stole abroad,
It was high-spring, and all the way
Primros'd, and hung with shade;
Yet, was it frost within,
And surly winds
Blasted my infant buds, and sinne
Like Clouds ecclips'd my mind.

II

Storm'd thus; I straight perceiv'd my spring
Meere stage, and show,
My walke a monstrous, mountain'd thing
Rough-cast with Rocks, and snow;
And as a Pilgrims Eye
Far from reliefe,
Measures the melancholy skye
Then drops, and rains for griefe,

III

So sigh'd I upwards still, at last
'Twixt steps, and falls
I reach'd the pinacle, where plac'd
I found a paire of scales,
I tooke them up and lay'd
In th'one late paines,
The other smoake, and pleasures weigh'd
But prov'd the heavier graines;

IV

With that, some cryed, Away; straight I
Obey'd, and led
Full East, a faire, fresh field could spy:
Some call'd it, Jacobs Bed;
A Virgin-soile, which no
Rude feet ere trod,
Where (since he stept there,) only go
Prophets, and friends of God.

V

Here, I repos'd; but scarse well set,
A grove descryed
Of stately height, whose branches met
And mixt on every side;
I entred, and once in
(Amaz'd to see't,)
Found all was chang'd, and a new spring
Did all my senses greet;

VI

The unthrift Sunne shot vitall gold
A thousand peeces,
And heaven its azure did unfold
Chequr'd with snowie fleeces,
The aire was all in spice
And every bush
A garland wore; Thus fed my Eyes
But all the Eare lay hush.

VII

Only a little Fountain lent
    Some use for Eares,
And on the dumbe shades language spent
  The Musick of her teares;
  I drew her neere, and found
    The Cisterne full
Of divers stones, some bright, and round
  Others ill-shap'd, and dull.

VIII

The first (pray marke), as quick as light
    Danc'd through the floud,
But, th'last more heavy then the night
  Nail'd to the Center stood;
  I wonder'd much, but tyr'd
    At last with thought,
My restless Eye that still desir'd
  As strange an object brought;

IX

It was a banke of flowers, where I descried
    (Though 'twas mid-day.)
Some fast asleepe, others broad-eyed
  And taking in the Ray,
  Here musing long, I heard
    A rushing wind
Which still increas'd, but whence it stirr'd
  No where I could not find;

X

I turn'd me round, and to each shade
Dispatch'd an Eye,
To see, if any leafe had made
Least motion, or Reply,
But while I listning sought
My mind to ease
By knowing, where 'twas, or where not,
It whisper'd; Where I please.

Lord, then said I, On me one breath,
And let me dye before my death!

Cant. Cap. v. ver. 17

Arise O North, and come thou South-wind, and blow upon my garden, that the spices thereof may flow out.

HENRY VAUGHAN.

EVENING QUATRAINS

I

THE Day's grown old, the fainting Sun
Has but a little way to run,
And yet his Steeds, with all his skill,
Scarce lug the Chariot down the Hill.

II

With Labour spent, and Thirst opprest,
Whilst they strain hard to gain the West,
From Fetlocks hot drops melted light,
Which turn to Meteors in the Night.

III

The Shadows now so long do grow,
That Brambles like tall Cedars show,
Mole-hills seem Mountains, and the Ant
Appears a monstrous Elephant.

IV

A very little little Flock
Shades thrice the ground that it would stock;
Whilst the small Stripling following them,
Appears a mighty Polypheme.

V

These being brought into the Fold,
And by the thrifty Master told,
He thinks his Wages are well paid,
Since none are either lost, or stray'd.

VI

Now lowing Herds are each-where heard,
Chains rattle in the Villains Yard,
The Cart's on Tayl set down to rest,
Bearing on high the Cuckolds Crest.

VII

The hedg is stript, the Clothes brought in,
Nought's left without should be within,
The Bees are hiv'd, and hum their Charm,
Whilst every House does seem a Swarm.

VIII

The Cock now to the Roost is prest:
For he must call up all the rest;
The Sow's fast pegg'd within the Sty,
To still her squeaking Progeny.

IX

Each one has had his Supping Mess,
The Cheese is put into the Press,
The Pans and Bowls clean scalded all,
Rear'd up against the Milk-house Wall.

X

And now on Benches all are sat
In the cool Air to sit and chat,
Till Phœbus, dipping in the West,
Shall lead the World the way to Rest.

CHARLES COTTON.

ENDYMION AND DIANA

I

On Bed of Flowers Endymion sleeping lay,
Tir'd with the Toyl of a long Summers-day,
Whilst softest Winds, and Season of the Year,
Agree to make his Graces all appear:
The wanton Cupids in a Troop descend,
Play with his Horn, and do his Bow unbend,
And Love, this small Assembly came to grace,
Wond'ring to see the Shepherd's charming Face.

II

The Air to view him could not chuse but stay,
And with his Locks upon his Forehead play.
The Cupids round about him were employ'd,
While some did into Curls his Hair divide;
Others of Flowers, of which they'd pick'd and brought
Their Hands-full, many various Fancies wrought;
Fetters, as if they would his Feet restrain,
Wreaths for his Head, and for his Wrists a Chai

III

This, with his Lips compar'd, a Piony,
Another, a Vermilion Emony;
Then at his Cheeks a Rose and Lily try'd,
The Rose it faded, and the Lily dy'd.
Still was the Wind, the Meadow, Field and Grov
The very Waters were not heard to move.
All things were hush'd, and did a silence keep,
As some had whisper'd, Peace, here's Love aslee

IV

When the bright Goddess of the lowest Orb,
Deck'd with the Rays of Sol her absent Lord,
Of Heav'n the dusky Mantle did unfold,
And silently Earth's wondrous Scene behold;
Then having first disperst in little Showres
The Pearly Dew upon the Grass and Flowres;
Spying this place which such delights could yield,
Came down to take the Pleasure of the Field.

V

Quickly the little Cupids disappear,
So soon as e're the Goddess drew but near;
Who seeing the sleeping Youth alone, she stays,
With Passion on his lovely face to gaze:
Till Virgin Modesty quench'd her bold Flame;
Of Folly then convinc'd, she blush'd for shame;
  And just was turning to have quit the place,
  But was recall'd by that alluring Face.

VI

In through her Eyes a Spark slid to her Heart,
Which fir'd her Soul; Nor could she thence depart,
But nearer by degrees, her steps does guide,
Till she sate down close by the Shepherd's side;
And of the Flowers with which the Cupids plaid,
When Gyves, and Fetters they in Sport had made:
  Such Snares she wove, her self was in them ta'ne,
  And as the Shepherd's Captive, wore his Chaine.

VII

Straight on his hand an eager Kiss she prest,
Then thousand on his Lips, Cheeks, Eyes and
        Breast;
Nor in this Transport could her self contain,
'Till she with Kisses wak'd the sleeping Swain,
Who being amaz'd at that Cœlestial Light,
With Reverence trembled at the Glorious Sight:
  He would have gone, when fre'd from his Sur-
        prise,
  But tho' he strove, she would not let him rise.

VIII

Fair Sleeper, would'st thou go, said she, so soon,
Be not afraid, Behold it is the Moon,
That comes to sport with thee in this sweet Grove,
Guided by Fate, Necessity and Love:
Be not disturb'd at this unusual Sight,
We silently in Joys will spend the Night:
  But if thou tell what I to thee have sed,
  Expect Heav'ns utmost Vengeance on thy Head.

IX

Goddess of Night, that tak'st from Sol thy Flame,
I, said the Youth, a silly Shepherd am;
But if thou promise me in Heav'n a Place,
To be translated hence from Humane Race,
Then of my Faith thou may'st assured live,
Of which this Mantle as a Pledge I'll give;
  The same my Father Etho gave the Night,
  That he his Faith to Calice did plight.

X

This said, his Mantle quickly he unbound,
That was with Flowers of Pearl embroyder'd round,
Which then he wore o'er his left shoulder slung,
And with two Ends beneath his right Arm hung;
Gave it the Goddess, who had now thrown by
All Sense of Honour and of Modesty:
  And like a Frost-nip'd Flower, she by his Charms
  Being thus o'rcome, dropt down into his Arms.

XI

Never more closely does the tender Vine,
About the shady Elm her Lover twine,

Nor the green Ivie more Affection bring
When she about her Pine does kindly cling,
Than these two vigorous Lovers there exprest,
Love having shot his Fire through eithers Breast:
With all their Art and Industry they strove,
How they might then enjoy their fill of Love.

XII

Thus Whilst in Wantonness they spend the Night,
And use all Skill that might promote delight;
Now tir'd with what before they ne'er had try'd,
These happy Lovers rested satisfy'd:
When Fair Diana lifting up her Eyes,
Accused her cruel Stars and Destinyes,
That her so long through so much Error drew,
And let her rather Beasts than Love pursue.

XIII

Ah, Fool! said she, How I too late repent,
That to the woods I e're a Hunting went;
How many Years have I consum'd since then,
Which I must never think to see agen?
How many pretious Minutes ev'ry Day,
Did I in that mad Pastime fool away!
And how much better is one sweet Embrace
Than all the toylsome pleasures of the Chase?

PHILIP AYRES.

A NIGHT-PIECE ON DEATH

By the blue Tapers trembling Light,
No more I waste the wakeful Night,

Intent with endless view to pore
The Schoolmen and the Sages o'er:
Their Books from Wisdom widely stray,
Or point at best the longest Way.
I'll seek a readier Path, and go
Where Wisdom's surely taught *below*.

How deep yon Azure dies the Sky!
Where Orbs of Gold unnumber'd lye,
While thro' their Ranks in silver pride
The nether Crescent seems to glide.
The slumb'ring Breeze forgets to breathe,
The Lake is smooth and clear beneath,
Where once again the spangled Show
Descends to meet our Eyes below.
The Grounds which on the right aspire,
In dimness from the View retire:
The Left presents a Place of Graves,
Whose Wall the silent Water laves.

That Steeple guides thy doubtful sight
Among the livid gleams of Night.
There pass with melancholy State,
By all the solemn Heaps of Fate,
And think, as softly-sad you tread
Above the venerable Dead,
Time was, like thee they Life possest,
And Time shall be, that thou shalt Rest.
Those Graves, with bending Osier bound,
That nameless heave the crumbled Ground,
Quick to the glancing Thought disclose
Where *Toil* and *Poverty* repose.

The flat smooth Stones that bear a Name,
The Chissels slender help to Fame,
(Which e'er our Sett of Friends decay
Their frequent Steps may wear away.)
A *middle Race* of Mortals own,
Men, half ambitious, all unknown.

The Marble Tombs that rise on high,
Whose Dead in vaulted Arches lye,
Whose Pillars swell with sculptur'd Stones,
Arms, Angels, Epitaphs and Bones.
These (all the poor Remains of State)
Adorn the *Rich*, or praise the *Great;*
Who while on Earth in Fame they live,
Are senseless of the Fame they give.

Ha! while I gaze, pale *Cynthia* fades,
The bursting Earth unveils the Shades!
All slow, and wan, and wrap'd with Shrouds,
They rise in visionary Crouds,
And all with sober Accent cry,
Think, Mortal, what it is to dye.

Now from yon black and fun'ral Yew,
That bathes the Charnel House with Dew,
Methinks I hear a *Voice* begin:
(Ye Ravens, cease your croaking Din,
Ye tolling Clocks, no Time resound
O'er the long Lake and midnight Ground)
It sends a Peal of hollow Groans,
Thus speaking from among the Bones.
When Men my Scythe and Darts supply,
How great a *King* of *Fears* am I!

They view me like the last of Things:
They make, and then they dread, my Stings.

Fools! if you less provok'd your Fears,
No more my Spectre-Form appears.
Death's but a Path that must be trod,
If Man wou'd ever pass to God:
A Port of Calms, a State of Ease
From the rough Rage of swelling Seas.

Why then thy flowing sable Stoles,
Deep pendent Cypress, mourning Poles,
Loose Scarfs to fall athwart thy Weeds,
Long Palls, drawn Herses, cover'd Steeds,
And Plumes of black, that as they tread,
Nod o'er the 'Scutcheons of the Dead?

Nor can the parted Body know,
Nor wants the Soul, these Forms of Woe:
As Men who long in Prison dwell,
With Lamps that glimmer round the Cell,
When e'er their suffering Years are run,
Spring forth to greet the glitt'ring Sun:
Such Joy, tho' far transcending Sense,
Have pious Souls at parting hence.
On Earth, and in the Body plac't,
A few, and evil Years, they wast:
But when their Chains are cast aside,
See the glad Scene unfolding wide,
Clap the glad Wing and tow'r away,
And mingle with the Blaze of Day.

THOMAS PARNELL.

THE UNIVERSAL PRAYER

Deo Opt. Max.

FATHER of All! in every Age,
In every Clime ador'd,
By Saint, by Savage, and by Sage,
Jehovah, Jove, or Lord!

Thou Great First Cause, least understood!
Who all my Sense confin'd
To know but this, — that Thou art Good,
And that myself am blind:

Yet gave me, in this dark Estate,
To see the Good from Ill;
And binding Nature fast in Fate,
Left Conscience free, and Will.

What Conscience dictates to be done,
Or warns me not to doe,
This, teaçh me more than Hell to shun,
That, more than Heav'n pursue.

What Blessings thy free Bounty gives,
Let me not cast away;
For God is pay'd when Man receives;
T'enjoy, is to obey.

Yet not to Earth's contracted Span,
Thy Goodness let me bound,
Or think thee Lord alone of Man,
When thousand Worlds are round.

Let not this weak, unknowing hand
  Presume Thy Bolts to throw,
And deal Damnation round the land,
  On each I judge thy Foe.

If I am right, thy Grace impart
  Still in the right to stay;
If I am wrong, oh teach my heart
  To find that better Way.

Save me alike from foolish Pride,
  Or impious Discontent,
At ought thy Wisdom has deny'd,
  Or ought thy Goodness lent.

Teach me to feel another's Woe;
  To hide the Fault I see;
That Mercy I to others show,
  That Mercy show to me.

Mean tho' I am, not wholly so
  Since quicken'd by thy Breath,
Oh lead me wheresoe'er I go,
  Thro' this day's Life, or Death:

This day, be Bread and Peace my Lot;
  All else beneath the Sun,
Thou know'st if best bestow'd, or not;
  And let Thy Will be done.

To Thee, whose Temple is all Space,
  Whose Altar, Earth, Sea, Skies;
One Chorus let all Being raise:
  All Nature's Incence rise!

ALEXANDER POPE.

ELEGY WRITTEN IN A COUNTRY CHURCH-YARD

The Curfew tolls the knell of parting day,
The lowing herd wind slowly o'er the lea,
The plowman homeward plods his weary way,
And leaves the world to darkness and to me.

Now fades the glimmering landscape on the sight,
And all the air a solemn stillness holds,
Save where the beetle wheels his droning flight,
And drowsy tinklings lull the distant folds;

Save that from yonder ivy-mantled tow'r
The mopeing owl does to the moon complain
Of such, as wand'ring near her secret bow'r,
Molest her ancient solitary reign.

Beneath those rugged elms, that yew-tree's shade,
Where heaves the turf in many a mould'ring heap,
Each in his narrow cell for ever laid,
The rude Forefathers of the hamlet sleep.

The breezy call of incense-breathing Morn,
The swallow twitt'ring from the straw-built shed,
The cock's shrill clarion, or the echoing horn,
No more shall rouse them from their lowly bed.

For them no more the blazing hearth shall burn,
Or busy housewife ply her evening care:
No children run to lisp their sire's return,
Or climb his knees the envied kiss to share.

Oft did the harvest to their sickle yield,
Their furrow oft the stubborn glebe has broke;
How jocund did they drive their team afield!
How bow'd the woods beneath their sturdy stroke!

Let not Ambition mock their useful toil,
Their homely joys, and destiny obscure;
Nor Grandeur hear with a disdainful smile,
The short and simple annals of the poor.

The boast of heraldry, the pomp of pow'r,
And all that beauty, all that wealth e'er gave,
Awaits alike th' inevitable hour,
The paths of glory lead but to the grave.

Nor you, ye Proud, impute to These the fault,
If Mem'ry o'er their Tomb no Trophies raise,
Where thro' the long-drawn isle and fretted vault
The pealing anthem swells the note of praise.

Can storied urn or animated bust
Back to its mansion call the fleeting breath?
Can Honour's voice provoke the silent dust,
Or Flatt'ry soothe the dull cold ear of Death?

Perhaps in this neglected spot is laid
Some heart once pregnant with celestial fire;
Hands, that the rod of empire might have sway'd,
Or wak'd to ecstasy the living lyre.

But Knowledge to their eyes her ample page
Rich with the spoils of time did ne'er unroll;

'hill Penury repress'd their noble rage,
nd froze the genial current of the soul.

ull many a gem of purest ray serene,
'he dark unfathom'd caves of ocean bear:
ull many a flower is born to blush unseen,
nd waste its sweetness on the desert air.

ome village-Hampden, that with dauntless breast
'he little Tyrant of his fields withstood;
ome mute inglorious Milton here may rest,
ome Cromwell guiltless of his country's blood.

'h' applause of list'ning senates to command,
'he threats of pain and ruin to despise,
'o scatter plenty o'er a smiling land,
nd read their hist'ry in a nation's eyes,

'heir lot forbad: nor circumscrib'd alone
'heir growing virtues, but their crimes confin'd;
orbad to wade through slaughter to a throne,
nd shut the gates of mercy on mankind,

'he struggling pangs of conscious truth to hide,
'o quench the blushes of ingenuous shame,
r heap the shrine of Luxury and Pride
Vith incense kindled at the Muse's flame.

ar from the madding crowd's ignoble strife,
heir sober wishes never learn'd to stray;
long the cool sequester'd vale of life
hey kept the noiseless tenor of their way.

Yet ev'n these bones from insult to protect
Some frail memorial still erected nigh,
With uncouth rhymes and shapeless sculpture
deck'd,
Implores the passing tribute of a sigh.

Their name, their years, spelt by th' unletter'd mus
The place of fame and elegy supply:
And many a holy text around she strews,
That teach the rustic moralist to die.

For who to dumb Forgetfulness a prey,
This pleasing anxious being e'er resign'd,
Left the warm precincts of the cheerful day,
Nor cast one longing ling'ring look behind?

On some fond breast the parting soul relies,
Some pious drops the closing eye requires;
Ev'n from the tomb the voice of Nature cries,
Ev'n in our Ashes live their wonted Fires.

For thee, who, mindful of th' unhonour'd Dead
Dost in these lines their artless tale relate;
If chance, by lonely contemplation led,
Some kindred Spirit shall inquire thy fate,

Haply some hoary-headed Swain may say,
"Oft have we seen him at the peep of dawn
"Brushing with hasty steps the dews away
"To meet the sun upon the upland lawn.

"There at the foot of yonder nodding beech
"That wreathes its old fantastic roots so high,

"His listless length at noontide would he stretch,
"And pore upon the brook that babbles by.

"Hard by yon wood, now smiling as in scorn,
"Mutt'ring his wayward fancies he would rove,
"Now drooping, woeful wan, like one forlorn,
"Or craz'd with care, or cross'd in hopeless love.

"One morn I miss'd him on the custom'd hill,
"Along the heath, and near his fav'rite tree;
"Another came; nor yet beside the rill,
"Nor up the lawn, nor at the wood was he;

"The next with dirges due in sad array
"Slow thro' the church-way path we saw him born.
"Approach and read (for thou can'st read) the lay,
"Grav'd on the stone beneath yon aged thorn."

THE EPITAPH

Here rests his head upon the lap of Earth
A Youth to Fortune and to Fame unknown.
Fair Science frown'd not on his humble birth,
And Melancholy mark'd him for her own.

Large was his bounty, and his soul sincere,
Heav'n did a recompense as largely send:
He gave to Mis'ry all he had, a tear,
He gain'd from Heav'n ('twas all he wish'd) a friend.

No farther seek his merits to disclose,
Or draw his frailties from their dread abode,
(There they alike in trembling hope repose,)
The bosom of his Father and his God.

THOMAS GRAY.

ODE TO EVENING

If aught of Oaten Stop, or Pastoral Song,
May hope, O pensive Eve, to soothe thine Ear,
Like thy own brawling Springs,
Thy Springs, and dying Gales,

O Nymph reserv'd, while now the bright-hair'd Sun
Sits in yon western Tent, whose cloudy Skirts,
With Brede ethereal wove,
O'erhang his wavy Bed:

Now Air is hush'd, save where the weak-ey'd Bat,
With short shrill Shriek flits by on leathern Wing,
Or where the Beetle winds
His small but sullen Horn,

As oft he rises 'midst the twilight Path,
Against the Pilgrim born in heedless Hum:
Now teach me, Maid compos'd,
To breathe some soften'd Strain,

Whose Numbers, stealing thro' thy darkening Vale,
May not unseemly with its Stillness suit,
As musing slow, I hail
Thy genial lov'd Return!

For when thy folding Star arising shews
His paly Circlet, at his warning Lamp
The fragrant Hours, and Elves
Who slept in Buds the Day,

And many a Nymph who wreathes her Brows
with Sedge,
And sheds the fresh'ning Dew, and lovelier still,
The Pensive Pleasures sweet
Prepare thy shadowy Car.

Then let me rove some wild and heathy Scene,
Or find some Ruin 'midst its dreary Dells,
Whose Walls more awful nod
By thy religious Gleams.

Or if chill blustring Winds, or driving Rain,
Prevent my willing Feet, be mine the Hut,
That from the Mountain's Side,
Views Wilds, and swelling Floods,

And Hamlets brown, and dim-discover'd Spires,
And hears their simple Bell, and marks o'er all
Thy Dewy Fingers draw
The gradual dusky Veil.

While Spring shall pour his Show'rs, as oft he
wont,
And bathe thy breathing Tresses, meekest Eve!
While Summer loves to sport,
Beneath thy ling'ring light:

While sallow Autumn fills thy Lap with Leaves,
Or Winter yelling thro' the troublous Air,
Affrights thy shrinking Train,
And rudely rends thy Robes.

So long regardful of thy quiet Rule,
Shall Fancy, Friendship, Science, smiling Peace,
Thy gentlest Influence own,
And love thy fav'rite Name!

WILLIAM COLLINS.

ON THE RECEIPT OF MY MOTHER'S PICTURE OUT OF NORFOLK

THE GIFT OF MY COUSIN ANN BODHAM

OH that those lips had language! Life has passed
With me but roughly since I heard thee last.
Those lips are thine — thy own sweet smiles I see,
The same that oft in childhood solaced me;
Voice only fails, else how distinct they say,
"Grieve not, my child, chase all thy fears away!"
The meek intelligence of those dear eyes
(Blest be the art that can immortalise,
The art that baffles time's tyrannic claim
To quench it) here shines on me still the same.
Faithful remembrancer of one so dear,
O welcome guest, though unexpected here!
Who bidst me honour with an artless song,
Affectionate, a mother lost so long.
I will obey, not willingly alone,
But gladly, as the precept were her own:
And, while that face renews my filial grief,
Fancy shall weave a charm for my relief,
Shall steep me in Elysian reverie,
A momentary dream that thou art she.
My mother! when I learned that thou wast dead
Say, wast thou conscious of the tears I shed?

Iovered thy spirit o'er thy sorrowing son,
Vretch even then, life's journey just begun?
'erhaps thou gavest me, though unfelt, a kiss:
'erhaps a tear, if souls can weep in bliss —
h, that maternal smile! it answers — Yes.
heard the bell tolled on thy burial day,
saw the hearse that bore thee slow away,
nd, turning from my nursery window, drew
long, long sigh, and wept a last adieu!
ut was it such? — It was. — Where thou art gone
dieus and farewells are a sound unknown.
lay I but meet thee on that peaceful shore,
he parting word shall pass my lips no more!
hy maidens, grieved themselves at my concern,
)ft gave me promise of thy quick return.
Vhat ardently I wished I long believed,
nd, disappointed still, was still deceived.
y expectation every day beguiled,
)upe of *to-morrow* even from a child.
hus many a sad to-morrow came and went,
'ill, all my stock of infant sorrow spent,
learned at last submission to my lot;
ut, though I less deplored thee, ne'er forgot.
Where once we dwelt our name is heard no more,
hildren not thine have trod my nursery floor;
nd where the gardener Robin, day by day,
)rew me to school along the public way,
)elighted with my bauble coach, and wrapped
n scarlet mantle warm, and velvet capped,
Tis now become a history little known
hat once we called the pastoral house our own
hort-lived possession! but the record fair
hat memory keeps, of all thy kindness there,

Still outlives many a storm that has effaced
A thousand other themes less deeply traced.
Thy nightly visits to my chamber made,
That thou mightst know me safe and warmly laid
Thy morning bounties ere I left my home,
The biscuit, or confectionary plum;
The fragrant waters on my cheeks bestowed
By thy own hand, till fresh they shone and glowed
All this, and more endearing still than all,
Thy constant flow of love, that knew no fall,
Ne'er roughened by those cataracts and brakes
That humour interposed too often makes:
All this still legible in memory's page,
And still to be so to my latest age,
Adds joy to duty, makes me glad to pay
Such honours to thee as my numbers may;
Perhaps a frail memorial, but sincere,
Not scorned in heaven, though little noticed here.
Could time, his flight reversed, restore the hours
When playing with thy vesture's tissued flowers,
The violet, the pink, and jessamine,
I pricked them into paper with a pin
(And thou wast happier than myself the while,
Wouldst softly speak, and stroke my head and smile)
Could those few pleasant hours again appear,
Might one wish bring them, would I wish them here
I would not trust my heart — the dear delight
Seems so to be desired, perhaps I might. —
But no — what here we call our life is such,
So little to be loved, and thou so much,
That I should ill requite thee to constrain
Thy unbound spirit into bonds again.
Thou, as a gallant bark from Albion's coast
(The storms all weathered and the ocean crossed)

ıoots into port at some well-havened isle,
'here spices breathe, and brighter seasons smile,
here sits quiescent on the floods that show
er beauteous form reflected clear below,
'hile airs impregnated with incense play
round her, fanning light her streamers gay;
› thou, with sails how swift! hast reached the shore
Where tempests never beat nor billows roar,"[1]
nd thy loved consort on the dangerous tide
f life long since has anchored at thy side.
ut me, scarce hoping to attain that rest,
lways from port withheld, always distressed —
[e howling winds drive devious, tempest tost,
ıils ripped, seams opening wide, and compass lost,
nd day by day some current's thwarting force
ets me more distant from a prosperous course.
ut, oh, the thought that thou art safe and he!
hat thought is joy, arrive what may to me.
[y boast is not, that I deduce my birth
rom loins enthroned and rulers of the earth;
ut higher far my proud pretensions rise —
he son of parents passed into the skies!
nd now farewell. Time unrevoked has run
is wonted course, yet what I wished is done
y contemplation's help, not sought in vain,
seem to have lived my childhood o'er again;
› have renewed the joys that once were mine,
'ithout the sin of violating thine:
nd, while the wings of fancy still are free
nd I can view this mimic show of thee,
ime has but half succeeded in his theft —
hyself removed, thy power to soothe me left.

WILLIAM COWPER.

[1] Garth.

RESOLUTION AND INDEPENDENCE

THERE was a roaring in the wind all night;
The rain came heavily and fell in floods;
But now the sun is rising calm and bright;
The birds are singing in the distant woods;
Over his own sweet voice the Stock-dove broods;
The Jay makes answer as the Magpie chatters;
And all the air is filled with pleasant noise of waters

All things that love the sun are out of doors;
The sky rejoices in the morning's birth;
The grass is bright with rain-drops; — on the moor
The hare is running races in her mirth;
And with her feet she from the plashy earth
Raises a mist; that, glittering in the sun,
Runs with her all the way, wherever she doth
run.

I was a Traveller then upon the moor;
I saw the hare that raced about with joy;
I heard the woods and distant waters roar;
Or heard them not, as happy as a boy:
The pleasant season did my heart employ:
My old remembrances went from me wholly;
And all the ways of men, so vain and melan-
choly.

But, as it sometimes chanceth, from the might
Of joy in minds that can no further go,
As high as we have mounted in delight
In our dejection do we sink as low;
To me that morning did it happen so;

.nd fears and fancies thick upon me came;
)im sadness — and blind thoughts, I knew not, nor
could name.

heard the sky-lark warbling in the sky;
.nd I bethought me of the playful hare:
;ven such a happy Child of earth am I;
;ven as these blissful creatures do I fare;
'ar from the world I walk, and from all care;
ut there may come another day to me —
olitude, pain of heart, distress, and poverty.

Ay whole life I have lived in pleasant thought,
\s if life's business were a summer mood;
\s if all needful things would come unsought
'o genial faith, still rich in genial good;
3ut how can He expect that others should
3uild for him, sow for him, and at his call
.ove him, who for himself will take no heed at all?

thought of Chatterton, the marvellous Boy,
'he sleepless Soul that perished in his pride;
)f Him who walked in glory and in joy
'ollowing his plough, along the mountain-side:
3y our own spirits are we deified:
Ve Poets in our youth begin in gladness;
3ut thereof come in the end despondency and madness.

Jow, whether it were by peculiar grace,
\ leading from above, a something given,
'et it befell that, in this lonely place,
Vhen I with these untoward thoughts had striven,

Beside a pool bare to the eye of heaven
I saw a Man before me unawares:
The oldest man he seemed that ever wore grey hairs.

As a huge stone is sometimes seen to lie
Couched on the bald top of an eminence;
Wonder to all who do the same espy,
By what means it could thither come, and whence;
So that it seems a thing endued with sense:
Like a sea-beast crawled forth, that on a shelf
Of rock or sand reposeth, there to sun itself;

Such seemed this Man, not all alive nor dead,
Nor all asleep — in his extreme old age:
His body was bent double, feet and head
Coming together in life's pilgrimage;
As if some dire constraint of pain, or rage
Of sickness felt by him in times long past,
A more than human weight upon his frame had cast.

Himself he propped, limbs, body, and pale face,
Upon a long grey staff of shaven wood:
And, still as I drew near with gentle pace,
Upon the margin of that moorish flood
Motionless as a cloud the old Man stood,
That heareth not the loud winds when they call;
And moveth all together, if it move at all.

At length, himself unsettling, he the pond
Stirred with his staff, and fixedly did look
Upon the muddy water, which he conned,
As if he had been reading in a book:
And now a stranger's privilege I took;

And, drawing to his side, to him did say,
"This morning gives us promise of a glorious day."

A gentle answer did the old Man make,
In courteous speech which forth he slowly drew:
And him with further words I thus bespake,
"What occupation do you there pursue?
This is a lonesome place for one like you."
Ere he replied, a flash of mild surprise
Broke from the sable orbs of his yet-vivid eyes.

His words came feebly, from a feeble chest,
But each in solemn order followed each,
With something of a lofty utterance drest —
Choice word and measured phrase, above the reach
Of ordinary men; a stately speech;
Such as grave Livers do in Scotland use,
Religious men, who give to God and man their dues.

He told, that to these waters he had come
To gather leeches, being old and poor:
Employment hazardous and wearisome!
And he had many hardships to endure:
From pond to pond he roamed, from moor to moor;
Housing, with God's good help, by choice or chance;
And in this way he gained an honest maintenance.

The old Man still stood talking by my side;
But now his voice to me was like a stream
Scarce heard; nor word from word could I divide;
And the whole body of the Man did seem
Like one whom I had met with in a dream;
Or like a man from some far region sent,
To give me human strength, by apt admonishment.

My former thoughts returned: the fear that kills;
And hope that is unwilling to be fed;
Cold, pain, and labour, and all fleshly ills;
And mighty Poets in their misery dead.
— Perplexed, and longing to be comforted,
My question eagerly did I renew,
"How is it that you live, and what is it you do?"

He with a smile did then his words repeat;
And said that, gathering leeches, far and wide
He travelled; stirring thus about his feet
The waters of the pools where they abide.
"Once I could meet with them on every side;
But they have dwindled long by slow decay;
Yet still I persevere, and find them where I may."

While he was talking thus, the lonely place,
The old Man's shape, and speech — all troubled me:
In my mind's eye I seemed to see him pace
About the weary moors continually,
Wandering about alone and silently.
While I these thoughts within myself pursued,
He, having made a pause, the same discourse
renewed.

And soon with this he other matter blended,
Cheerfully uttered, with demeanour kind,
But stately in the main; and, when he ended,
I could have laughed myself to scorn to find
In that decrepit Man so firm a mind.
"God," said I, "be my help and stay secure;
I'll think of the Leech-gatherer on the lonely moor!"

WILLIAM WORDSWORTH.

THE ISLES OF GREECE

The Isles of Greece, the Isles of Greece!
  Where burning Sappho loved and sung,
Where grew the arts of War and Peace,
  Where Delos rose, and Phœbus sprung!
Eternal summer gilds them yet,
But all, except their Sun, is set.

The Scian and the Teian muse,
  The Hero's harp, the Lover's lute,
Have found the fame your shores refuse:
  Their place of birth alone is mute
To sounds which echo further west
Than your Sires' "Islands of the Blest."

The mountains look on Marathon —
  And Marathon looks on the sea;
And musing there an hour alone,
  I dreamed that Greece might still be free;
For standing on the Persians' grave,
I could not deem myself a slave.

A King sate on the rocky brow
  Which looks o'er sea-born Salamis;
And ships, by thousands, lay below,
  And men in nations; — all were his!
He counted them at break of day —
And, when the Sun set, where were they?

And where are they? and where art thou
  My Country? On thy voiceless shore

The heroic lay is tuneless now —
  The heroic bosom beats no more!
And must thy Lyre, so long divine,
Degenerate into hands like mine?

'Tis something, in the dearth of Fame,
  Though linked among a fettered race,
To feel at least a patriot's shame,
  Even as I sing, suffuse my face;
For what is left the poet here?
For Greeks a blush — for Greece a tear.

Must *we* but weep o'er days more blest?
  Must *we* but blush? — Our fathers bled.
Earth! render back from out thy breast
  A remnant of our Spartan dead!
Of the three hundred grant but three,
To make a new Thermopylæ!

What, silent still? and silent all?
  Ah! no; — the voices of the dead
Sound like a distant torrent's fall,
  And answer, "Let one living head,
But one arise, — we come, we come!"
'Tis but the living who are dumb.

In vain — in vain: strike other chords;
  Fill high the cup with Samian wine!
Leave battles to the Turkish hordes,
  And shed the blood of Scio's vine!
Hark! rising to the ignoble call —
How answers each bold Bacchanal!

You have the Pyrrhic dance as yet;
  Where is the Pyrrhic phalanx gone?
Of two such lessons, why forget
  The nobler and the manlier one?
You have the letters Cadmus gave —
Think ye he meant them for a slave?

Fill high the bowl with Samian wine!
  We will not think of themes like these!
It made Anacreon's song divine:
  He served — but served Polycrates —
A Tyrant; but our masters then
Were still, at least, our countrymen.

The Tyrant of the Chersonese
  Was Freedom's best and bravest friend;
That tyrant was Miltiades!
  Oh! that the present hour would lend
Another despot of the kind!
Such chains as his were sure to bind.

Fill high the bowl with Samian wine!
  On Suli's rock, and Parga's shore,
Exists the remnant of a line
  Such as the Doric mothers bore;
And there, perhaps, some seed is sown,
The Heracleidan blood might own.

Trust not for freedom to the Franks —
  They have a king who buys and sells;
In native swords, and native ranks,
  The only hope of courage dwells;

But Turkish force, and Latin fraud,
Would break your shield, however broad.

Fill high the bowl with Samian wine!
  Our virgins dance beneath the shade —
I see their glorious black eyes shine;
  But gazing on each glowing maid,
My own the burning tear-drop laves,
To think such breasts must suckle slaves.

Place me on Sunium's marbled steep,
  Where nothing, save the waves and I,
May hear our mutual murmurs sweep;
  There, swan-like, let me sing and die:
A land of slaves shall ne'er be mine —
Dash down yon cup of Samian wine!

LORD BYRON.

ODE TO THE WEST WIND

I

O WILD West Wind, thou breath of Autumn's being,
Thou, from whose unseen presence the leaves dead
Are driven, like ghosts from an enchanter fleeing,

Yellow, and black, and pale, and hectic red,
Pestilence-stricken multitudes: O thou,
Who chariotest to their dark wintry bed

The wingèd seeds, where they lie cold and low,
Each like a corpse within its grave, until
Thine azure sister of the Spring shall blow

Her clarion o'er the dreaming earth, and fill
(Driving sweet buds like flocks to feed in air)
With living hues and odours plain and hill:

Wild Spirit, which art moving everywhere;
Destroyer and preserver; hear, oh, hear!

II

Thou on whose stream, mid the steep sky's commo-
tion
Loose clouds like earth's decaying leaves are shed,
Shook from the tangled boughs of Heaven and Ocean,

Angels of rain and lightning: they are spread
On the blue surface of thine aëry surge,
Like the bright hair uplifted from the head

Of some fierce Mænad, even from the dim verge
Of the horizon to the zenith's height,
The locks of the approaching storm. Thou dirge

Of the dying year, to which this closing night
Will be the dome of a vast sepulchre,
Vaulted with all thy congregated might

Of vapours, from whose solid atmosphere
Black rain, and fire, and hail will burst: oh, hear!

III

Thou who didst waken from his summer dreams
The blue Mediterranean, where he lay,
Lulled by the coil of his crystàlline streams,

Beside a pumice isle in Baiae's bay,
And saw in sleep old palaces and towers
Quivering within the wave's intenser day,

All overgrown with azure moss and flowers
So sweet, the sense faints picturing them! Thou
For whose path the Atlantic's level powers

Cleave themselves into chasms, while far below
The sea-blooms and the oozy woods which wear
The sapless foliage of the ocean, know

Thy voice, and suddenly grow gray with fear,
And tremble and despoil themselves: oh, hear!

IV

If I were a dead leaf thou mightest bear;
If I were a swift cloud to fly with thee;
A wave to pant beneath thy power, and share

The impulse of thy strength, only less free
Than thou, O uncontrollable! If even
I were as in my boyhood, and could be

The comrade of thy wanderings over Heaven,
As then, when to outstrip thy skiey speed
Scarce seemed a vision; I would ne'er have striven

As thus with thee in prayer in my sore need.
Oh, lift me as a wave, a leaf, a cloud!
I fall upon the thorns of life! I bleed!

A heavy weight of hours has chained and bowed
One too like thee: tameless, and swift, and proud.

V

Make me thy lyre, even as the forest is:
What if my leaves are falling like its own!
The tumult of thy mighty harmonies

Will take from both a deep, autumnal tone,
Sweet though in sadness. Be thou, Spirit fierce,
My spirit! Be thou me, impetuous one!

Drive my dead thoughts over the universe
Like withered leaves to quicken a new birth!
And, by the incantation of this verse,

Scatter, as from an unextinguished hearth
Ashes and sparks, my words among mankind!
Be through my lips to unawakened earth

The trumpet of a prophecy! O, Wind,
If Winter comes, can Spring be far behind?

PERCY BYSSHE SHELLEY.

ODE TO A NIGHTINGALE

MY heart aches, and a drowsy numbness pains
  My sense, as though of hemlock I had drunk,
Or emptied some dull opiate to the drains
  One minute past, and Lethe-wards had sunk:
'Tis not through envy of thy happy lot,
  But being too happy in thine happiness,—

That thou, light-winged Dryad of the trees,
In some melodious plot
Of beechen green, and shadows numberless,
Singest of summer in full-throated ease.

O, for a draught of vintage! that hath been
Cool'd a long age in the deep-delved earth,
Tasting of Flora and the country green,
Dance, and Provençal song, and sun-burnt mirth
O for a beaker full of the warm South,
Full of the true, the blushful Hippocrene,
With beaded bubbles winking at the brim,
And purple-stained mouth;
That I might drink, and leave the world unseen,
And with thee fade away into the forest dim:

Fade far away, dissolve, and quite forget
What thou among the leaves hast never known,
The weariness, the fever, and the fret
Here, where men sit and hear each other groan;
Where palsy shakes a few, sad, last gray hairs,
Where youth grows pale, and spectre-thin, and dies;
Where but to think is to be full of sorrow
And leaden-eyed despairs,
Where Beauty cannot keep her lustrous eyes,
Or new Love pine at them beyond to-morrow

Away! away! for I will fly to thee,
Not charioted by Bacchus and his pards,
But on the viewless wings of Poesy,
Though the dull brain perplexes and retards:

Already with thee! tender is the night,
 And haply the Queen-Moon is on her throne,
  Cluster'd around by all her starry Fays;
   But here there is no light,
 Save what from heaven is with the breezes blown
  Through verdurous glooms and winding mossy ways.

I cannot see what flowers are at my feet,
 Nor what soft incense hangs upon the boughs,
But, in embalmed darkness, guess each sweet
 Wherewith the seasonable month endows
The grass, the thicket, and the fruit-tree wild;
 White hawthorn, and the pastoral eglantine;
  Fast-fading violets cover'd up in leaves;
   And mid-May's eldest child,
 The coming musk-rose, full of dewy wine,
  The murmurous haunt of flies on summer eves.

Darkling I listen; and for many a time
 I have been half in love with easeful Death,
Call'd him soft names in many a mused rhyme,
 To take into the air my quiet breath;
Now more than ever seems it rich to die,
 To cease upon the midnight with no pain,
  While thou art pouring forth thy soul abroad
   In such an ecstasy!
 Still would'st thou sing, and I have ears in vain —
  To thy high requiem become a sod.

Thou wast not born for death, immortal Bird!
 No hungry generations tread thee down;

The voice I hear this passing night was heard
  In ancient days by emperor and clown:
Perhaps the self-same song that found a path
  Through the sad heart of Ruth, when, sick for home,
    She stood in tears amid the alien corn;
        The same that oft-times hath
  Charm'd magic casements, opening on the foam
    Of perilous seas, in faery lands forlorn.

Forlorn! the very word is like a bell
  To toll me back from thee to my sole self.
Adieu! the fancy cannot cheat so well
  As she is fam'd to do, deceiving elf.
Adieu! adieu! thy plaintive anthem fades
  Past the near meadows, over the still stream,
    Up the hill-side; and now 'tis buried deep
        In the next valley-glades:
  Was it a vision, or a waking dream?
    Fled is that music: — do I wake or sleep?

JOHN KEATS.

ODE ON A GRECIAN URN

THOU still unravish'd bride of quietness,
  Thou foster-child of silence and slow time,
Sylvan historian, who canst thus express
  A flowery tale more sweetly than our rhyme:
What leaf-fring'd legend haunts about thy shape
  Of deities or mortals, or of both,
    In Tempe or the dales of Arcady?
  What men or gods are these? What maidens loth?
What mad pursuit? What struggle to escape?
  What pipes and timbrels? What wild ecstasy?

Heard melodies are sweet, but those unheard
  Are sweeter; therefore, ye soft pipes, play on;
Not to the sensual ear, but, more endear'd,
  Pipe to the spirit ditties of no tone:
Fair youth, beneath the trees, thou canst not leave
  Thy song, nor ever can those trees be bare;
    Bold Lover, never, never canst thou kiss,
Though winning near the goal — yet, do not grieve;
    She cannot fade, though thou hast not thy
      bliss,
  For ever wilt thou love, and she be fair!

Ah, happy, happy boughs! that cannot shed
  Your leaves, nor ever bid the Spring adieu;
And, happy melodist, unwearied,
  For ever piping songs for ever new;
More happy love! more happy, happy love!
  For ever warm and still to be enjoy'd,
    For ever panting and for ever young;
All breathing human passion far above,
  That leaves a heart high sorrowful and cloy'd,
    A burning forehead, and a parching tongue.

Who are these coming to the sacrifice?
  To what green altar, O mysterious priest,
Lead'st thou that heifer lowing at the skies,
  And all her silken flanks with garlands drest?
What little town by river or sea shore,
  Or mountain-built with peaceful citadel,
    Is emptied of its folk, this pious morn?
And, little town, thy streets for evermore
  Will silent be; and not a soul to tell
    Why thou art desolate, can e'er return.

O Attic shape! Fair attitude! with brede
  Of marble men and maidens overwrought,
With forest branches and the trodden weed;
  Thou, silent form, dost tease us out of thought
As doth eternity: Cold Pastoral!
  When old age shall this generation waste,
    Thou shalt remain, in midst of other woe
  Than ours, a friend to man, to whom thou say'st,
"Beauty is truth, truth beauty," — that is all
    Ye know on earth, and all ye need to know.

JOHN KEATS.

LA BELLE DAME SANS MERCI

O WHAT can ail thee, Knight at arms,
  Alone and palely loitering?
The sedge has withered from the Lake,
  And no birds sing!

O what can ail thee, Knight at arms,
  So haggard, and so woe begone?
The Squirrel's granary is full
  And the harvest's done.

I see a lily on thy brow,
  With anguish moist and fever dew;
And on thy cheeks a fading rose
  Fast withereth too —

I met a Lady in the Meads
  Full beautiful — a faery's child;
Her hair was long, her foot was light,
  And her eyes were wild —

I made a Garland for her head,
  And bracelets too, and fragrant Zone;
She look'd at me as she did love,
  And made sweet moan.

I set her on my pacing steed,
  And nothing else saw all day long;
For sidelong would she bend and sing
  A faery's song.

She found me roots of relish sweet,
  And honey wild and manna dew;
And sure in language strange she said,
  "I love thee true."

She took me to her elfin grot
  And there she wept and sigh'd full sore;
And there I shut her wild wild eyes
  With kisses four.

And there she lulled me asleep,
  And there I dream'd — Ah! woe betide!
The latest dream I ever dreamt,
  On the cold hill's side.

I saw pale Kings, and Princes too,
  Pale warriors — death pale were they all;
They cried, "La belle dame sans merci
  Thee hath in thrall!"

I saw their starv'd lips in the gloam,
  With horrid warning gaped wide;

And I awoke, and found me here
  On the cold hill's side.

And this is why I sojourn here,
  Alone and palely loitering;
Though the sedge is withered from the Lake,
  And no birds sing.

JOHN KEATS.

ULYSSES

IT little profits that an idle king,
By this still hearth, among these barren crags,
Match'd with an aged wife, I mete and dole
Unequal laws unto a savage race,
That hoard, and sleep, and feed, and know not me.
I cannot rest from travel: I will drink
Life to the lees: all times I have enjoy'd
Greatly, have suffer'd greatly, both with those
That loved me, and alone; on shore, and when
Thro' scudding drifts the rainy Hyades
Vext the dim sea: I am become a name;
For always roaming with a hungry heart
Much have I seen and known; cities of men
And manners, climates, councils, governments,
Myself not least, but honour'd of them all;
And drunk delight of battle with my peers,
Far on the ringing plains of windy Troy.
I am a part of all that I have met;
Yet all experience is an arch wherethro'
Gleams that untravell'd world, whose margin fades
For ever and for ever when I move.
How dull it is to pause, to make an end,

To rust unburnish'd, not to shine in use!
As tho' to breathe were life. Life piled on life
Were all too little, and of one to me
Little remains: but every hour is saved
From that eternal silence, something more,
A bringer of new things; and vile it were
For some three suns to store and hoard myself,
And this gray spirit yearning in desire
To follow knowledge, like a sinking star,
Beyond the utmost bound of human thought.
  This is my son, mine own Telemachus,
To whom I leave the sceptre and the isle —
Well-loved of me, discerning to fulfil
This labour, by slow prudence to make mild
A rugged people, and thro' soft degrees
Subdue them to the useful and the good.
Most blameless is he, centred in the sphere
Of common duties, decent not to fail
In offices of tenderness, and pay
Meet adoration to my household gods,
When I am gone. He works his work, I mine.
  There lies the port: the vessel puffs her sail:
There gloom the dark broad seas. My mariners,
Souls that have toil'd, and wrought, and thought
    with me —
That ever with a frolic welcome took
The thunder and the sunshine, and opposed
Free hearts, free foreheads — you and I are old
Old age hath yet his honour and his toil;
Death closes all: but something ere the end,
Some work of noble note, may yet be done,
Not unbecoming men that strove with Gods.
The lights begin to twinkle from the rocks:

The long day wanes: the slow moon climbs: the deep
Moans round with many voices. Come, my friends,
'Tis not too late to seek a newer world.
Push off, and sitting well in order smite
The sounding furrows; for my purpose holds
To sail beyond the sunset, and the baths
Of all the western stars, until I die.
It may be that the gulfs will wash us down:
It may be we shall touch the Happy Isles,
And see the great Achilles, whom we knew.
Tho' much is taken, much abides; and tho'
We are not now that strength which in old days
Moved earth and heaven; that which we are, we
are;
One equal temper of heroic hearts,
Made weak by time and fate, but strong in will
To strive, to seek, to find, and not to yield.

LORD TENNYSON.

A LIGHT WOMAN

I

So far as our story approaches the end,
Which do you pity the most of us three? —
My friend, or the mistress of my friend
With her wanton eyes, or me?

II

My friend was already too good to lose,
And seemed in the way of improvement yet,
When she crossed his path with her hunting-noose
And over him drew her net.

III

When I saw him tangled in her toils,
  A shame, said I, if she adds just him
To her nine-and-ninety other spoils,
  The hundredth, for a whim!

IV

And before my friend be wholly hers,
  How easy to prove to him, I said,
An eagle's the game her pride prefers,
  Though she snaps at the wren instead!

V

So, I gave her eyes my own eyes to take,
  My hand sought hers as in earnest need,
And round she turned for my noble sake,
  And gave me herself indeed.

VI

The eagle am I, with my fame in the world,
  The wren is he, with his maiden face.
— You look away and your lip is curled?
  Patience, a moment's space!

VII

For see, my friend goes shaking and white:
  He eyes me as the basilisk:
I have turned, it appears, his day to night,
  Eclipsing his sun's disk.

VIII

And I did it, he thinks, as a very thief:
 "Though I love her — that he comprehends —
One should master one's passions (love, in chief)
 And be loyal to one's friends!"

IX

And she, — she lies in my hand as tame
 As a pear late basking over a wall;
Just a touch to try and off it came;
 'Tis mine, — can I let it fall?

X

With no mind to eat it, that's the worst!
 Were it thrown in the road, would the case assist
'Twas quenching a dozen blue-flies' thirst
 When I gave its stalk a twist.

XI

And I, — what I seem to my friend, you see:
 What I soon shall seem to his love, you guess:
What I seem to myself, do you ask of me?
 No hero, I confess.

XII

'Tis an awkward thing to play with souls,
 And matter enough to save one's own:
Yet think of my friend, and the burning coals
 He played with for bits of stone!

XIII

One likes to show the truth for the truth;
  That the woman was light is very true:
But suppose she says, — Never mind that youth!
  What wrong have I done to you?

XIV

Well, any how, here the story stays,
  So far at least as I understand;
And, Robert Browning, you writer of plays,
  Here's a subject made to your hand!

ROBERT BROWNING.

SHOP

I

So, friend, your shop was all your house!
  Its front, astonishing the street,
Invited view from man and mouse
  To what diversity of treat
  Behind its glass — the single sheet!

II

What gimcracks, genuine Japanese:
  Gape-jaw and goggle-eye, the frog;
Dragons, owls, monkeys, beetles, geese;
  Some crush-nosed human-hearted dog:
  Queer names, too, such a catalogue!

III

I thought, "And he who owns the wealth
  Which blocks the window's vastitude,

— Ah, could I peep at him by stealth
Behind his ware, pass shop, intrude
On house itself, what scenes were viewed!

IV

"If wide and showy thus the shop,
What must the habitation prove?
The true house with no name a-top —
The mansion, distant one remove,
Once get him off his traffic-groove!

V

"Pictures he likes, or books perhaps;
And as for buying most and best,
Commend me to these City chaps!
Or else he's social, takes his rest
On Sundays, with a Lord for guest.

VI

"Some suburb-palace, parked about
And gated grandly, built last year:
The four-mile walk to keep off gout;
Or big seat sold by bankrupt peer:
But then he takes the rail, that's clear.

VII

"Or stop! I wager, taste selects
Some out o' the way, some all-unknown
Retreat: the neighbourhood suspects
Little that he who rambles lone
Makes Rothschild tremble on his throne!"

VIII

Nowise! Nor Mayfair residence
  Fit to receive and entertain, —
Nor Hampstead villa's kind defence
  From noise and crowd, from dust and drain, —
  Nor country-box was soul's domain!

IX

Nowise! At back of all that spread
  Of merchandise, woe's me, I find
A hole i' the wall where, heels by head,
  The owner couched, his ware behind,
  — In cupboard suited to his mind.

X

For why? He saw no use of life
  But, while he drove a roaring trade,
To chuckle "Customers are rife!"
  To chafe "So much hard cash outlaid
  Yet zero in my profits made!

XI

"This novelty costs pains, but — takes?
  Cumbers my counter! Stock no more!
This article, no such great shakes,
  Fizzes like wildfire? Underscore
  The cheap thing — thousands to the fore!"

XII

'Twas lodging best to live most nigh
  (Cramp, coffinlike as crib might be)

Receipt of Custom; ear and eye
  Wanted no outworld: "Hear and see
  The bustle in the shop!" quoth he.

XIII

My fancy of a merchant-prince
  Was different. Through his wares we groped
Our darkling way to — not to mince
  The matter — no black den where moped
  The master if we interloped!

XIV

Shop was shop only: household-stuff?
  What did he want with comforts there?
"Walls, ceiling, floor, stay blank and rough,
  So goods on sale show rich and rare!
  '*Sell and send home*' be shop's affair!"

XV

What might he deal in? Gems, suppose!
  Since somehow business must be done
At cost of trouble, — see, he throws
  You choice of jewels, everyone,
  Good, better, best, star, moon and sun!

XVI

Which lies within your power of purse?
  This ruby that would tip aright
Solomon's sceptre? Oh, your nurse
  Wants simply coral, the delight
  Of teething baby, — stuff to bite!

XVII

Howe'er your choice fell, straight you took
 Your purchase, prompt your money rang
On counter, — scarce the man forsook
 His study of the *Times*, just swang
 Till-ward his hand that stopped the clang,

XVIII

Then off made buyer with a prize,
 Then seller to his *Times* returned
And so did day wear, wear, till eyes
 Brightened apace, for rest was earned:
 He locked door long ere candle burned.

XIX

And whither went he? Ask himself,
 Not me! To change of scene, I think.
Once sold the ware and pursed the pelf,
 Chaffer was scarce his meat and drink,
 Nor all his music — money-chink.

XX

Because a man has shop to mind
 In time and place, since flesh must live,
Needs spirit lack all life behind,
 All stray thoughts, fancies fugitive,
 All loves except what trade can give?

XXI

I want to know a butcher paints,
 A baker rhymes for his pursuit,

Candlestick-maker much acquaints
His soul with song, or, haply mute,
Blows out his brains upon the flute!

XXII

But — shop each day and all day long!
Friend, your good angel slept, your star
Suffered eclipse, fate did you wrong!
From where these sorts of treasures are,
There should our hearts be — Christ, how far!

ROBERT BROWNING.

EVELYN HOPE

I

BEAUTIFUL Evelyn Hope is dead!
Sit and watch by her side an hour.
That is her book-shelf, this her bed;
She plucked that piece of geranium-flower,
Beginning to die too, in the glass;
Little has yet been changed, I think:
The shutters are shut, no light may pass
Save two long rays thro' the hinge's chink.

II

Sixteen years old when she died!
Perhaps she had scarcely heard my name;
It was not her time to love; beside,
Her life had many a hope and aim,
Duties enough and little cares,
And now was quiet, now astir,

Till God's hand beckoned unawares, —
  And the sweet white brow is all of her.

III

Is it too late then, Evelyn Hope?
  What, your soul was pure and true,
The good stars met in your horoscope,
  Made you of spirit, fire and dew —
And, just because I was thrice as old
  And our paths in the world diverged so wide,
Each was nought to each, must I be told?
  We were fellow mortals, nought beside?

IV

No, indeed! for God above
  Is great to grant, as mighty to make,
And creates the love to reward the love:
  I claim you still, for my own love's sake!
Delayed it may be for more lives yet,
  Through worlds I shall traverse, not a few:
Much is to learn, and much to forget
  Ere the time be come for taking you.

V

But the time will come, — at last it will,
  When, Evelyn Hope, what meant (I shall say),
In the lower earth, in the years long still,
  That body and soul so pure and gay?
Why your hair was amber, I shall divine,
  And your mouth of your own geranium's red —
And what you would do with me, in fine,
  In the new life come in the old one's stead.

VI

I have lived (I shall say) so much since then,
Given up myself so many times,
Gained me the gains of various men,
Ransacked the ages, spoiled the climes;
Yet one thing, one, in my soul's full scope,
Either I missed or itself missed me:
And I want and find you, Evelyn Hope!
What is the issue? let us see!

VII

I loved you, Evelyn, all the while.
My heart seemed full as it could hold?
There was place and to spare for the frank young smile,
And the red young mouth, and the hair's young gold.
So, hush, — I will give you this leaf to keep:
See, I shut it inside the sweet cold hand!
There, that is our secret: go to sleep!
You will wake, and remember, and understand.

ROBERT BROWNING.

THE BLESSED DAMOZEL

THE blessed damozel leaned out
From the gold bar of Heaven;
Her eyes were deeper than the depth
Of waters stilled at even;
She had three lilies in her hand,
And the stars in her hair were seven.

Her robe, ungirt from clasp to hem,
  No wrought flowers did adorn,
But a white rose of Mary's gift,
  For service meetly worn;
Her hair that lay along her back
  Was yellow like ripe corn.

Herseemed she scarce had been a day
  One of God's choristers;
The wonder was not yet quite gone
  From that still look of hers;
Albeit, to them she left, her day
  Had counted as ten years.

(To one, it is ten years of years.
  . . . Yet now, and in this place,
Surely she leaned o'er me — her hair
  Fell all about my face. . . .
Nothing: the autumn fall of leaves.
  The whole year sets apace.)

It was the rampart of God's house
  That she was standing on;
By God built over the sheer depth
  The which is Space begun;
So high, that looking downward thence
  She scarce could see the sun.

It lies in Heaven, across the flood
  Of ether, as a bridge.
Beneath, the tides of day and night
  With flame and darkness ridge

The void, as low as where this earth
  Spins like a fretful midge.

Heard hardly, some of her new friends
  Amid their loving games
Spake evermore among themselves
  Their virginal chaste names;
And the souls mounting up to God
  Went by her like thin flames.

And still she bowed herself and stooped
  Out of the circling charm;
Until her bosom must have made
  The bar she leaned on warm,
And the lilies lay as if asleep
  Along her bended arm.

From the fixed place of Heaven she saw
  Time like a pulse shake fierce
Through all the worlds. Her gaze still strove
  Within the gulf to pierce
Its path; and now she spoke as when
  The stars sang in their spheres.

The sun was gone now; the curled moon
  Was like a little feather
Fluttering far down the gulf; and now
  She spoke through the still weather.
Her voice was like the voice the stars
  Had when they sang together.

(Ah sweet! Even now, in that bird's song,
  Strove not her accents there,

Fain to be hearkened? When those bells
  Possessed the mid-day air,
Strove not her steps to reach my side
  Down all the echoing stair?)

"I wish that he were come to me,
  For he will come," she said.
"Have I not prayed in Heaven? — on earth,
  Lord, Lord, has he not prayed?
Are not two prayers a perfect strength?
  And shall I feel afraid?

"When round his head the aureole clings,
  And he is clothed in white,
I'll take his hand and go with him
  To the deep wells of light;
We will step down as to a stream,
  And bathe there in God's sight.

"We two will stand beside that shrine,
  Occult, withheld, untrod,
Whose lamps are stirred continually
  With prayer sent up to God;
And see our old prayers, granted, melt
  Each like a little cloud.

"We two will lie i' the shadow of
  That living mystic tree
Within whose secret growth the Dove
  Is sometimes felt to be,
While every leaf that His plumes touch
  Saith His Name audibly.

"And I myself will teach to him,
I myself, lying so,
The songs I sing here; which his voice
Shall pause in, hushed and slow,
And find some knowledge at each pause,
Or some new thing to know."

(Alas! We two, we two, thou say'st!
Yea, one wast thou with me
That once of old. But shall God lift
To endless unity
The soul whose likeness with thy soul
Was but its love for thee?)

"We two," she said, "will seek the groves
Where the lady Mary is,
With her five handmaidens, whose names
Are five sweet symphonies,
Cecily, Gertrude, Magdalen,
Margaret and Rosalys.

"Circlewise sit they, with bound locks
And foreheads garlanded;
Into the fine cloth white like flame
Weaving the golden thread,
To fashion the birth-robes for them
Who are just born, being dead.

"He shall fear, haply, and be dumb:
Then will I lay my cheek
To his, and tell about our love,
Not once abashed or weak:

And the dear Mother will approve
  My pride, and let me speak.

"Herself shall bring us, hand in hand,
  To Him round whom all souls
Kneel, the clear-ranged unnumbered heads
  Bowed with their aureoles:
And angels meeting us shall sing
  To their citherns and citoles.

"There will I ask of Christ the Lord
  Thus much for him and me: —
Only to live as once on earth
  With Love, — only to be,
As then awhile, for ever now
  Together, I and he."

She gazed and listened and then said,
  Less sad of speech than mild, —
"All this is when he comes." She ceased.
  The light thrilled towards her, fill'd
With angels in strong level flight.
  Her eyes prayed, and she smil'd.

(I saw her smile.) But soon their path
  Was vague in distant spheres:
And then she cast her arms along
  The golden barriers,
And laid her face between her hands,
  And wept. (I heard her tears.)

DANTE GABRIEL ROSSETTI.

LOVE IN THE VALLEY

UNDER yonder beech-tree single on the green-sward,
  Couched with her arms behind her golden head,
Knees and tresses folded to slip and ripple idly,
  Lies my young love sleeping in the shade.
Had I the heart to slide an arm beneath her,
  Press her parting lips as her waist I gather slow,
Waking in amazement she could not but embrace
      me:
  Then would she hold me and never let me go?
. . . .

Shy as the squirrel and wayward as the swallow,
  Swift as the swallow along the river's light
Circleting the surface to meet his mirrored winglets,
  Fleeter she seems in her stay than in her flight.
Shy as the squirrel that leaps among the pine-tops,
  Wayward as the swallow overhead at set of sun,
She whom I love is hard to catch and conquer,
  Hard, but O the glory of the winning were she
      won.

When her mother tends her before the laughing
      mirror,
  Tying up her laces, looping up her hair,
Often she thinks, were this wild thing wedded,
  More love should I have, and much less care.
When her mother tends her before the lighted
      mirror,
  Loosening her laces, combing down her curls,
Often she thinks, were this wild thing wedded,
  I should miss but one for many boys and girls.
. . . .

Heartless she is as the shadow in the meadows
  Flying to the hills on a blue and breezy noon.
No, she is athirst and drinking up her wonder:
  Earth to her is young as the slip of the new
      moon.
Deals she an unkindness, 'tis but her rapid measure,
  Even as in a dance; and her smile can heal no less:
Like the swinging May-cloud that pelts the flowers
      with hailstones
  Off a sunny border, she was made to bruise and
      bless.

Lovely are the curves of the white owl sweeping
  Wavy in the dusk lit by one large star.
Lone on the fir-branch, his rattle-note unvaried,
  Brooding o'er the gloom, spins the brown evejar.
Darker grows the valley, more and more forgetting:
  So were it with me if forgetting could be willed.
Tell the grassy hollow that holds the bubbling well-
      spring.
  Tell it to forget the source that keeps it filled.

. . . .

Stepping down the hill with her fair companions,
  Arm in arm, all against the raying West,
Boldly she sings, to the merry tune she marches,
  Brave is her shape, and sweeter unpossessed.
Sweeter, for she is what my heart first awaking
  Whispered the world was; morning light is she.
Love that so desires would fain keep her changeless,
  Fain would fling the net, and fain have her free.

Happy happy time, when the white star hovers
  Low over dim fields fresh with bloomy dew,

Near the face of dawn, that draws athwart the dark-
ness,
Threading it with colour, like yewberries the yew.
Thicker crowd the shades as the grave East deepens
Glowing, and with crimson a long cloud swells.
Maiden still the morn is; and strange she is, and
secret;
Strange her eyes; her cheeks are cold as cold sea-
shells.

. . . .

Sunrays, leaning on our southern hills and lighting
Wild cloud-mountains that drag the hills along,
Oft ends the day of your shifting brilliant laughter
Chill as a dull face frowning on a song.
Ay, but shows the South-West a ripple-feathered
bosom
Blown to silver while the clouds are shaken and
ascend
Scaling the mid-heavens as they stream, there comes
a sunset
Rich, deep like love in beauty without end.

When at dawn she sighs, and like an infant to the
window
Turns grave eyes craving light, released from
dreams,
Beautiful she looks, like a white water-lily
Bursting out of bud in havens of the streams.
When from bed she rises clothed from neck to ankle
In her long nightgown sweet as boughs of May,
Beautiful she looks, like a tall garden lily
Pure from the night, and splendid for the day.

. . . .

Mother of the dews, dark-lashed twilight,
  Low-lidded twilight, o'er the valley's brim,
Rounding on thy breast sings the dew-delighted sky-
    lark,
  Clear as though the dewdrops had their voice in
    him.
Hidden where the rose-flush drinks the rayless
    planet,
  Fountain-full he pours the spraying fountain-
    showers.
Let me hear her laughter, I would have her ever
  Cool as dew in twilight, the lark above the flowers.

All the girls are out with their baskets for the
    primrose;
  Up lanes, woods through, they troop in joyful
    bands.
My sweet leads: she knows not why, but now she
    loiters,
  Eyes the bent anemones, and hangs her hands.
Such a look will tell that the violets are peeping,
  Coming the rose: and unaware a cry
Springs in her bosom for odours and for colour,
  Covert and the nightingale; she knows not why.
. . . .

Kerchiefed head and chin she darts between her
    tulips,
  Streaming like a willow grey in arrowy rain:
Some bend beaten cheek to gravel, and their angel
  She will be; she lifts them, and on she speeds
    again.
Black the driving raincloud breasts the iron gateway:
  She is forth to cheer a neighbour lacking mirth.

So when sky and grass met rolling dumb for thunder
Saw I once a white dove, sole light of earth.

Prim little scholars are the flowers of her garden,
Trained to stand in rows, and asking if they please.
I might love them well but for loving more the wild ones:
O my wild ones! they tell me more than these.
You, my wild one, you tell of honied field-rose,
Violet, blushing eglantine in life; and even as they,
They by the wayside are earnest of your goodness,
You are of life's, on the banks that line the way.
. . . .

Peering at her chamber the white crowns the red rose,
Jasmine winds the porch with stars two and three.
Parted is the window; she sleeps; the starry jasmine
Breathes a falling breath that carries thoughts of me.
Sweeter unpossessed, have I said of her my sweetest?
Not while she sleeps: while she sleeps the jasmine breathes,
Luring her to love; she sleeps; the starry jasmine
Bears me to her pillow under white rose-wreaths.

Yellow with birdfoot-trefoil are the grass-glades;
Yellow with cinquefoil of the dew-grey leaf;
Yellow with stonecrop; the moss-mounds are yellow:
Blue-necked the wheat sways, yellowing to the sheaf.
Green-yellow bursts from the copse the laughing yaffle;
Sharp as a sickle is the edge of shade and shine:

Earth in her heart laughs looking at the heavens,
  Thinking of the harvest: I look and think of mine.
. . . .

This I may know: her dressing and undressing
  Such a change of light shows as when the skies in sport
Shift from cloud to moonlight; or edging over thunder
  Slips a ray of sun; or sweeping into port
White sails furl; or on the ocean borders
  White sails lean along the waves leaping green.
Visions of her shower before me, but from eyesight
  Guarded she would be like the sun were she seen.

Front door and back of the mossed old farmhouse
  Open with the morn, and in a breezy link
Freshly sparkles garden to stripe-shadowed orchard,
  Green across a rill where on sand the minnows wink.
Busy in the grass the early sun of summer
  Swarms, and the blackbird's mellow fluting notes
Call my darling up with round and roguish challenge:
  Quaintest, richest carol of all the singing throats!
. . . .

Cool was the woodside; cool as her white dairy
  Keeping sweet the cream-pan; and there the boys from school,
Cricketing below, rushed brown and red with sunshine;
  O the dark translucence of the deep-eyed cool!
Spying from the farm, herself she fetched a pitcher
  Full of milk, and tilted for each in turn the beak.

Then a little fellow, mouth up and on tiptoe,
Said, "I will kiss you": she laughed and leaned her cheek.

Doves of the firwood walling high our red roof
Through the long noon coo, crooning through the coo.
Loose droop the leaves, and down the sleepy roadway
Sometimes pipes a chaffinch; loose drops the blue.
Cows flap a slow tail knee-deep in the river,
Breathless, given up to sun and gnat and fly.
Nowhere is she seen; and if I see her nowhere,
Lightning may come, straight rains and tiger sky.
. . . .

O the golden sheaf, the rustling treasure-armful!
O the nutbrown tresses nodding interlaced!
O the treasure-tresses one another over
Nodding! O the girdle slack about the waist!
Slain are the poppies that shot their random scarlet
Quick amid the wheatears: wound about the waist,
Gathered, see these brides of Earth one blush of ripeness!
O the nutbrown tresses nodding interlaced!

Large and smoky red the sun's cold disk drops,
Clipped by naked hills, on violet shaded snow:
Eastward large and still lights up a bower of moonrise,
Whence at her leisure steps the moon aglow.
Nightlong on black print-branches our beech-tree
Gazes in this whiteness: nightlong could I.

Iere may life on death or death on life be painted.
Let me clasp her soul to know she cannot die!

. . . .

;ossips count her faults; they scour a narrow chamber
Where there is no window, read not heaven or her.
When she was tiny," one aged woman quavers,
Plucks at my heart and leads me by the ear.
'aults she had once as she learnt to run and tumbled:
Faults of feature some see, beauty not complete.
'et, good gossips, beauty that makes holy
Earth and air, may have faults from head to feet.

Iither she comes; she comes to me; she lingers,
Deepens her brown eyebrows, while in new surprise
Iigh rise the lashes in wonder of a stranger;
Yet am I the light and living of her eyes.
;omething friends have told her fills her heart to brimming,
Nets her in her blushes, and wounds her, and tames.—
;ure of her haven, O like a dove alighting,
Arms up, she dropped: our souls were in our names.

. . . .

;oon will she lie like a white frost sunrise.
Yellow oats and brown wheat, barley pale as rye,
.ong since your sheaves have yielded to the thresher,
Felt the girdle loosened, seen the tresses fly.
;oon she will lie like a blood-red sunset.
Swift with the to-morrow, green-winged Spring!

Sing from the South-West, bring her back the tru
ants,
Nightingale and swallow, song and dipping win

Soft new beech-leaves, up to beamy April
Spreading bough on bough a primrose mountain
you
Lucid in the moon, raise lilies to the skyfields,
Youngest green transfused in silver shining
through:
Fairer than the lily, than the wild white cherry:
Fair as in image my seraph love appears
Borne to me by dreams when dawn is at my eyelids
Fair as in the flesh she swims to me on tears.

. . . .

Could I find a place to be alone with heaven,
I would speak my heart out: heaven is my need
Every woodland tree is flushing like the dogwood
Flashing like the whitebeam, swaying like the
reed.
Flushing like the dogwood crimson in October;
Streaming like the flag-reed South-West blown;
Flashing as in gusts the sudden-lighted whitebeam
All seem to know what is for heaven alone.

GEORGE MEREDITH.

CHORUS FROM
ATALANTA IN CALYDON

BEFORE the beginning of years
There came to the making of man
Time, with a gift of tears;
Grief, with a glass that ran;

Pleasure, with pain for leaven;
  Summer, with flowers that fell;
Remembrance fallen from heaven,
  And madness risen from hell;
Strength without hands to smite;
  Love that endures for a breath;
Night, the shadow of light,
  And life, the shadow of death.

And the high gods took in hand
  Fire, and the falling of tears,
And a measure of sliding sand
  From under the feet of the years;
And froth and drift of the sea;
  And dust of the labouring earth;
And bodies of things to be
  In the houses of death and of birth;
And wrought with weeping and laughter,
  And fashioned with loathing and love,
With life before and after
  And death beneath and above,
For a day and a night and a morrow,
  That his strength might endure for a span
With travail and heavy sorrow,
  The holy spirit of man.

From the winds of the north and the south
  They gathered as unto strife;
They breathed upon his mouth,
  They filled his body with life;
Eyesight and speech they wrought
  For the veils of the soul therein,

A time for labour and thought,
A time to serve and to sin;
They gave him light in his ways,
And love, and a space for delight,
And beauty and length of days,
And night, and sleep in the night.
His speech is a burning fire;
With his lips he travaileth;
In his heart is a blind desire,
In his eyes foreknowledge of death;
He weaves, and is clothed with derision;
Sows, and he shall not reap;
His life is a watch or a vision
Between a sleep and a sleep.

ALGERNON SWINBURNE.

DAISY

WHERE the thistle lifts a purple crown
Six foot out of the turf,
And the harebell shakes on the windy hill —
O the breath of the distant surf! —

The hills look over on the South,
And southward dreams the sea;
And with the sea-breeze hand in hand
Came innocence and she.

Where 'mid the gorse the raspberry
Red for the gatherer springs,
Two children did we stray and talk
Wise, idle, childish things.

She listened with big-lipped surprise,
  Breast-deep 'mid flower and spine:
Her skin was like a grape, whose veins
  Run snow instead of wine.

She knew not those sweet words she spake,
  Nor knew her own sweet way;
But there's never a bird, so sweet a song
  Thronged in whose throat that day.

O, there were flowers in Storrington
  On the turf and on the spray;
But the sweetest flower on Sussex hills
  Was the Daisy-flower that day!

Her beauty smoothed earth's furrowed face.
  She gave me tokens three:—
A look, a word of her winsome mouth,
  And a wild raspberry.

A berry red, a guileless look,
  A still word,—strings of sand!
And yet they made my wild, wild heart
  Fly down to her little hand.

For standing artless as the air,
  And candid as the skies,
She took the berries with her hand,
  And the love with her sweet eyes.

The fairest things have fleetest end,
  Their scent survives their close:

But the rose's scent is bitterness
  To him that loved the rose.

She looked a little wistfully,
  Then went her sunshine way:—
The sea's eye had a mist on it,
  And the leaves fell from the day.

She went her unremembering way,
  She went and left in me
The pang of all the partings gone,
  And partings yet to be.

She left me marvelling why my soul
  Was sad that she was glad;
At all the sadness in the sweet,
  The sweetness in the sad.

Still, still I seemed to see her, still
  Look up with soft replies,
And take the berries with her hand,
  And the love with her lovely eyes.

Nothing begins, and nothing ends,
  That is not paid with moan;
For we are born in others' pain
  And perish in our own.

FRANCIS THOMPSON.

AN ANCIENT TO ANCIENTS

Where once we danced, where once we sang,
Gentlemen,
The floors are sunken, cobwebs hang,
And cracks creep; worms have fed upon
The doors. Yea, sprightlier times were then
Than now, with harps and tabrets gone,
Gentlemen!

Where once we rowed, where once we sailed,
Gentlemen,
And damsels took the tiller, veiled
Against too strong a stare (God wot
Their fancy, then or anywhen!)
Upon that shore we are clean forgot,
Gentlemen!

We have lost somewhat, afar and near,
Gentlemen,
The thinning of our ranks each year
Affords a hint we are nigh undone,
That we shall not be ever again
The marked of many, loved of one,
Gentlemen.

In dance the polka hit our wish,
Gentlemen,
The paced quadrille, the spry schottische,
"Sir Roger." — And in opera spheres
The "Girl" (the famed "Bohemian"),
And "Trovatore," held the ears,
Gentlemen.

This season's paintings do not please,
Gentlemen,
Like Etty, Mulready, Maclise;
Throbbing romance has waned and wanned;
No wizard wields the witching pen
Of Bulwer, Scott, Dumas, and Sand,
Gentlemen.

The bower we shrined to Tennyson,
Gentlemen,
Is roof-wrecked; damps there drip upon
Sagged seats, the creeper-nails are rust,
The spider is sole denizen;
Even she who read those rhymes is dust,
Gentlemen!

We who met sunrise sanguine-souled,
Gentlemen,
Are wearing weary. We are old;
These younger press; we feel our rout
Is imminent to Aïdes' den,—
That evening's shades are stretching out,
Gentlemen!

And yet, though ours be failing frames,
Gentlemen,
So were some others' history names,
Who trod their track light-limbed and fast
As these youth, and not alien
From enterprise, to their long last,
Gentlemen.

Sophocles, Plato, Socrates,
Gentlemen,
Pythagoras, Thucydides,
Herodotus, and Homer, — yea,
Clement, Augustin, Origen,
Burnt brightlier towards their setting-day,
Gentlemen.

And ye, red-lipped and smooth-browed; list
Gentlemen;
Much is there waits you we have missed;
Much lore we leave you worth the knowing,
Much, much has lain outside our ken:
Nay, rush not: time serves: we are going,
Gentlemen.

THOMAS HARDY.

THE BRIDE

THE book was dull, its pictures
As leaden as its lore,
But one glad, happy picture
Made up for all and more;
'Twas that of you, sweet peasant,
Beside your grannie's door —
I never stopped so startled
Inside a book before.

Just so had I sat spell-bound,
Quite still with staring eyes,
If some great shiny hoopoe
Or moth of song-bird size
Had drifted to my window

And trailed its fineries —
Just so had I been startled,
Spelled with the same surprise.

It pictured you when springtime
In part had given place
But not surrendered wholly
To summer in your face;
When still your slender body
Was all a childish grace
Though woman's richest glories
Were building there apace.

'Twas blissful so to see you,
Yet not without a sigh
I dwelt upon the people
Who saw you not as I,
But in your living sweetness,
Beneath your native sky;
Ah, bliss to be the people
When you went tripping by!

I sat there, thinking, wondering,
About your life and home,
The happy days behind you,
The happy days to come,
Your grannie in her corner,
Upstairs the little room
Where you wake up each morning
To dream all day — of Whom?

That ring upon your finger,
Who gave you that to wear?

What blushing smith or farm lad
Came stammering at your ear
A million-time-told story
No maid but burns to hear,
And went about his labours
Delighting in his dear!

I thought of you sweet lovers,
The things you say and do,
The pouts and tears and partings
And swearings to be true,
The kissings in the barley —
You brazens, both of you!
I nearly burst out crying
With thinking of you two.

It put me in a frenzy
Of pleasure nearly pain,
A host of blurry faces
'Gan shaping in my brain,
I shut my eyes to see them
Come forward clear and plain,
I saw them come full flower,
And blur and fade again.

One moment so I saw them,
One sovereign moment so,
A host of girlish faces
All happy and aglow
With Life and Love it dealt them
Before it laid them low,
A hundred years, a thousand,
Ten thousand years ago.

One moment so I saw them
Come back with time full tide,
The host of girls, your grannies,
Who lived and loved and died
To give your mouth its beauty,
Your soul its gentle pride,
Who wrestled with the ages
To give the world a bride.

RALPH HODGSON.

BOOK III

EPITHALAMION

YE learned sisters which haue oftentimes
Beene to me ayding, others to adorne:
Whom ye thought worthy of your gracefull rymes,
That euen the greatest did not greatly scorne
To heare theyr names sung in your simple layes,
But ioyed in theyr prayse.
And when ye list your owne mishaps to mourne,
Which death, or loue, or fortunes wreck did rayse,
Your string could soone to sadder tenor turne,
And teach the woods and waters to lament
Your dolefull dreriment.
Now lay those sorrowfull complaints aside,
And hauing all your heads with girland crownd,
Helpe me mine owne loues prayses to resound,
Ne let the same of any be enuide:
So Orpheus did for his owne bride,
So I vnto my selfe alone will sing,
The woods shall to me answer and my Eccho ring.

Early before the worlds light giuing lampe,
His golden beame vpon the hils doth spred,
Hauing disperst the nights vnchearefull dampe,
Doe ye awake, and with fresh lusty hed,
Go to the bowre of my beloued loue,
My truest turtle doue,
Bid her awake; for Hymen is awake,
And long since ready forth his maske to moue,

With his bright Tead that flames with many a flake,
And many a bachelor to waite on him,
In theyr fresh garments trim.
Bid her awake therefore and soone her dight,
For lo the wished day is come at last,
That shall for al the paynes and sorrowes past,
Pay to her vsury of long delight:
And whylest she doth her dight,
Doe ye to her ioy and solace sing,
That all the woods may answer and your eccho ring.

Bring with you all the Nymphes that you can heare
Both of the riuers and the forrests greene:
And of the sea that neighbours to her neare,
Al with gay girlands goodly wel beseene.
And let them also with them bring in hand,
Another gay girland
For my fayre loue of lillyes and of roses,
Bound trueloue wize with a blew silke riband.
And let them make great store of bridale poses,
And let them eke bring store of other flowers
To deck the bridale bowers.
And let the ground whereas her foot shall tread,
For feare the stones her tender foot should wrong
Be strewed with fragrant flowers all along,
And diapred lyke the discolored mead.
Which done, doe at her chamber dore awayt,
For she will waken strayt,
The whiles doe ye this song vnto her sing,
The woods shall to you answer and your Eccho ring.

Ye Nymphes of Mulla which with carefull heed,
The siluer scaly trouts doe tend full well,

And greedy pikes which vse therein to feed,
(Those trouts and pikes all others doo excell)
And ye likewise which keepe the rushy lake,
Where none doo fishes take,
Bynd vp the locks the which hang scatterd light,
And in his waters which your mirror make,
Behold your faces as the christall bright,
That when you come whereas my loue doth lie,
No blemish she may spie.
And eke ye lightfoot mayds which keepe the deere,
That on the hoary mountayne vse to towre
And the wylde wolues which seeke them to deuoure,
With your steele darts doo chace from comming neer
Be also present heere,
To helpe to decke her and to help to sing,
That all the woods may answer and your eccho ring.

Wake, now my loue, awake; for it is time,
The Rosy Morne long since left Tithones bed,
All ready to her siluer coche to clyme,
And Phœbus gins to shew his glorious hed.
Hark how the cheerefull birds do chaunt theyr laies
And carroll of loues praise.
The merry Larke hir mattins sings aloft,
The thrush replyes, the Mauis descant playes,
The Ouzell shrills, the Ruddock warbles soft,
So goodly all agree with sweet consent,
To this dayes merriment.
Ah my deere loue why doe ye sleepe thus long,
When meeter were that ye should now awake,
T'awayt the comming of your ioyous make,
And hearken to the birds louelearned song,
The deawy leaues among.

For they of ioy and pleasance to you sing,
That all the woods them answer and theyr eccho
ring.

My loue is now awake out of her dreame,
And her fayre eyes like stars that dimmed were
With darksome cloud, now shew theyr goodly
beams
More bright then Hesperus his head doth rere.
Come now ye damzels, daughters of delight,
Helpe quickly her to dight,
But first come ye fayre houres which were begot
In loues sweet paradice, of Day and Night,
Which doe the seasons of the yeare allot,
And al that euer in this world is fayre
Doe make and still repayre.
And ye three handmayds of the Cyprian Queene,
The which doe still adorne her beauties pride,
Helpe to addorne my beautifullest bride:
And as ye her array, still throw betweene
Some graces to be seene,
And as ye vse to Venus, to her sing,
The whiles the woods shal answer and your eccho
ring.

Now is my loue all ready forth to come,
Let all the virgins therefore well awayt,
And ye fresh boyes that tend vpon her groome
Prepare your selues; for he is comming strayt.
Set all your things in seemely good aray
Fit for so ioyfull day,
The ioyfulst day that euer sunne did see.
Faire Sun, shew forth thy fauourable ray,

And let thy lifull heat not feruent be
For feare of burning her sunshyny face,
Her beauty to disgrace.
O fayrest Phœbus, father of the Muse,
If euer I did honour thee aright,
Or sing the thing, that mote thy mind delight,
Doe not thy seruants simple boone refuse,
But let this day let this one day be myne,
Let all the rest be thine.
Then I thy souerayne prayses loud wil sing,
That all the woods shal answer and theyr eccho
ring.

Harke how the Minstrels gin to shrill aloud
Their merry Musick that resounds from far,
The pipe, the tabor, and the trembling Croud,
That well agree withouten breach or iar,
But most of all the Damzels doe delite,
When they their tymbrels smyte,
And thereunto doe daunce and carrol sweet,
That all the sences they doe rauish quite,
The whyles the boyes run vp and downe the street,
Crying aloud with strong confused noyce,
As if it were one voyce.
Hymen io Hymen, Hymen they do shout,
That euen to the heauens theyr shouting shrill
Doth reach, and all the firmament doth fill,
To which the people standing all about,
As in approuance doe thereto applaud
And loud aduaunce her laud,
And euermore they Hymen Hymen sing,
That al the woods them answer and theyr eccho
ring.

Loe where she comes along with portly pace
Like Phœbe from her chamber of the East,
Arysing forth to run her mighty race,
Clad all in white, that seemes a virgin best.
So well it her beseemes that ye would weene
Some angell she had beene.
Her long loose yellow locks lyke golden wyre,
Sprinckled with perle, and perling flowres a tweene,
Doe lyke a golden mantle her attyre,
And being crowned with a girland greene,
Seeme lyke some mayden Queene.
Her modest eyes abashed to behold
So many gazers, as on her do stare,
Vpon the lowly ground affixed are.
Ne dare lift vp her countenance too bold,
But blush to heare her prayses sung so loud,
So farre from being proud.
Nathlesse doe ye still loud her prayses sing,
That all the woods may answer and your eccho ring

Tell me ye merchants daughters did ye see
So fayre a creature in your towne before,
So sweet, so louely, and so mild as she,
Adornd with beautyes grace and vertues store,
Her goodly eyes lyke Saphyres shining bright,
Her forehead yuory white,
Her cheekes lyke apples which the sun hath rudded,
Her lips lyke cherryes charming men to byte,
Her brest like to a bowle of creame vncrudded,
Her paps lyke lyllies budded,
Her snowie necke lyke to a marble towre,
And all her body like a pallace fayre,
Ascending vppe with many a stately stayre,

'o honours seat and chastities sweet bowre.
Vhy stand ye still ye virgins in amaze,
'pon her so to gaze,
Vhiles ye forget your former lay to sing,
'o which the woods did answer and your eccho ring.

3vt if ye saw that which no eyes can see,
'he inward beauty of her liuely spright,
ǐarnisht with heauenly guifts of high degree,
Auch more then would ye wonder at that sight,
and stand astonisht lyke to those which red
Aedusaes mazeful hed.
There dwels sweet loue and constant chastity,
'nspotted fayth and comely womanhood,
Regard of honour and mild modesty,
There vertue raynes as Queene in royal throne,
And giueth lawes alone.
The which the base affections doe obay,
And yeeld theyr seruices vnto her will,
Ne thought of thing vncomely euer may
Thereto approch to tempt her mind to ill.
Had ye once seene these her celestial threasures,
And vnreuealed pleasures,
Then would ye wonder and her prayses sing,
That al the woods should answer and your echo ring.

Open the temple gates vnto my loue,
Open them wide that she may enter in,
And all the postes adorne as doth behoue,
And all the pilours deck with girlands trim,
For to recyue this Saynt with honour dew,
That commeth in to you.
With trembling steps and humble reuerence,

She commeth in, before th' almighties vew,
Of her ye virgins learne obedience,
When so ye come into those holy places,
To humble your proud faces:
Bring her vp to th' high altar, that she may
The sacred ceremonies there partake,
The which do endlesse matrimony make,
And let the roring Organs loudly play
The praises of the Lord in liuely notes,
The whiles with hollow throates
The Choristers the ioyous Antheme sing,
That al the woods may answere and their eccho ring.

Behold whiles she before the altar stands
Hearing the holy priest that to her speakes
And blesseth her with his two happy hands,
How the red roses flush vp in her cheekes,
And the pure snow with goodly vermill stayne,
Like crimsin dyde in grayne,
That euen th' Angels which continually,
About the sacred Altare doe remaine,
Forget their seruice and about her fly,
Ofte peeping in her face that seemes more fayre,
The more they on it stare.
But her sad eyes still fastened on the ground,
Are gouerned with goodly modesty,
That suffers not one looke to glaunce awry,
Which may let in a little thought vnsownd.
Why blush ye loue to giue to me your hand,
The pledge of all our band?
Sing ye sweet Angels, Alleluya sing,
That all the woods may answere and your eccho
ring.

Now al is done; bring home the bride againe,
Bring home the triumph of our victory,
Bring home with you the glory of her gaine,
With ioyance bring her and with iollity.
Neuer had man more ioyfull day then this,
Whom heauen would heape with blis.
Make feast therefore now all this liue long day,
This day for euer to me holy is,
Poure out the wine without restraint or stay,
Poure not by cups, but by the belly full,
Poure out to all that wull,
And sprinkle all the postes and wals with wine,
That they may sweat, and drunken be withall.
Crowne ye God Bacchus with a coronall,
And Hymen also crowne with wreathes of vine,
And let the Graces daunce vnto the rest;
For they can doe it best:
The whiles the maydens doe theyr carroll sing,
To which the woods shall answer and theyr eccho
ring.

Ring ye the bels, ye yong men of the towne,
And leaue your wonted labors for this day:
This day is holy; doe ye write it downe,
That ye for euer it remember may.
This day the sunne is in his chiefest hight,
With Barnaby the bright,
From whence declining daily by degrees,
He somewhat loseth of his heat and light,
When once the Crab behind his back he sees.
But for this time it ill ordained was,
To chose the longest day in all the yeare,
And shortest night, when longest fitter weare:

Yet neuer day so long, but late would pass.
Ring ye the bels, to make it weare away,
And bonefiers make all day,
And daunce about them, and about them sing:
That all the woods may answer, and your eccho ring

Ah when will this long weary day haue end,
And lende me leaue to come vnto my loue?
How slowly do the houres theyr numbers spend?
How slowly does sad Time his feathers moue?
Hast thee O fayrest Planet to thy home
Within the Westerne fome:
Thy tyred steedes long since haue need of rest.
Long though it be, at last I see it gloome,
And the bright euening star with golden creast
Appeare out of the East.
Fayre childe of beauty, glorious lampe of loue
That all the host of heauen in rankes doost lead,
And guydest louers through the nightes dread,
How chearefully thou lookest from aboue,
And seemst to laugh atweene thy twinkling light
As ioying in the sight
Of these glad many which for ioy doe sing,
That all the woods them answer and their echo rin

Now cease ye damsels your delights forepast;
Enough is it, that all the day was youres:
Now day is doen, and night is nighing fast:
Now bring the Bryde into the brydall boures.
Now night is come, now soone her disarray,
And in her bed her lay:
Lay her in lillies and in violets,
And silken courteins ouer her display,

And odourd sheetes, and Arras couerlets.
Behold how goodly my faire loue does ly,
In proud humility;
Like vnto Maia, when as Ioue her tooke,
In Tempe, lying on the flowry gras,
Twixt sleepe and wake, after she weary was,
With bathing in the Acidalian brooke.
Now it is night, ye damsels may be gon,
And leaue my loue alone,
And leaue likewise your former lay to sing:
The woods no more shal answere, nor your eccho
ring.

Now welcome night, thou night so long expected,
That long daies labour doest at last defray,
And all my cares, which cruell loue collected,
Hast sumd in one, and cancelled for aye:
Spread thy broad wing ouer my loue and me,
That no man may vs see,
And in thy sable mantle vs enwrap,
From feare of perrill and foule horror free.
Let no false treason seeks vs to entrap,
Nor any dread disquiet once annoy
The safety of our ioy:
But let the night be calme and quietsome,
Without tempestuous storms or sad afray:
Lyke as when Ioue with fayre Alcmena lay,
When he begot the great Tirynthian groome:
Or lyke as when he with thy selfe did lie,
And begot Maiesty.
And let the mayds and yongmen cease to sing:
Ne let the woods them answer, nor theyr eccho
ring.

Let no lamenting cryes, nor dolefull teares,
Be heard all night within nor yet without:
Ne let false whispers, breeding hidden feares,
Breake gentle sleepe with misconceiued dout.
Let no deluding dreames, nor dreadful sights
Make sudden sad affrights;
Ne let housefyres, nor lightnings helpelesse harmes,
Ne let the Pouke, nor other euill sprights,
Ne let mischiuous witches with theyr charmes,
Ne let hob Goblins, names whose sence we see not,
Fray vs with things that be not.
Let not the shriech Oule, nor the Storke be heard:
Nor the night Rauen that still deadly yels,
Nor damned ghosts cald vp with mighty spels,
Nor griesly vultures make vs once affeard:
Ne let th' unpleasant Quyre of Frogs still croking
Make vs to wish theyr choking.
Let none of these theyr drery accents sing;
Ne let the woods them answer, nor theyr eccho ring.

Bvt let stil Silence trew night watches keepe,
That sacred peace may in assurance rayne,
And tymely sleep, when it is tyme to sleepe,
May poure his limbs forth on your pleasant playne,
The whiles an hundred little winged loues,
Like diuers fethered doues,
Shall fly and flutter round about your bed,
And in the secret darke, that none reproues,
Their prety stealthes shall worke, and snares shal
spread
To filch away sweet snatches of delight,
Conceald through couert night.
Ye sonnes of Venus, play your sports at will,

For greedy pleasure, carelesse of your toyes,
Thinks more vpon her paradise or ioyes,
Then what ye do, albeit good or ill.
All night therefore attend your merry play,
For it will soone be day:
Now none doth hinder you, that say or sing,
Ne will the woods now answer, nor your Eccho ring.

Who is the same, which at my window peepes?
Or whose is that faire face, that shines so bright,
Is it not Cinthia, she that neuer sleepes,
But walkes about high heauen al the night?
O fayrest goddesse, do thou not enuy
My loue with me to spy:
For thou likewise didst loue, though now vnthought,
And for a fleece of woll, which priuily,
The Latmian shephard once vnto thee brought,
His pleasures with thee wrought.
Therefore to vs be fauourable now;
And sith of wemens labours thou hast charge,
And generation goodly dost enlarge,
Encline thy will t'effect our wishfull vow,
And the chast wombe informe with timely seed,
That may our comfort breed:
Till which we cease our hopefull hap to sing,
Ne let the woods vs answere, nor our Eccho ring.

And thou great Iuno, which with awful might
The lawes of wedlock still dost patronize,
And the religion of the faith first plight
With sacred rites hast taught to solemnize:
And ekke for comfort often called art
Of women in their smart,

Eternally bind thou this louely band,
And all thy blessings vnto vs impart.
And thou glad Genius, in whose gentle hand,
The bridale bowre and geniall bed remaine,
Without blemish or staine,
And the sweet pleasures of theyr loues delight
With secret ayde doest succour and supply,
Till they bring forth the fruitfull progeny,
Send vs the timely fruit of this same night.
And thou fayre Hebe, and thou Hymen free,
Grant that it may so be.
Til which we cease your further prayse to sing,
Ne any woods shal answer, nor your Eccho ring.

And ye high heauens, the temple of the gods,
In which a thousand torches flaming bright
Doe burne, that to vs wretched earthly clods,
In dreadful darknesse lend desired light;
And all ye powers which in the same remayne,
More then we men can fayne,
Poure out your blessing on vs plentiously,
And happy influence vpon vs raine,
That we may raise a large posterity,
Which from the earth, which they may long possesse,
With lasting happinesse,
Vp to your haughty pallaces may mount,
And for the guerdon of theyr glorious merit
May heauenly tabernacles there inherit,
Of blessed Saints for to increase the count.
So let vs rest, sweet loue, in hope of this,
And cease till then our tymely ioyes to sing,
The woods no more vs answer, nor our eccho
ring.

Song made in lieu of many ornaments,
With which my loue should duly haue bene dect,
Which cutting off through hasty accidents,
Ye would not stay your dew time to expect,
But promist both to recompens,
Be vnto her a goodly ornament,
And for short time an endlesse moniment.

EDMUND SPENSER.

TO THE CAMBRO-BRITANS, AND THEIR HARPE, HIS BALLAD OF AGINCOURT

FAIRE stood the Wind for France,
When we our Sayles aduance,
Nor now to proue our chance,
Longer will tarry;
But putting to the Mayne,
At Kaux, the Mouth of Sene,
With all his Martiall Trayne,
Landed King Harry.

And taking many a Fort,
Furnish'd in Warlike sort,
Marcheth tow'rds Agincourt,
In happy howre;
Skirmishing day by day,
With those that stop'd his way,
Where the French Gen'rall lay,
With all his Power.

Which in his Hight of Pride,
King Henry to deride,

His Ransome to prouide
    To the King sending.
Which he neglects the while,
As from a Nation vile,
Yet with an angry smile,
    Their fall portending.

And turning to his Men,
Quoth our braue Henry then,
Though they to one be ten,
    Be not amazed.
Yet haue we well begunne,
Battels so brauely wonne,
Haue euer to the Sonne,
    By Fame beene raysed.

And for my Selfe (quoth he,)
This my full rest shall be,
England ne'r mourne for Me,
    Nor more esteeme me.
Victor I will remaine,
Or on this Earth lie slaine,
Neuer shall Shee sustaine,
    Losse to redeeme me.

Poiters and Cressy tell,
When most their Pride did swell,
Vnder our Swords they fell,
    No lesse our skill is,
Then when our Grandsire Great,
Clayming the Regall Seate,
By many a Warlike feate,
    Lop'd the French Lillies.

The Duke of Yorke so dread,
The eager Vaward led;
With the maine, Henry sped,
    Among'st his Hench-men.
Excester had the Rere,
A Brauer man not there,
O Lord, how hot they were,
    On the false French-men!

They now to fight are gone,
Armour on Armour shone,
Drumme now to Drumme did grone,
    To heare, was wonder;
That with Cryes they make,
The very Earth did shake,
Trumpet to Trumpet spake,
    Thunder to Thunder.

Well it thine Age became,
O Noble Erpingham,
Which didst the Signall ayme,
    To our hid Forces;
When from a Medow by,
Like a Storme suddenly,
The English Archery
    Stuck the French Horses.

With Spanish Ewgh so strong,
Arrowes a Cloth-yard long,
That like to Serpents stung,
    Piercing the Weather;
None from his fellow starts,
But playing Manly parts,

And like true English hearts,
    Stuck close together.

When downe their Bowes they threw,
And forth their Bilbowes drew,
And on the French they flew,
    Not one was tardie;
Armes were from shoulders sent,
Scalpes to the Teeth were rent,
Downe the French Pesants went,
    Our Men were hardie.

This while our Noble King,
His broad Sword brandishing,
Downe the French Hoast did ding,
    As to o'r-whelme it;
And many a deepe Wound lent,
His Armes with Bloud besprent,
And many a cruell Dent
    Bruised his Helmet.

Gloster, that Duke so good,
Next of the Royall Blood,
For famous England stood,
    With his braue Brother;
Clarence, his Steele so bright,
Though but a Maiden Knight,
Yet in that furious Fight,
    Scarce such another.

Warwick in Bloud did wade,
Oxford the Foe inuade,

And cruell slaughter made,
    Still as they ran vp;
Svffolke his Axe did ply,
Beavmont and Willovghby
Bare them right doughtily,
    Ferrers and Fanhope.

Vpon Saint Crispin's day
Fought was this Noble Fray,
Which Fame did not delay,
    To England to carry;
O, when shall English Men,
With such Acts fill a Pen,
Or England Breed againe,
    Such a King Harry?

MICHAEL DRAYTON.

IL PENSEROSO

HENCE, vain deluding joyes,
  The brood of folly without father bred,
How little you bested,
  Or fill the fixed mind with all your toyes;
Dwell in som idle brain,
  And fancies fond with gaudy shapes possess,
As thick and numberless
  As the gay motes that people the Sun Beams,
Or likest hovering dreams
  The fickle Pensioners of Morpheus train.
But hail thou Goddes, sage and holy,
Hail divinest Melancholy,
Whose Saintly visage is too bright
To hit the Sense of human sight;

And therfore to our weaker view,
Ore laid with black staid Wisdoms hue.
Black, but such as in esteem,
Prince Memnons sister might beseem,
Or that Starr'd Ethiope Queen that strove
To set her beauties praise above
The Sea Nymphs, and their powers offended.
Yet thou art higher far descended,
Thee bright-hair'd Vesta long of yore,
To solitary Saturn bore;
His daughter she (in Saturns raign,
Such mixture was not held a stain.)
Oft in glimmering Bowres, and glades
He met her, and in secret shades
Of woody Ida's inmost grove,
While yet there was no fear of Jove.
Com pensive Nun, devout and pure,
Sober, stedfast, and demure,
All in a robe of darkest grain,
Flowing with majestick train,
And sable stole of Cipres Lawn,
Over thy decent shoulders drawn.
Com, but keep thy wonted state,
With eev'n step, and musing gate,
And looks commercing with the skies,
Thy rapt soul sitting in thine eyes:
There held in holy passion still,
Forget thy self, to Marble, till
With a sad Leaden downward cast,
Thou fix them on the earth as fast.
And joyn with thee calm Peace, and Quiet,
Spare Fast, that oft with gods doth diet,
And hears the Muses in a ring,

Ay round about Joves Altar sing.
And adde to these retired Leasure,
That in trim Gardens takes his pleasure;
But first, and chiefest, with thee bring,
Him that yon soars on golden wing,
Guiding the fiery-wheeled throne,
The Cherub Contemplation,
And the mute Silence hist along,
'Less Philomel will daign a Song,
In her sweetest, saddest plight,
Smoothing the rugged brow of night,
While Cynthia checks her Dragon yoke,
Gently o're th' accustom'd Oke;
Sweet Bird that shunn'st the noise of folly,
Most musicall, most melancholy!
Thee Chauntress oft the Woods among,
I woo to hear thy eeven-Song;
And missing thee, I walk unseen
On the dry smooth-shaven Green,
To behold the wandring Moon,
Riding neer her highest noon,
Like one that had bin led astray
Through the Heav'ns wide pathles way;
And oft, as if her head she bow'd,
Stooping, through a fleecy cloud.
Oft on a Plat of rising ground,
I hear the far-off Curfeu sound,
Over som wide-water'd shoar,
Swinging slow with sullen roar;
Or if the Ayr will not permit,
Som still removed place will fit,
Where glowing Embers through the room
Teach light to counterfeit a gloom,

Far from all resort of mirth,
Save the Cricket on the hearth,
Or the Belmans drousie charm,
To bless the dores from nightly harm:
Or let my lamp at midnight hour,
Be seen in som high lonely Towr,
Where I may oft out-watch the Bear,
With thrice great Hermes, or upsphear
The spirit of Plato to unfold
What Worlds, or what vast Regions hold
The immortal mind that hath forsook
Her mansion in this fleshly nook:
And of those Dæmons that are found
In fire, air, flood, or under ground,
Whose power hath a true consent
With Planet, or with Element.
Som time let Gorgeous Tragedy
In Scepter'd Pall com sweeping by,
Presenting Thebs, or Pelops line,
Or the tale of Troy divine.
Or what (though rare) of later age,
Ennobled hath the Buskind stage.
But, O sad Virgin, that thy power
Might raise Musæus from his bower,
Or bid the soul of Orpheus sing
Such notes as warbled to the string,
Drew Iron tears down Pluto's cheek,
And made Hell grant what Love did seek.
Or call up him that left half told
The story of Cambuscan bold,
Of Camball, and of Algarsife,
And who had Canace to wife,
That own'd the vertuous Ring and Glass,

And of the wondrous Hors of Brass,
On which the Tartar King did ride;
And if ought els, great Bards beside,
In sage and solemn tunes have sung,
Of Turneys and of Trophies hung;
Of Forests, and inchantments drear,
Where more is meant then meets the ear.
Thus night oft see me in thy pale career,
Till civil-suited Morn appeer,
Not trickt and frounc't as she was wont,
With the Attick Boy to hunt,
But Cherchef't in a comly Cloud,
While rocking Winds are Piping loud,
Or usher'd with a shower still,
When the gust hath blown his fill,
Ending on the russling Leaves,
With minute drops from off the Eaves.
And when the Sun begins to fling
His flaring beams, me Goddes bring
To arched walks of twilight groves,
And shadows brown that Sylvan loves
Of Pine, or monumental Oake,
Where the rude Ax with heaved stroke,
Was never heard the Nymphs to daunt,
Or fright them from their hallow'd haunt.
There in close covert by som Brook,
Where no profaner eye may look,
Hide me from Day's garish eie,
While the Bee with Honied thie,
That at her flowry work doth sing,
And the Waters murmuring
With such consort as they keep,
Entice the dewy-feather'd Sleep;

And let som strange mysterious dream,
Wave at his Wings in Airy stream,
Of lively portrature display'd,
Softly on my eye-lids laid.
And as I wake, sweet musick breath
Above, about, or underneath,
Sent by som spirit to mortals good,
Or th'unseen Genius of the Wood.
But let my due feet never fail,
To walk the studious Cloysters pale,
And love the high embowed Roof,
With antick Pillars massy proof,
And storied Windows richly dight,
Casting a dimm religious light.
There let the pealing Organ blow,
To the full voic'd Quire below,
In Service high, and Anthems cleer,
As may with sweetnes, through mine ear,
Dissolve me into extasies,
And bring all Heav'n before mine eyes.
And may at last my weary age
Find out the peacefull hermitage,
The Hairy Gown and Mossy Cell,
Where I may sit and rightly spell
Of Every Star that Heav'n doth shew,
And every Herb that sips the dew;
Till old experience do attain
To somthing like Prophetic strain.
These pleasures Melancholy give,
And I with thee will choose to live.

JOHN MILTON.

AN HORATIAN ODE UPON CROMWELL'S RETURN FROM IRELAND

The forward youth that would appear
Must now forsake his Muses dear,
Nor in the shadows sing
His numbers languishing:

'Tis time to leave the books in dust,
And oil the unusèd armour's rust;
Removing from the wall
The corselet of the hall.

So restless Cromwell could not cease
In the inglorious arts of peace,
But through adventurous war
Urgèd his active star;

And, like the three-forked lightning, first
Breaking the clouds where it was nursed,
Did thorough his own side
His fiery way divide:

(For 'tis all one to courage high,
The emulous, or enemy;
And with such, to enclose
Is more than to oppose;)

Then burning through the air he went
And palaces and temples rent;
And Cæsar's head at last
Did through his laurels blast.

'Tis madness to resist or blame
The face of angry Heaven's flame;
    And if we would speak true,
    Much to the man is due,

Who, from his private gardens, where
He lived reservèd and austere,
    (As if his highest plot
    To plant the bergamot;)

Could by industrious valour climb
To ruin the great work of Time,
    And cast thy kingdoms old,
    Into another mould;

Though Justice against Fate complain,
And plead the ancient rights in vain;
    (But those do hold or break,
    As men are strong or weak.)

Nature that hateth emptiness,
Allows of penetration less,
    And therefore must make room
    Where greater spirits come.

What field of all the civil war,
Where his were not the deepest scar?
    And Hampton shows what part
    He had of wiser art;

Where, twining subtle fears with hope,
He wove a net of such a scope

That Charles himself might chase
To Caresbrooke's narrow case,

That thence the royal actor borne,
The tragic scaffold might adorn;
While round the armèd bands
Did clap their bloody hands.

He nothing common did, or mean,
Upon that memorable scene,
But with his keener eye
The axe's edge did try;

Nor call'd the gods with vulgar spite
To vindicate his helpless right;
But bow'd his comely head
Down, as upon a bed.

This was that memorable hour,
Which first assured the forcèd power;
So, when they did design
The capitol's first line,

A bleeding head, where they begun,
Did fright the architects to run;
And yet in that the state
Foresaw its happy fate.

And now the Irish are ashamed
To see themselves in one year tamed;
So much one man can do,
That does both act and know

They can affirm his praises best,
And have, though overcome, confessed
    How good he is, how just,
    And fit for highest trust.

Nor yet grown stiffer with command,
But still in the republic's hand —
    How fit he is to sway,
    That can so well obey!

He to the Commons' feet presents
A kingdom for his first year's rents;
    And, what he may, forbears
    His fame, to make it theirs;

And has his sword and spoils ungirt,
To lay them at the public's skirt:
    So, when the falcon high
    Falls heavy from the sky,

She, having killed, no more doth search,
But on the next green bough to perch;
    Where, when he first does lure,
    The falconer has her sure.

What may not then our isle presume,
While victory his crest does plume?
    What may not others fear,
    If thus he crowns each year?

As Cæsar, he, ere long, to Gaul,
To Italy an Hannibal,

And to all States not free,
Shall climactèric be.

The Pict no shelter now shall find
Within his parti-coloured mind,
But, from his valour sad,
Shrink underneath the plaid;

Happy, if in the tufted brake,
The English hunter him mistake,
Nor lay his hounds in near
The Caledonian deer.

But thou, the war's and fortune's son,
March indefatigably on;
And for the last effect,
Still keep the sword erect;

Besides the force it has to fright
The spirits of the shady night,
The same arts that did gain
A power, must it maintain.

ANDREW MARVELL.

ALEXANDER'S FEAST

I

'TWAS at the Royal Feast, for Persia won
By Philip's Warlike Son:
Aloft in awful State
The God-like Heroe sate
On his Imperial Throne:

His valiant Peers were plac'd around;
Their brows with Roses and with Myrtles bound.
(So shou'd Desert in Arms be Crown'd:)
The Lovely Thais by his side,
Sate like a blooming Eastern Bride
In Flow'r of Youth and Beauty's Pride.
Happy, happy, happy Pair!
None but the Brave
None but the Brave
None but the Brave deserves the Fair.

Chorus:

Happy, happy, happy Pair!
None but the Brave
None but the Brave
None but the Brave deserves the Fair.

II

Timotheus plac'd on high
Amid the tuneful Quire,
With flying Fingers touch'd the Lyre:
The trembling Notes ascend the Sky,
And Heav'nly Joys inspire.
The Song began from Jove;
Who left his blissful Seats above,
(Such is the Pow'r of mighty Love.)
A Dragon's fiery Form bely'd the God:
Sublime on Radiant Spires He rode,
When He to fair Olympia press'd:
And while He sought her snowy Breast:
Then, round her slender Waist he curl'd,
And stamp'd an Image of himself, a Sov'raign of the World.

The list'ning Crowd admire the lofty Sound,
A present Deity, they shout around;
A present Deity the vaulted Roofs rebound.
With ravish'd Ears
The Monarch hears,
Assumes the God,
Affects to nod,
And seems to shake the Spheres.

Chorus:

With ravish'd Ears
The Monarch hears,
Assumes the God,
Affects to nod,
And seems to shake the Spheres.

III

The Praise of Bacchus then, the sweet Musician sung;
Of Bacchus ever Fair, and ever Young.
The jolly God in Triumph comes;
Sound the Trumpets; beat the Drums;
Flush'd with a purple Grace
He shows his honest Face,
Now give the Hautboys breath; He comes, He comes,
Bacchus ever Fair and Young,
Drinking Joys did first ordain:
Bacchus Blessings are a Treasure;
Drinking is the Soldiers Pleasure;
Rich the Treasure;
Sweet the Pleasure;
Sweet is Pleasure after Pain.

Chorus:

Bacchus Blessings are a Treasure,
Drinking is the Soldier's Pleasure;
Rich the Treasure,
Sweet the Pleasure;
Sweet is Pleasure after Pain.

IV

Sooth'd with the Sound the King grew vain;
Fought all his Battails o'er again;
And thrice He routed all his Foes; and thrice he slew the slain.
The Master saw the Madness rise;
His glowing Cheeks, his ardent Eyes;
And while He Heav'n and Earth defy'd,
Chang'd his Hand, and check'd his Pride.
He chose a Mournful Muse,
Soft Pity to infuse:
He sung Darius Great and Good,
By too severe a Fate,
Fallen, fallen, fallen, fallen,
Fallen from his high Estate,
And weltring in his Blood;
Deserted at his utmost Need,
By those his former Bounty fed:
On the bare Earth expos'd He lies,
With not a Friend to close his Eyes.

With down-cast looks the joyless Victor sate,
Revolving in his alter'd Soul
The various Turns of Chance below;
And, now and then, a Sigh he stole;
And tears began to flow.

Chorus:

Revolving in his alter'd Soul
The various Turns of Chance below;
And, now and then, a Sigh he stole;
And Tears began to flow.

V

The Mighty Master smil'd to see
That love was in the next Degree:
'Twas but a Kindred-Sound to move;
For Pity melts the Mind to Love.
Softly, sweet, in Lydian Measures,
Soon he sooth'd his Soul to Pleasures.
War, he sung, is Toil and Trouble;
Honour, but an empty Bubble;
Never ending, still beginning,
Fighting still, and still destroying,
If the World be worth thy Winning,
Think, O think it worth Enjoying.
Lovely Thais sits beside thee,
Take the Good the Gods provide thee.

The many rend the Skies with loud Applause;
So Love was Crown'd, but Musique won the Cause.
The Prince, unable to conceal his Pain,
Gaz'd on the Fair
Who caus'd his Care,
And sigh'd and look'd, sigh'd and look'd,
Sigh'd and look'd, and sigh'd again:
At length, with Love and Wine at once oppress'd,
The vanquish'd Victor sunk upon her Breast.

Chorus:

The Prince, unable to conceal his Pain,
Gaz'd on the Fair
Who caus'd his Care,
And sigh'd and look'd, sigh'd and look'd,
Sigh'd and look'd, and sigh'd again:
At length, with Love and Wine at once oppress'd,
The vanquish'd Victor sunk upon her Breast.

VI

Now strike the Golden lyre again:
A lowder yet, and yet a lowder Strain.
Break his Bands of Sleep asunder,
And rouze him, like a rattling Peal of Thunder.
Hark, hark, the horrid Sound
Has rais'd up his Head;
As awak'd from the Dead,
And amaz'd, he stares around.
Revenge, Revenge, Timotheus cries,
See the Furies arise!
See the Snakes that they rear,
How they hiss in their Hair,
And the Sparkles that flash from their Eyes!
Behold a ghastly Band,
Each a Torch in his Hand!
Those are Grecian Ghosts, that in Battail were slain
And unbury'd remain
Inglorious on the Plain:
Give the Vengeance due
To the Valiant Crew.
Behold how they toss their Torches on high,
How they point to the Persian Abodes,

And glitt'ring Temples of their Hostile Gods!
The Princes applaud, with a furious Joy;
And the King seiz'd a Flambeau with Zeal to destroy;
    Thais led the Way,
    To light him to his Prey,
And, like another Hellen, fir'd another Troy.

Chorus:

And the King seiz'd a Flambeau with Zeal to destroy;
    Thais led the Way,
    To light him to his Prey,
And, like another Hellen, fir'd another Troy.

VII

      Thus, long ago
  Ere heaving Bellows learn'd to blow,
    While Organs yet were mute;
    Timotheus, to his breathing Flute,
      And sounding Lyre,
Cou'd swell the Soul to rage, or kindle soft Desire.
  At last Divine Cecilia came,
  Inventress of the Vocal Frame;
The sweet Enthusiast, from her Sacred Store,
  Enlarg'd the former narrow Bounds,
  And added Length to solemn Sounds,
With Nature's Mother-Wit, and Arts unknown
    before.
  Let old Timotheus yield the Prize,
    Or both divide the Crown:
  He rais'd a Mortal to the Skies;
    She drew an Angel down.

Grand Chorus:

At last, Divine Cecilia came,
Inventress of the Vocal Frame;
The sweet Enthusiast, from her Sacred Store,
Enlarg'd the former narrow Bounds,
And added Length to solemn Sounds,
With Nature's Mother-Wit, and Arts unknown before.
Let old Timotheus yield the Prize,
Or both divide the Crown;
He raised a Mortal to the Skies;
She drew an Angel down.

JOHN DRYDEN.

TAM O' SHANTER

A TALE

Of Brownyis and of Bogillis full is this Buke.

GAWIN DOUGLAS.

WHEN chapman billies leave the street,
And drouthy neebors neebors meet;
As market-days are wearing late,
An' folk begin to tak the gate;
While we sit bousing at the nappy,
An' getting fou and unco happy,
We think na on the lang Scots miles,
The mosses, waters, slaps, and styles,
That lie between us and our hame,
Whare sits our sulky, sullen dame,
Gathering her brows like gathering storm,
Nursing her wrath to keep it warm.

This truth fand honest Tam o' Shanter,
As he frae Ayr ae night did canter:
(Auld Ayr, wham ne'er a town surpasses,
For honest men and bonie lasses).

O Tam, had'st thou but been sae wise,
As taen thy ain wife Kate's advice!
She tauld thee weel thou was a skellum,
A blethering, blustering, drunken blellum
That frae November till October,
Ae market-day thou was nae sober;
That ilka melder wi' the miller,
Thou sat as lang as thou had siller;
That ev'ry naig was ca'd a shoe on,
The smith and thee gat roaring fou on;
That at the Lord's house, even on Sunday,
Thou drank wi' Kirkton Jean till Monday.
She prophesied that, late or soon,
Thou would be found deep drown'd in Doon,
Or catch'd wi' warlocks in the mirk
By Alloway's auld, haunted kirk.

Ah! gentle dames, it gars me greet,
To think how monie counsels sweet,
How monie lengthen'd, sage advices
The husband frae the wife despises!

But to our tale: — Ae market-night,
Tam had got planted unco right,
Fast by an ingle, bleezing finely,
Wi' reaming swats, that drank divinely;
And at his elbow, Souter Johnie,
His ancient, trusty, drouthy cronie:

Tam lo'ed him like a very brither;
They had been fou for weeks thegither.
The night drave on wi' sangs and clatter;
And ay the ale was growing better:
The landlady and Tam grew gracious
Wi' secret favours, sweet and precious;
The Souter tauld his queerest stories;
The landlord's laugh was ready chorus:
The storm without might rair and rustle,
Tam did na mind the storm a whistle.

Care, mad to see a man sae happy,
E'en drown'd himself amang the nappy.
As bees flee hame wi' lades o' treasure,
The minutes wing'd their way wi' pleasure:
Kings may be blest but Tam was glorious,
O'er a' the ills o' life victorious!

But pleasures are like poppies spread:
You seize the flow'r, its bloom is shed;
Or like the snow falls in the river,
A moment white — then melts for ever;
Or like the borealis race,
That flit ere you can point their place;
Or like the rainbow's lovely form
Evanishing amid the storm.
Nae man can tether time or tide;
The hour approaches Tam maun ride:
That hour, o' night's black arch the keystane,
That dreary hour Tam mounts his beast in;
And sic a night he taks the road in,
As ne'er poor sinner was abroad in.

The wind blew as 'twad blawn its last;
The rattling showers rose on the blast;
The speedy gleams the darkness swallow'd;
Loud, deep, and lang the thunder bellow'd:
That night, a child might understand,
The Deil had business on his hand.

Weel mounted on his gray mare Meg,
A better never lifted leg,
Tam skelpit on thro' dub and mire,
Despising wind, and rain, and fire;
Whiles holding fast his guid blue bonnet,
Whiles crooning o'er some auld Scots sonnet,
Whiles glow'ring round wi' prudent cares,
Lest bogles catch him unawares:
Kirk-Alloway was drawing nigh,
Whare ghaists and houlets nightly cry.

By this time he was cross the ford,
Whare in the snaw the chapman smoor'd;
And past the birks and meikle stane,
Whare drunken Charlie brak's neck-bane;
And thro' the whins and by the cairn,
Whare hunters fand the murder'd bairn;
And near the thorn, aboon the well,
Whare Mungo's mither hang'd hersel.
Before him Doon pours all his floods;
The doubling storm roars thro' the woods;
The lightnings flash from pole to pole;
Near and more near the thunders roll:
When, glimmering thro' the groaning trees,
Kirk-Alloway seem'd in a bleeze,

Thro' ilka bore the beams were glancing,
And loud resounded mirth and dancing.

Inspiring bold John Barleycorn,
What dangers thou canst make us scorn!
Wi' tippenny, we fear nae evil;
Wi' usquabae, we'll face the Devil!
The swats sae ream'd in Tammie's noddle,
Fair play, he car'd na deils a boddle.
But Maggie stood, right sair astonish'd,
Till, by the heel and hand admonish'd,
She ventur'd forward on the light;
And, wow! Tam saw an unco sight!

Warlocks and witches in a dance:
Nae cotillion, brent new frae France,
But hornpipes, jigs, strathspeys, and reels,
Put life and mettle in their heels.
A winnock-bunker in the east,
There sat Auld Nick, in shape o' beast;
A tousie tyke, black, grim, and large,
To gie them music was his charge:
He screw'd the pipes and gart them skirl,
Till roof and rafters a' did dirl.
Coffins stood round, like open presses,
That shaw'd the dead in their last dresses;
And, by some devilish cantraip sleight,
Each in its cauld hand held a light:
By which heroic Tam was able
To note upon the haly table,
A murderer's banes, in gibbet-airns;
Twa span-lang, wee, unchristen'd bairns;
A thief new-cutted frae a rape —

Wi' his last gasp his gab did gape;
Five tomahawks wi' bluid red-rusted;
Five scymitars wi' murder crusted;
A garter which a babe had strangled;
A knife a father's throat had mangled —
Whom his ain son o' life bereft —
The grey-hairs yet stack to the heft;
Wi' mair of horrible and awefu',
Which even to name wad be unlawfu'.

As Tammie glowr'd, amaz'd, and curious,
The mirth and fun grew fast and furious;
The piper loud and louder blew,
The dancers quick and quicker flew,
They reel'd, they set, they cross'd, they cleekit,
Till ilka carlin swat and reekit,
And coost her duddies to the wark,
And linket at it in her sark!

Now Tam, O Tam! had thae been queans,
A' plump and strapping in their teens!
Their sarks, instead o' creeshie flannen,
Been snaw-white seventeen hunder linen! —
Thir breeks o' mine, my only pair,
That ance were plush, o' guid blue hair,
I wad hae gi'en them off my hurdies
For ae blink o' the bonie burdies!

But wither'd beldams, auld and droll,
Rigwoodie hags wad spean a foal,
Louping and flinging on a crummock,
I wonder did na turn thy stomach!

But Tam kend what was what fu' brawlie:
There was ae winsome wench and wawlie,
That night enlisted in the core,
Lang after kend on Carrick shore
(For monie a beast to dead she shot,
An' perish'd monie a bonie boat,
And shook baith meikle corn and bear,
And kept the country-side in fear).
Her cutty sark, o' Paisley harn,
That while a lassie she had worn,
In longitude tho' sorely scanty,
It was her best, and she was vauntie. . . .
Ah! little kend thy reverend grannie,
That sark she coft for her wee Nannie,
Wi' twa pund Scots ('twas a' her riches),
Wad ever grac'd a dance of witches!

But here my Muse her wing maun cour,
Sic flights are far beyond her power:
To sing how Nannie lap and flang
(A souple jade she was and strang),
And how Tam stood like ane bewitch'd,
And thought his very een enrich'd;
Even Satan glowr'd, and fidg'd fu' fain,
And hotch'd and blew wi' might and main;
Till first ae caper, syne anither,
Tam tint his reason a' thegither,
And roars out: "Weel done, Cutty-sark!"
And in an instant all was dark;
And scarcely had he Maggie rallied,
When out the hellish legion sallied.

As bees bizz out wi' angry fyke,
When plundering herds assail their byke;

As open pussie's mortal foes,
When, pop! she starts before their nose;
As eager runs the market-crowd,
When "Catch the thief!" resounds aloud:
So Maggie runs, the witches follow,
Wi' monie an eldritch skriech and hollo.

Ah, Tam! Ah, Tam! thou'll get thy fairin!
In hell they'll roast thee like a herrin!
In vain thy Kate awaits thy comin!
Kate soon will be a woefu' woman!
Now, do thy speedy utmost, Meg,
And win the keystane of the brig;
There, at them thou thy tail may toss,
A running stream they dare na cross!
But ere the keystane she could make,
The fient a tail she had to shake;
For Nannie, far before the rest,
Hard upon noble Maggie prest,
And flew at Tam wi' furious ettle;
But little wist she Maggie's mettle!
Ae spring brought off her master hale,
But left behind her ain grey tail:
The carlin claught her by the rump,
And left poor Maggie scarce a stump.

Now, wha this tale o' truth shall read,
Ilk man, and mother's son, take heed:
Whene'er to drink you are inclin'd,
Or cutty sarks run in your mind,
Think! ye may buy the joys o'er dear:
Remember Tam o' Shanter's mare.

ROBERT BURNS.

MICHAEL

A PASTORAL POEM

If from the public way you turn your steps
Up the tumultuous brook of Green-head Ghyll,
You will suppose that with an upright path
Your feet must struggle; in such bold ascent
The pastoral mountains front you, face to face.
But, courage! for around that boisterous brook
The mountains have all opened out themselves,
And made a hidden valley of their own.
No habitation can be seen; but they
Who journey thither find themselves alone
With a few sheep, with rocks and stones, and kites
That overhead are sailing in the sky.
It is in truth an utter solitude;
Nor should I have made mention of this Dell,
But for one object which you might pass by,
Might see and notice not. Beside the brook
Appears a straggling heap of unhewn stones!
And to that simple object appertains
A story — unenriched with strange events,
Yet not unfit, I deem, for the fireside,
Or for the summer shade. It was the first
Of those domestic tales that spake to me
Of Shepherds, dwellers in the valleys, men
Whom I already loved; — not verily
For their own sakes, but for the fields and hills
Where was their occupation and abode.
And hence this Tale, while I was yet a Boy
Careless of books, yet having felt the power
Of Nature, by the gentle agency
Of natural objects, led me on to feel

For passions that were not my own, and think
(At random and imperfectly indeed)
On man, the heart of man, and human life.
Therefore, although it be a history
Homely and rude, I will relate the same
For the delight of a few natural hearts;
And, with yet fonder feeling, for the sake
Of youthful Poets, who among these hills
Will be my second self when I am gone.

Upon the forest-side in Grasmere Vale
There dwelt a Shepherd, Michael was his name;
An old man, stout of heart, and strong of limb.
His bodily frame had been from youth to age
Of an unusual strength: his mind was keen,
Intense, and frugal, apt for all affairs,
And in his shepherd's calling he was prompt
And watchful more than ordinary men.
Hence had he learned the meaning of all winds,
Of blasts of every tone; and oftentimes,
When others heeded not, He heard the South
Make subterraneous music, like the noise
Of bagpipers on distant Highland hills.
The Shepherd, at such warning, of his flock
Bethought him, and he to himself would say,
"The winds are now devising work for me!"
And, truly, at all times, the storm, that drives
The traveller to a shelter, summoned him
Up to the mountains: he had been alone
Amid the heart of many thousand mists,
That came to him, and left him, on the heights.
So lived he till his eightieth year was past.
And grossly that man errs, who should suppose

That the green valleys, and the streams and rocks,
Were things indifferent to the Shepherd's thoughts.
Fields, where with cheerful spirits he had breathed
The common air; hills, which with vigorous step
He had so often climbed; which had impressed
So many incidents upon his mind
Of hardship, skill or courage, joy or fear;
Which, like a book, preserved the memory
Of the dumb animals, whom he had saved,
Had fed or sheltered, linking to such acts
The certainty of honourable gain;
Those fields, those hills — what could they less? had laid
Strong hold on his affections, were to him
A pleasurable feeling of blind love,
The pleasure which there is in life itself.

His days had not been passed in singleness.
His Helpmate was a comely matron, old —
Though younger than himself full twenty years.
She was a woman of a stirring life,
Whose heart was in her house: two wheels she had
Of antique form: this large, for spinning wool;
That small, for flax; and, if one wheel had rest,
It was because the other was at work.
The Pair had but one inmate in their house,
An only Child, who had been born to them
When Michael, telling o'er his years, began
To deem that he was old, — in shepherd's phrase,
With one foot in the grave. This only Son,
With two brave sheep-dogs tried in many a storm,
The one of an inestimable worth,
Made all their household. I may truly say,

That they were as a proverb in the vale
For endless industry. When day was gone,
And from their occupations out of doors
The Son and Father were come home, even then,
Their labour did not cease; unless when all
Turned to the cleanly supper-board, and there,
Each with a mess of pottage and skimmed milk,
Sat round the basket piled with oaten cakes,
And their plain home-made cheese. Yet when the
meal
Was ended, Luke (for so the Son was named)
And his old Father both betook themselves
To such convenient work as might employ
Their hands by the fireside; perhaps to card
Wool for the Housewife's spindle, or repair
Some injury done to sickle, flail, or scythe,
Or other implement of house or field.

Down from the ceiling, by the chimney's edge,
That in our ancient uncouth country style
With huge and black projection overbrowed
Large space beneath, as duly as the light
Of day grew dim the Housewife hung a lamp;
An aged utensil, which had performed
Service beyond all others of its kind.
Early at evening did it burn — and late,
Surviving comrade of uncounted hours,
Which, going by from year to year, had found,
And left, the couple neither gay perhaps
Nor cheerful, yet with objects and with hopes,
Living a life of eager industry.
And now, when Luke had reached his eighteenth
year,

There by the light of this old lamp they sate,
Father and Son, while far into the night
The Housewife plied her own peculiar work,
Making the cottage through the silent hours
Murmur as with the sound of summer flies.
This light was famous in its neighbourhood,
And was a public symbol of the life
That thrifty Pair had lived. For, as it chanced,
Their cottage on a plot of rising ground
Stood single, with large prospect, north and south,
High into Easedale, up to Dunmail-Raise,
And westward to the village near the lake;
And from this constant light, so regular,
And so far seen, the House itself, by all
Who dwelt within the limits of the vale,
Both old and young, was named THE EVENING STAR.

Thus living on through such a length of years,
The Shepherd, if he loved himself, must needs
Have loved his Helpmate; but to Michael's heart
This son of his old age was yet more dear —
Less from instinctive tenderness, the same
Fond spirit that blindly works in the blood of all —
Than that a child, more than all other gifts
That earth can offer to declining man,
Brings hope with it, and forward-looking thoughts,
And stirrings of inquietude, when they
By tendency of nature needs must fail.
Exceeding was the love he bare to him,
His heart and his heart's joy! For oftentimes
Old Michael, while he was a babe in arms,
Had done him female service, not alone
For pastime and delight, as is the use

Of fathers, but with patient mind enforced
To acts of tenderness; and he had rocked
His cradle, as with a woman's gentle hand.

And in a later time, ere yet the Boy
Had put on boy's attire, did Michael love,
Albeit of a stern unbending mind,
To have the Young-one in his sight, when he
Wrought in the field, or on his shepherd's stool
Sate with a fettered sheep before him stretched
Under the large old oak, that near his door
Stood single, and, from matchless depth of shade,
Chosen for the Shearer's covert from the sun,
Thence in our rustic dialect was called
The CLIPPING TREE, a name which yet it bears.
There, while they two were sitting in the shade,
With others round them, earnest all and blithe,
Would Michael exercise his heart with looks
Of fond correction and reproof bestowed
Upon the Child, if he disturbed the sheep
By catching at their legs, or with his shouts
Scared them, while they lay still beneath the shears.

And when by Heaven's good grace the boy grew up
A healthy Lad, and carried in his cheek
Two steady roses that were five years old;
Then Michael from a winter coppice cut
With his own hand a sapling, which he hooped
With iron, making it throughout in all
Due requisites a perfect shepherd's staff,
And gave it to the Boy; wherewith equipt
He as a watchman oftentimes was placed

At gate or gap, to stem or turn the flock;
And, to his office prematurely called,
There stood the urchin, as you will divine,
Something between a hindrance and a help;
And for this cause not always, I believe,
Receiving from his Father hire of praise;
Though nought was left undone which staff, or voice,
Or looks, or threatening gestures, could perform.

But soon as Luke, full ten years old, could stand
Against the mountain blasts; and to the heights,
Not fearing toil, nor length of weary ways,
He with his Father daily went, and they
Were as companions, why should I relate
That objects which the Shepherd loved before
Were dearer now? that from the Boy there came
Feelings and emanations — things which were
Light to the sun and music to the wind;
And that the old Man's heart seemed born again?

Thus in his Father's sight the Boy grew up:
And now, when he had reached his eighteenth year,
He was his comfort and his daily hope.

While in this sort the simple household lived
From day to day, to Michael's ear there came
Distressful tidings. Long before the time
Of which I speak, the Shepherd had been bound
In surety for his brother's son, a man
Of an industrious life, and ample means;
But unforeseen misfortunes suddenly
Had prest upon him; and old Michael now
Was summoned to discharge the forfeiture,

A grievous penalty, but little less
Than half his substance. This unlooked-for claim,
At the first hearing, for a moment took
More hope out of his life than he supposed
That any old man ever could have lost.
As soon as he had armed himself with strength
To look his trouble in the face, it seemed
The Shepherd's sole resource to sell at once
A portion of his patrimonial fields.
Such was his first resolve; he thought again,
And his heart failed him. "Isabel," said he,
Two evenings after he had heard the news,
"I have been toiling more than seventy years,
And in the open sunshine of God's love
Have we all lived; yet, if these fields of ours
Should pass into a stranger's hand, I think
That I could not lie quiet in my grave.
Our lot is a hard lot; the sun himself
Has scarcely been more diligent than I;
And I have lived to be a fool at last
To my own family. An evil man
That was, and made an evil choice, if he
Were false to us; and, if he were not false,
There are ten thousand to whom loss like this
Had been no sorrow. I forgive him; — but
'Twere better to be dumb than to talk thus.

"When I began, my purpose was to speak
Of remedies and of a cheerful hope.
Our Luke shall leave us, Isabel; the land
Shall not go from us, and it shall be free;
He shall possess it, free as is the wind
That passes over it. We have, thou know'st,

Another kinsman — he will be our friend
In this distress. He is a prosperous man,
Thriving in trade — and Luke to him shall go,
And with his kinsman's help and his own thrift
He quickly will repair this loss, and then
He may return to us. If here he stay,
What can be done? Where every one is poor,
What can be gained?"
At this the old Man paused
And Isabel sat silent, for her mind
Was busy, looking back into past times.
There's Richard Bateman, thought she to herself,
He was a parish boy — at the church-door
They made a gathering for him, shillings, pence,
And halfpennies, wherewith the neighbours bought
A basket, which they filled with pedlar's wares;
And, with this basket on his arm, the lad
Went up to London, found a master there,
Who, out of many, chose the trusty boy
To go and overlook his merchandise
Beyond the seas; where he grew wondrous rich,
And left estates and monies to the poor,
And, at his birth-place, built a chapel floored
With marble, which he sent from foreign lands.
These thoughts, and many others of like sort,
Passed quickly through the mind of Isabel,
And her face brightened. The old Man was glad,
And thus resumed: — "Well, Isabel! this scheme
These two days has been meat and drink to me.
Far more than we have lost is left us yet.
We have enough — I wish indeed that I
Were younger; — but this hope is a good hope.
Make ready Luke's best garments, of the best

uy for him more, and let us send him forth
o-morrow, or the next day, or to-night:
If he *could* go, the Boy should go to-night."

Here Michael ceased, and to the fields went forth
/ith a light heart. The Housewife for five days
/as restless morn and night, and all day long
/rought on with her best fingers to prepare
'hings needful for the journey of her son.
ut Isabel was glad when Sunday came
'o stop her in her work: for, when she lay
;y Michael's side, she through the last two nights
Ieard him, how he was troubled in his sleep:
.nd when they rose at morning she could see
'hat all his hopes were gone. That day at noon
he said to Luke, while they two by themselves
Vere sitting at the door, "Thou must not go:
Ve have no other Child but thee to lose,
Jone to remember — do not go away,
'or if thou leave thy Father he will die."
Ihe Youth made answer with a jocund voice;
\nd Isabel, when she had told her fears,
Recovered heart. That evening her best fare
)id she bring forth, and all together sat
.ike happy people round a Christmas fire.

With daylight Isabel resumed her work;
\nd all the ensuing week the house appeared
\s cheerful as a grove in Spring: at length
The expected letter from their kinsman came
With kind assurances that he would do
His utmost for the welfare of the Boy;
To which, requests were added, that forthwith

He might be sent to him. Ten times or more
The letter was read over; Isabel
Went forth to show it to the neighbours round;
Nor was there at that time on English land
A prouder heart than Luke's. When Isabel
Had to her house returned, the old Man said,
"He shall depart to-morrow." To this word
The Housewife answered, talking much of things
Which, if at such short notice he should go,
Would surely be forgotten. But at length
She gave consent, and Michael was at ease.

Near the tumultuous brook of Green-head Ghyll
In that deep valley, Michael had designed
To build a Sheep-fold; and, before he heard
The tidings of his melancholy loss,
For this same purpose he had gathered up
A heap of stones, which by the streamlet's edge
Lay thrown together, ready for the work.
With Luke that evening thitherward he walked:
And soon as they had reached the place he stopped
And thus the old Man spake to him:—"My son
To-morrow thou wilt leave me: with full heart
I look upon thee, for thou art the same
That wert a promise to me ere thy birth,
And all thy life hast been my daily joy.
I will relate to thee some little part
Of our two histories; 'twill do thee good
When thou art from me, even if I should touch
On things thou canst not know of.—— After thou
First cam'st into the world — as oft befalls
To new-born infants — thou didst sleep away
Two days, and blessings from thy Father's tongue

Then fell upon thee. Day by day passed on,
And still I loved thee with increasing love.
Never to living ear came sweeter sounds
Than when I heard thee by our own fireside
First uttering, without words, a natural tune;
While thou, a feeding babe, didst in thy joy
Sing at thy Mother's breast. Month followed month,
And in the open fields my life was passed
And on the mountains; else I think that thou
Hadst been brought up upon thy Father's knees.
But we were playmates, Luke: among these hills,
As well thou knowest, in us the old and young
Have played together, nor with me didst thou
Lack any pleasure which a boy can know."
Luke had a manly heart; but at these words
He sobbed aloud. The old Man grasped his hand,
And said, "Nay, do not take it so — I see
That these are things of which I need not speak.
— Even to the utmost I have been to thee
A kind and a good Father: and herein
I but repay a gift which I myself
Received at others' hands; for, though now old
Beyond the common life of man, I still
Remember them who loved me in my youth.
Both of them sleep together: here they lived,
As all their Forefathers had done; and, when
At length their time was come, they were not loth
To give their bodies to the family mould.
I wished that thou shouldst live the life they lived,
But 'tis a long time to look back, my Son,
And see so little gain from threescore years.
These fields were burthened when they came to me;
Till I was forty years of age, not more

Than half of my inheritance was mine.
I toiled and toiled; God blessed me in my work,
And till these three weeks past the land was free.
— It looks as if it never could endure
Another Master. Heaven forgive me, Luke,
If I judge ill for thee, but it seems good
That thou shouldst go."
At this the old Man paused;
Then, pointing to the stones near which they stood,
Thus, after a short silence, he resumed:
"This was a work for us; and now, my Son,
It is a work for me. But, lay one stone —
Here, lay it for me, Luke, with thine own hands.
Nay, Boy, be of good hope; — we both may live
To see a better day. At eighty-four
I still am strong and hale; — do thou thy part;
I will do mine. — I will begin again
With many tasks that were resigned to thee;
Up to the heights, and in among the storms,
Will I without thee go again, and do
All works which I was wont to do alone,
Before I knew thy face. — Heaven bless thee, Boy!
Thy heart these two weeks has been beating fast
With many hopes; it should be so — yes — yes —
I knew that thou couldst never have a wish
To leave me, Luke; thou hast been bound to me
Only by links of love: when thou art gone,
What will be left to us! — But I forget
My purposes. Lay now the corner-stone,
As I requested; and hereafter, Luke,
When thou art gone away, should evil men
Be thy companions, think of me, my Son,
And of this moment; hither turn thy thoughts,

And God will strengthen thee: amid all fear
And all temptation, Luke, I pray that thou
May'st bear in mind the life thy Fathers lived,
Who, being innocent, did for that cause
Bestir them in good deeds. Now, fare thee well —
When thou return'st, thou in this place wilt see
A work which is not here: a covenant
'Twill be between us; but, whatever fate
Befall thee, I shall love thee to the last,
And bear thy memory with me to the grave."

The Shepherd ended here; and Luke stooped down,
And, as his Father had requested, laid
The first stone of the Sheep-fold. At the sight
The old Man's grief broke from him; to his heart
He pressed his Son, he kissèd him and wept;
And to the house together they returned.
— Hushed was that House in peace, or seeming peace,
Ere the night fell: — with morrow's dawn the Boy
Began his journey, and, when he had reached
The public way, he put on a bold face;
And all the neighbours, as he passed their doors,
Came forth with wishes and with farewell prayers,
That followed him till he was out of sight.

A good report did from their Kinsman come,
Of Luke and his well-doing: and the Boy
Wrote loving letters, full of wondrous news,
Which, as the Housewife phrased it, were throughout
"The prettiest letters that were ever seen."

Both parents read them with rejoicing hearts.
So, many months passed on: and once again
The Shepherd went about his daily work
With confident and cheerful thoughts; and now
Sometimes when he could find a leisure hour
He to that valley took his way, and there
Wrought at the Sheep-fold. Meantime Luke
    began
To slacken in his duty; and, at length,
He in the dissolute city gave himself
To evil courses: ignominy and shame
Fell on him, so that he was driven at last
To seek a hiding-place beyond the seas.

There is a comfort in the strength of love;
'Twill make a thing endurable, which else
Would overset the brain, or break the heart:
I have conversed with more than one who well
Remember the old Man, and what he was
Years after he had heard this heavy news.
His bodily frame had been from youth to age
Of an unusual strength. Among the rocks
He went, and still looked up to sun and cloud,
And listened to the wind; and, as before,
Performed all kinds of labour for his sheep
And for the land, his small inheritance.
And to that hollow dell from time to time
Did he repair, to build the Fold of which
His flock had need. 'Tis not forgotten yet
The pity which was then in every heart
For the old Man — and 'tis believed by all
That many and many a day he thither went,
And never lifted up a single stone.

There, by the Sheep-fold, sometimes was he seen
Sitting alone, or with his faithful Dog,
Then old, beside him, lying at his feet.
The length of full seven years, from time to time,
He at the building of this Sheep-fold wrought,
And left the work unfinished when he died.
Three years, or little more, did Isabel
Survive her Husband: at her death the estate
Was sold, and went into a stranger's hand.
The Cottage which was named THE EVENING STAR
Is gone — the ploughshare has been through the
  ground
On which it stood; great changes have been wrought
In all the neighbourhood: — yet the oak is left
That grew beside their door; and the remains
Of the unfinished Sheep-fold may be seen
Beside the boisterous brook of Green-head Ghyll.

WILLIAM WORDSWORTH.

THE RIME OF THE ANCIENT MARINER

IN SEVEN PARTS

ARGUMENT

How a Ship having passed the Line was driven by storms to the cold Country towards the South Pole; and how from thence she made her course to the tropical Latitude of the Great Pacific Ocean; and of the strange things that befell; and in what manner the Ancyent Marinere came back to his own Country.

PART I

An ancient Mariner meeteth three Gallants bidden to a wedding-feast, and detaineth one.

It is an ancient Mariner,
And he stoppeth one of three.
"By thy long grey beard and glittering eye,
Now wherefore stopp'st thou me?

The Bridegroom's doors are opened wide,
And I am next of kin;
The guests are met, the feast is set:
May'st hear the merry din."

He holds him with his skinny hand,
"There was a ship," quoth he.
"Hold off! unhand me, grey-beard loon!"
Eftsoons his hand dropt he.

The Wedding-Guest is spell-bound by the eye of the old seafaring man, and constrained to hear his tale.

He holds him with his glittering eye—
The Wedding-Guest stood still,
And listens like a three years' child:
The Mariner hath his will.

The Wedding-Guest sat on a stone:
He cannot choose but hear;
And thus spake on that ancient man,
The bright-eyed Mariner.

"The ship was cheered, the harbour
cleared,
Merrily did we drop
Below the kirk, below the hill,
Below the lighthouse top.

The Mariner tells how the ship sailed southward with a good wind and fair weather, till it reached the line.

The Sun came up upon the left,
Out of the sea came he!
And he shone bright, and on the right
Went down into the sea.

The Wedding-Guest heareth the bridal music; but the Mariner continueth his tale.

Higher and higher every day,
Till over the mast at noon ——"
The Wedding-Guest here beat his breast,
For he heard the loud bassoon.

The bride hath paced into the hall,
Red as a rose is she;
Nodding their heads before her goes
The merry minstrelsy.

The Wedding-Guest he beat his breast,
Yet he cannot choose but hear;
And thus spake on that ancient man,
The bright-eyed Mariner.

The ship driven by a storm toward the south pole.

"And now the STORM-BLAST came,
and he
Was tyrannous and strong:

He struck with his o'ertaking wings,
And chased us south along.

With sloping masts and dipping prow,
As who pursued with yell and blow
Still treads the shadow of his foe,
And forward bends his head,
The ship drove fast, loud roared the
blast,
And southward aye we fled.

And now there came both mist and
snow,
And it grew wondrous cold:
And ice, mast-high, came floating by,
As green as emerald.

The land of ice, and of fearful sounds, where no living thing was to be seen.

And through the drifts the snowy clifts
Did send a dismal sheen:
Nor shapes of men nor beasts we ken —
The ice was all between.

The ice was here, the ice was there,
The ice was all around:
It cracked and growled, and roared and
howled,
Like noises in a swound!

Till a great sea-bird, called the Albatross, came through the snow-fog, and was received with great joy and hospitality.

At length did cross an Albatross,
Thorough the fog it came;
As if it had been a Christian soul,
We hailed it in God's name.

And lo! the Albatross proveth a bird of good omen, and followeth the ship as it returned northward through fog and floating ice.

It ate the food it ne'er had eat,
And round and round it flew.
The ice did split with a thunder-fit;
The helmsman steered us through!

And a good south wind sprung up behind;
The Albatross did follow,
And every day, for food or play,
Came to the mariners' hollo!

In mist or cloud, on mast or shroud,
It perched for vespers nine;
Whiles all the night, through fog-smoke white,
Glimmered the white Moon-shine."

The ancient Mariner inhospitably killeth the pious bird of good omen.

"God save thee, ancient Mariner!
From the fiends, that plague thee thus!—
Why look'st thou so?"—"With my cross-bow
I shot the Albatross.

Part II

The Sun now rose upon the right:
Out of the sea came he,
Still hid in mist, and on the left
Went down into the sea.

And the good south wind still blew behind,
But no sweet bird did follow,

Nor any day for food or play
Came to the mariners' hollo!

His shipmates cry out against the ancient Mariner, for killing the bird of good luck.

And I had done an hellish thing,
And it would work 'em woe:
For all averred, I had killed the bird
That made the breeze to blow.
Ah wretch! said they, the bird to slay,
That made the breeze to blow!

But when the fog cleared off, they justify the same, and thus make themselves accomplices in the crime.

Nor dim nor red, like God's own head,
The glorious Sun uprist:
Then all averred, I had killed the bird
That brought the fog and mist.
'Twas right, said they, such birds to slay,
That bring the fog and mist.

The fair breeze continues; the ship enters the Pacific Ocean and sails northward, even till it reaches the Line.

The fair breeze blew, the white foam flew,
The furrow followed free;
We were the first that ever burst
Into that silent sea.

The ship hath been suddenly becalmed.

Down dropt the breeze, the sails dropt down,
'Twas sad as sad could be;
And we did speak only to break
The silence of the sea!

All in a hot and copper sky,
The bloody Sun, at noon,

Right up above the mast did stand,
No bigger than the Moon.

Day after day, day after day,
We stuck, nor breath nor motion;
As idle as a painted ship
Upon a painted ocean.

nd the Albatross begins o be avenged.

Water, water, every where,
And all the boards did shrink;
Water, water, every where,
Nor any drop to drink;

The very deep did rot: O Christ!
That ever this should be!
Yea, slimy things did crawl with legs
Upon the slimy sea.

Spirit had ollowed them; ne of the invisible inhabtants of this lanet, neither eparted souls or angels; oncerning whom the earned Jew, osephus, and ne Platonic Constantinoolitan, Michael sellus, may be onsulted. They re very numerus, and there s no climate or lement without ne or more.

About, about, in reel and rout
The death-fires danced at night;
The water, like a witch's oils,
Burnt green, and blue and white.

And some in dreams assuréd were
Of the Spirit that plagued us so;
Nine fathom deep he had followed us
From the land of mist and snow.

And every tongue, through utter
    drought,
Was withered at the root;
We could not speak, no more than if
We had been choked with soot.

The shipmates, in their sore distress, would fain throw the whole guilt on the ancient Mariner; in sign whereof they hang the dead sea-bird round his neck.

Ah! well-a-day! what evil looks
Had I from old and young!
Instead of the cross, the Albatross
About my neck was hung.

Part III

There passed a weary time. Each throat
Was parched, and glazed each eye.
A weary time! a weary time!
How glazed each weary eye,
When looking westward, I beheld
A something in the sky.

The ancient Mariner beholdeth a sign in the element afar off.

At first it seemed a little speck,
And then it seemed a mist;
It moved and moved, and took at last
A certain shape, I wist.

A speck, a mist, a shape, I wist!
And still it neared and neared:
As if it dodged a water-sprite,
It plunged and tacked and veered.

At its nearer approach, it seemeth him to be a ship; and at a dear ransom he freeth his speech from the bonds of thirst.

With throats unslaked, with black lips
baked,
We could not laugh nor wail;
Through utter drought all dumb we
stood!
I bit my arm, I sucked the blood,
And cried, A sail! a sail!

A flash of joy;

With throats unslaked, with black lips
baked,
Agape they heard me call:
Gramercy! they for joy did grin,
And all at once their breath drew in,
As they were drinking all.

And horror follows. For can it be a ship that comes onward without wind or tide?

See! See! (I cried) she tacks no more!
Hither to work us weal;
Without a breeze, without a tide,
She steadies with upright keel!

The western wave was all a-flame.
The day was well nigh done!
Almost upon the western wave
Rested the broad bright Sun;
When that strange shape drove suddenly
Betwixt us and the Sun.

It seemeth him but the skeleton of a ship.

And straight the Sun was flecked with
bars,

And its ribs are seen as bars on the face of the setting Sun.

(Heaven's Mother send us grace!)
As if through a dungeon-grate he peered
With broad and burning face.

Alas! (thought I, and my heart beat
loud)
How fast she nears and nears!
Are those *her* sails that glance in the
Sun,
Like restless gossameres?

Are those *her* ribs through which the Sun
Did peer, as through a grate?
And is that Woman all her crew?
Is that a Death? and are there two?
Is Death that woman's mate?

The Spectre-Woman and her Death-mate, and no other on board the skeleton-ship. Like vessel, like crew!

Her lips were red, *her* looks were free,
Her locks were yellow as gold:
Her skin was as white as leprosy,
The Night-mare Life-in-Death was she,
Who thicks man's blood with cold.

Death and Life-in-Death have diced for the ship's crew, and she (the latter) winneth the ancient Mariner.

The naked hulk alongside came,
And the twain were casting dice;
"The game is done! I've won, I've won!"
Quoth she, and whistles thrice.

No twilight within the courts of the Sun.

The Sun's rim dips; the stars rush out:
At one stride comes the dark;
With far-heard whisper, o'er the sea,
Off shot the spectre-bark.

We listened and looked sideways up!
Fear at my heart, as at a cup,
My life-blood seemed to sip!
The stars were dim, and thick the night,
The steersman's face by his lamp gleamed white;
From the sails the dew did drip —
Till clomb above the eastern bar
The hornéd Moon, with one bright star
Within the nether tip.

At the rising of the Moon.

One after another,

One after one, by the star-dogged Moon,
Too quick for groan or sigh,
Each turned his face with a ghastly
pang,
And cursed me with his eye.

His shipmates drop down dead.

Four times fifty living men,
(And I heard nor sigh nor groan)
With heavy thump, a lifeless lump,
They dropped down one by one.

But Life-in-Death begins her work on the ancient Mariner.

The souls did from their bodies fly,—
They fled to bliss or woe!
And every soul, it passed me by,
Like the whizz of my cross-bow!"

Part IV

The Wedding-Guest feareth that a Spirit is talking to him;

"I fear thee, ancient Mariner!
I fear thy skinny hand!
And thou art long, and lank, and brown,
As is the ribbed sea-sand.

I fear thee and thy glittering eye,
And thy skinny hand, so brown."—

But the ancient Mariner assureth him of his bodily life, and proceedeth to relate his horrible penance.

"Fear not, fear not, thou Wedding-Guest!
This body dropt not down.

Alone, alone, all, all alone,
Alone on a wide wide sea!
And never a saint took pity on
My soul in agony.

He despiseth the creatures of the calm,

The many men, so beautiful!
And they all dead did lie:

And envieth that *they* should live, and so many lie dead.

And a thousand thousand slimy things
Lived on; and so did I.

I looked upon the rotting sea.
And drew my eyes away;
I looked upon the rotting deck,
And there the dead men lay.

I looked to heaven, and tried to pray
But or ever a prayer had gusht,
A wicked whisper came, and made
My heart as dry as dust.

I closed my lids, and kept them close,
And the balls like pulses beat;
For the sky and the sea, and the sea an
the sky
Lay like a load on my weary eye,
And the dead were at my feet.

But the curse liveth for him in the eye of the dead men.

The cold sweat melted from their limbs
Nor rot nor reek did they;
The look with which they looked on m
Had never passed away.

An orphan's curse would drag to hell
A spirit from on high;
But oh! more horrible than that
Is a curse in a dead man's eye!
Seven days, seven nights, I saw that curse
And yet I could not die.

his loneliness nd fixedness he yearneth towards the journeying Moon, and the stars that still sojourn, yet still move onward; and every where the blue sky belongs to them, and is their appointed rest, and their native country and their own natural homes, which they enter unannounced, as lords that are certainly expected, and yet there is a silent joy at their arrival.

The moving Moon went up the sky,
And no where did abide:
Softly she was going up,
And a star or two beside —

Her beams bemocked the sultry main,
Like April hoar-frost spread;
But where the ship's huge shadow lay,
The charméd water burnt alway
A still and awful red.

By the light of the Moon he beholdeth God's creatures of the great calm.

Beyond the shadow of the ship,
I watched the water-snakes:
They moved in tracks of shining white,
And when they reared, the elfish light
Fell off in hoary flakes.

Within the shadow of the ship
I watched their rich attire:
Blue, glossy green, and velvet black,
They coiled and swam; and every track
Was a flash of golden fire.

Their beauty and their happiness.

O happy living things! no tongue
Their beauty might declare:
A spring of love gushed from my heart,
And I blessed them unaware:

He blesseth them in his heart.

Sure my kind saint took pity on me,
And I blessed them unaware.

The spell begins to break.

The self-same moment I could pray;
And from my neck so free
The Albatross fell off, and sank
Like lead into the sea.

Part V

Oh sleep! it is a gentle thing,
Beloved from pole to pole!
To Mary Queen the praise be given!
She sent the gentle sleep from Heaven
That slid into my soul.

The silly buckets on the deck,
That had so long remained,
I dreamt that they were filled with dew
And when I awoke, it rained.

By grace of the holy Mother, the ancient Mariner is refreshed with rain.

My lips were wet, my throat was cold
My garments all were dank;
Sure I had drunken in my dreams,
And still my body drank.

I moved, and could not feel my limbs:
I was so light — almost
I thought that I had died in sleep
And was a blesséd ghost.

He heareth sounds and seeth strange sights and commotions in the sky and the element.

And soon I heard a roaring wind:
It did not come anear;
But with its sound it shook the sails,
That were so thin and sere.

The upper air burst into life!
And a hundred fire-flags sheen,
To and fro they were hurried about!
And to and fro, and in and out,
The wan stars danced between.

And the coming wind did roar more
  loud,
And the sails did sigh like sedge;
And the rain poured down from one
  black cloud;
The Moon was at its edge.

The thick black cloud was cleft, and
  still
The Moon was at its side:
Like waters shot from some high crag,
The lightning fell with never a jag,
A river steep and wide.

he bodies of
ıe ship's crew
re inspired,
nd the ship
ıoves on;

The loud wind never reached the ship,
Yet now the ship moved on!
Beneath the lightning and the Moon
The dead men gave a groan.

They groaned, they stirred, they all up-
  rose,
Nor spake, nor moved their eyes;
It had been strange, even in a dream,
To have seen those dead men rise.

The helmsman steered, the ship moved
  on;
Yet never a breeze up-blew;
The mariners all 'gan work the ropes
Where they were wont to do;
They raised their limbs like lifeless
  tools —
We were a ghastly crew.

But not by the souls of the men, nor by daemons of earth or middle air, but by a blessed troop of angelic spirits, sent down by the invocation of the guardian saint.

The body of my brother's son
Stood by me, knee to knee:
The body and I pulled at one rope,
But he said nought to me."

"I fear thee, ancient Mariner!"
"Be calm, thou Wedding-Guest!
'Twas not those souls that fled i
pain,
Which to their corses came again,
But a troop of spirits blest:

For when it dawned — they droppe
their arms,
And clustered round the mast;
Sweet sounds rose slowly through the
mouths,
And from their bodies passed.

Around, around, flew each sweet soun
Then darted to the Sun;
Slowly the sounds came back again,
Now mixed, now one by one.

Sometimes a-dropping from the sky
I heard the sky-lark sing;
Sometimes all little birds that are,
How they seemed to fill the sea an
air
With their sweet jargoning!

And now 'twas like all instruments,
Now like a lonely flute;

And now it is an angel's song,
That makes the heavens be mute.

It ceased; yet still the sails made on
A pleasant noise till noon,
A noise like of a hidden brook
In the leafy month of June,
That to the sleeping woods all night
Singeth a quiet tune.

Till noon we quietly sailed on,
Yet never a breeze did breathe:
Slowly and smoothly went the ship,
Moved onward from beneath.

The lonesome Spirit from the south-pole carries on the ship as far as the Line, in obedience to the angelic troop, but still requireth vengeance.

Under the keel nine fathom deep,
From the land of mist and snow,
The spirit slid: and it was he
That made the ship to go.
The sails at noon left off their tune,
And the ship stood still also.

The Sun, right up above the mast,
Had fixed her to the ocean:
But in a minute she 'gan stir,
With a short uneasy motion —
Backwards and forwards half her length
With a short uneasy motion.

Then, like a pawing horse let go,
She made a sudden bound:
It flung the blood into my head,
And I fell down in a swound.

The Polar Spirit's fellow-daemons, the invisible inhabitants of the element, take part in his wrong; and two of them relate, one to the other, that penance long and heavy for the ancient Mariner hath been accorded to the Polar Spirit, who returneth southward.

How long in that same fit I lay,
I have not to declare;
But ere my living life returned,
I heard and in my soul discerned
Two voices in the air.

"Is it he?" quoth one, "Is this the man?
By him who died on cross,
With his cruel bow he laid full low
The harmless Albatross.

The spirit who bideth by himself
In the land of mist and snow,
He loved the bird that loved the man
Who shot him with his bow."

The other was a softer voice,
As soft as honeydew:
Quoth he, "The man hath penance done,
And penance more will do."

PART VI

First Voice

"But tell me, tell me! speak again,
Thy soft response renewing —
What makes that ship drive on so fast?
What is the ocean doing?"

Second Voice

"Still as a slave before his lord,
The ocean hath no blast;
His great bright eye most silently
Up to the Moon is cast —

If he may know which way to go;
For she guides him smooth or grim.
See, brother, see! how graciously
She looketh down on him!"

First Voice

The Mariner hath been cast into a trance; for the angelic power causeth the vessel to drive northward faster than human life could endure.

"But why drives on that ship so fast,
Without or wave or wind?"

Second Voice

"The air is cut away before,
And closes from behind.

Fly, brother, fly! more high, more high!
Or we shall be belated:
For slow and slow that ship will go,
When the Mariner's trance is abated."

The supernatural motion is retarded; the Mariner awakes, and his penance begins anew.

I woke, and we were sailing on
As in a gentle weather:
'Twas night, calm night, the Moon was
high;
The dead men stood together.

All stood together on the deck,
For a charnel-dungeon fitter:
All fixed on me their stony eyes,
That in the Moon did glitter.

The pang, the curse, with which they died.
Had never passed away:
I could not draw my eyes from theirs,
Nor turn them up to pray.

The curse is finally expiated.

And now this spell was snapt: once more
I viewed the ocean green,
And looked far forth, yet little saw
Of what had else been seen —

Like one, that on a lonesome road
Doth walk in fear and dread,
And having once turned round walks
on,
And turns no more his head;
Because he knows, a frightful fiend
Doth close behind him tread.

But soon there breathed a wind on me,
Nor sound nor motion made:
Its path was not upon the sea,
In ripple or in shade.

It raised my hair, it fanned my cheek
Like a meadow-gale of spring —
It mingled strangely with my fears,
Yet it felt like a welcoming.

Swiftly, swiftly flew the ship,
Yet she sailed softly too:
Sweetly, sweetly blew the breeze —
On me alone it blew.

And the ancient Mariner beholdeth his native country.

Oh! dream of joy! is this indeed
The lighthouse top I see?
Is this the hill? is this the kirk?
Is this mine own countree?

We drifted o'er the harbour-bar,
And I with sobs did pray —
O let me be awake, my God!
Or let me sleep alway.

The harbour-bay was clear as glass,
So smoothly it was strewn!
And on the bay the moonlight lay,
And the shadow of the Moon.

The rock shone bright, the kirk no less,
That stands above the rock:
The moonlight steeped in silentness
The steady weathercock.

And the bay was white with silent light,
Till rising from the same,
Full many shapes, that shadows were,
In crimson colours came.

The angelic spirits leave the dead bodies.

A little distance from the prow
Those crimson shadows were:
I turned my eyes upon the deck —
Oh, Christ! what saw I there!

And appear in their own forms of light.

Each corse lay flat, lifeless and flat,
And, by the holy rood!
A man all light, a seraph-man,
On every corse there stood.

This seraph-band, each waved his hand:
It was a heavenly sight!
They stood as signals to the land,
Each one a lovely light;

This seraph-band, each waved his hand,
No voice did they impart —
No voice; but oh! the silence sank
Like music on my heart.

But soon I heard the dash of oars,
I heard the Pilot's cheer;
My head was turned perforce away,
And I saw a boat appear.

The Pilot and the Pilot's boy,
I heard them coming fast:
Dear Lord in Heaven! it was a joy
The dead men could not blast.

I saw a third — I heard his voice:
It is the Hermit good!
He singeth loud his godly hymns
That he makes in the wood.
He'll shrieve my soul, he'll wash away
The Albatross's blood.

Part VII

The Hermit of the Wood.

This Hermit good lives in that wood
Which slopes down to the sea.
How loudly his sweet voice he rears!
He loves to talk with marineres
That come from a far countree.

He kneels at morn, and noon, and eve —
He hath a cushion plump:

It is the moss that wholly hides
The rotted old oak-stump.

The skiff-boat neared: I heard them
talk,
"Why this is strange, I trow!
Where are those lights so many and fair,
That signal made but now?"

Approacheth the ship with wonder.

"Strange, by my faith!" the Hermit
said —
"And they answered not our cheer!
The planks look warped! and see those
sails,
How thin they are and sere!
I never saw aught like to them,
Unless perchance it were

Brown skeletons of leaves that lag
My forest-brook along;
When the ivy-tod is heavy with snow,
And the owlet whoops to the wolf below,
That eats the she-wolf's young."

"Dear Lord! it hath a fiendish look —
(The Pilot made reply)
I am a-feared" — "Push on, push on!"
Said the Hermit cheerily.

The boat came closer to the ship,
But I nor spake nor stirred;
The boat came close beneath the ship,
And straight a sound was heard.

Under the water it rumbled on,
Still louder and more dread:
It reached the ship, it split the bay;
The ship went down like lead.

The ship suddenly sinketh.

Stunned by that loud and dreadful sound,
Which sky and ocean smote,
Like one that hath been seven days drowned
My body lay afloat;
But swift as dreams, myself I found
Within the Pilot's boat.

The ancient Mariner is saved in the Pilot's boat.

Upon the whirl, where sank the ship,
The boat spun round and round;
And all was still, save that the hill
Was telling of the sound.

I moved my lips — the Pilot shrieked
And fell down in a fit;
The holy Hermit raised his eyes,
And prayed where he did sit.

I took the oars: the Pilot's boy,
Who now doth crazy go,
Laughed loud and long, and all the while
His eyes went to and fro.
"Ha! ha!" quoth he, "full plain I see,
The Devil knows how to row."

And now, all in my own countree,
I stood on the firm land!

The Hermit stepped forth from the boat,
And scarcely he could stand.

The ancient Mariner earnestly entreateth the Hermit to shrieve him; and the penance of life falls on him.

"O shrieve me, shrieve me, holy man!"
The Hermit crossed his brow.
"Say quick," quoth he, "I bid thee say —
What manner of man art thou?"

Forthwith this frame of mine was wrenched
With a woful agony,
Which forced me to begin my tale;
And then it left me free.

And ever and anon throughout his future life an agony constraineth him to travel from land to land;

Since then, at an uncertain hour,
That agony returns:
And till my ghastly tale is told,
This heart within me burns.

I pass, like night, from land to land;
I have strange power of speech;
That moment that his face I see,
I know the man that must hear me:
To him my tale I teach.

What loud uproar bursts from that door!
The wedding-guests are there:
But in the garden-bower the bride
And bride-maids singing are:
And hark the little vesper bell,
Which biddeth me to prayer!

O Wedding-Guest! this soul hath been
Alone on a wide wide sea:

So lonely 'twas, that God Himself
Scarce seeméd there to be.

O sweeter than the marriage-feast,
'Tis sweeter far to me,
To walk together to the kirk
With a goodly company!—

To walk together to the kirk,
And all together pray,
While each to his great Father bends,
Old men, and babes, and loving friends
And youths and maidens gay!

And to teach, by his own example, love and reverence to all things that God made and loveth.

Farewell, farewell! but this I tell
To thee, thou Wedding-Guest!
He prayeth well, who loveth well
Both man and bird and beast.

He prayeth best, who loveth best
All things both great and small;
For the dear God who loveth us,
He made and loveth all."

The Mariner, whose eye is bright,
Whose beard with age is hoar,
Is gone: and now the Wedding-Guest
Turned from the bridegroom's door.

He went like one that hath been stunned,
And is of sense forlorn:
A sadder and a wiser man,
He rose the morrow morn.

SAMUEL TAYLOR COLERIDGE.

ADONAIS

N ELEGY ON THE DEATH OF JOHN KEATS, AUTHOR OF ENDYMION, HYPERION, ETC.

Ἀστὴρ πρὶν μὲν ἔλαμπες ἐνὶ ζώοισιν Ἑῷος·
νῦν δὲ θανὼν λάμπεις Ἕσπερος ἐν φθιμένοις.— PLATO.

I

I WEEP for Adonais — he is dead!
O, weep for Adonais! though our tears
Thaw not the frost which binds so dear a head!
And thou, sad Hour, selected from all years
To mourn our loss, rouse thy obscure compeers,
And teach them thine own sorrow, say: "With me
Died Adonais; till the Future dares
Forget the Past, his fate and fame shall be
An echo and a light unto eternity!"

II

Where wert thou, mighty Mother, when he lay,
When thy Son lay, pierced by the shaft which flies
In darkness? where was lorn Urania
When Adonais died? With veilèd eyes,
'Mid listening Echoes, in her Paradise
She sate, while one, with soft enamoured breath,
Rekindled all the fading melodies,
With which, like flowers that mock the corse
beneath,
He had adorned and hid the coming bulk of Death.

III

Oh, weep for Adonais — he is dead!
Wake, melancholy Mother, wake and weep!

Yet wherefore? Quench within their burning bed
Thy fiery tears, and let thy loud heart keep
Like his, a mute and uncomplaining sleep;
For he is gone, where all things wise and fair
Descend; — oh, dream not that the amorous
Deep
Will yet restore him to the vital air;
Death feeds on his mute voice, and laughs at our
despair.

IV

Most musical of mourners, weep again!
Lament anew, Urania! — He died,
Who was the Sire of an immortal strain,
Blind, old, and lonely, when his country's pride
The priest, the slave, and the liberticide
Trampled and mocked with many a loathèd rite
Of lust and blood; he went, unterrified,
Into the gulf of death; but his clear Sprite
Yet reigns o'er earth; the third among the sons of
light.

V

Most musical of mourners, weep anew!
Not all to that bright station dared to climb;
And happier they their happiness who knew,
Whose tapers yet burn through that night of time
In which suns perished; others more sublime,
Struck by the envious wrath of man or god,
Have sunk, extinct in their refulgent prime;
And some yet live, treading the thorny road,
Which leads, through toil and hate, to Fame's serene
abode.

VI

But now, thy youngest, dearest one, has perished —
The nursling of thy widowhood, who grew,
Like a pale flower by some sad maiden cherished,
And fed with true-love tears, instead of dew;
Most musical of mourners, weep anew!
Thy extreme hope, the loveliest and the last,
The bloom, whose petals nipped before they blew
Died on the promise of the fruit, is waste;
The broken lily lies — the storm is overpast.

VII

To that high Capital, where kingly Death
Keeps his pale court in beauty and decay,
He came; and bought, with price of purest breath,
A grave among the eternal. — Come away!
Haste, while the vault of blue Italian day
Is yet his fitting charnel-roof! while still
He lies, as if in dewy sleep he lay;
Awake him not! surely he takes his fill
Of deep and liquid rest, forgetful of all ill.

VIII

He will awake no more, oh, never more! —
Within the twilight chamber spreads apace
The shadow of white Death, and at the door
Invisible Corruption waits to trace
His extreme way to her dim dwelling-place;
The eternal Hunger sits, but pity and awe
Soothe her pale rage, nor dares she to deface
So fair a prey, till darkness, and the law
Of change, shall o'er his sleep the mortal curtain draw.

IX

Oh, weep for Adonais! — The quick Dreams,
The passion-wingèd Ministers of thought,
Who were his flocks, whom near the living streams
Of his young spirit he fed, and whom he taught
The love which was its music, wander not, —
Wander no more, from kindling brain to brain,
But droop there, whence they sprung; and mourn their lot
Round the cold heart, where, after their sweet pain,
They ne'er will gather strength, or find a home again.

X

And one with trembling hands clasps his cold head,
And fans him with her moonlight wings, and cries;
"Our love, our hope, our sorrow, is not dead;
See, on the silken fringe of his faint eyes,
Like dew upon a sleeping flower, there lies
A tear some Dream has loosened from his brain."
Lost Angel of a ruined Paradise!
She knew not 'twas her own; as with no stain
She faded, like a cloud which had outwept its rain.

XI

One from a lucid urn of starry dew
Washed his light limbs as if embalming them;
Another clipped her profuse locks, and threw
The wreath upon him, like an anadem,
Which frozen tears instead of pearls begem;

Another in her wilful grief would break
Her bow and wingèd reeds, as if to stem
A greater loss with one which was more weak
And dull the barbèd fire against his frozen cheek.

XII

Another Splendour on his mouth alit,
That mouth, whence it was wont to draw the breath
Which gave it strength to pierce the guarded wit,
And pass into the panting heart beneath
With lightning and with music: the damp death
Quenched its caress upon his icy lips;
And, as a dying meteor stains a wreath
Of moonlight vapour, which the cold night clips,
It flushed through his pale limbs, and passed to its eclipse.

XIII

And others came . . . Desires and Adorations,
Wingèd Persuasions and veiled Destinies,
Splendours, and Glooms, and glimmering Incarnations
Of hopes and fears, and twilight Phantasies;
And Sorrow, with her family of Sighs,
And Pleasure, blind with tears, led by the gleam
Of her own dying smile instead of eyes,
Came in slow pomp; — the moving pomp might seem
Like pageantry of mist on an autumnal stream.

XIV

All he had loved, and moulded into thought,
From shape, and hue, and odour, and sweet sound,
Lamented Adonais. Morning sought
Her eastern watch-tower, and her hair unbound,
Wet with the tears which should adorn the ground,
Dimmed the aëreal eyes that kindle day;
Afar the melancholy thunder moaned,
Pale Ocean in unquiet slumber lay,
And the wild Winds flew round, sobbing in their dismay.

XV

Lost Echo sits amid the voiceless mountains,
And feeds her grief with his remembered lay,
And will no more reply to winds or fountains,
Or amorous birds perched on the young green spray,
Or herdsman's horn, or bell at closing day;
Since she can mimic not his lips, more dear
Than those for whose disdain she pined away
Into a shadow of all sounds: — a drear
Murmur, between their songs, is all the woodmen hear.

XVI

Grief made the young Spring wild, and she threw down
Her kindling buds, as if she Autumn were,
Or they dead leaves; since her delight is flown,
For whom should she have waked the sullen year?
To Phoebus was not Hyacinth so dear

Nor to himself Narcissus, as to both
Thou, Adonais: wan they stand and sere
Amid the faint companions of their youth,
With dew all turned to tears; odour, to sighing ruth.

XVII

Thy spirit's sister, the lorn nightingale
Mourns not her mate with such melodious pain;
Not so the eagle, who like thee could scale
Heaven, and could nourish in the sun's domain
Her mighty youth with morning, doth complain,
Soaring and screaming round her empty nest,
As Albion wails for thee: the curse of Cain
Light on his head who pierced thy innocent breast
And scared the angel soul that was its earthly guest!

XVIII

Ah, woe is me! Winter is come and gone,
But grief returns with the revolving year;
The airs and streams renew their joyous tone;
The ants, the bees, the swallows reappear;
Fresh leaves and flowers deck the dead Seasons'
bier;
The amorous birds now pair in every brake,
And build their mossy homes in field and brere;
And the green lizard, and the golden snake,
Like unimprisoned flames, out of their trance awake.

XIX

Through wood and stream and field and hill and
Ocean
A quickening life from the Earth's heart has burst

As it has ever done, with change and motion,
From the great morning of the world when first
God dawned on Chaos; in its stream immersed,
The lamps of Heaven flash with a softer light;
All baser things pant with life's sacred thirst;
Diffuse themselves; and spend in love's delight,
The beauty and the joy of their renewèd might.

XX

The leprous corpse, touched by this spirit tender,
Exhales itself in flowers of gentle breath;
Like incarnations of the stars, when splendour
Is changed to fragrance, they illumine death
And mock the merry worm that wakes beneath;
Nought we know, dies. Shall that alone which
knows
Be as a sword consumed before the sheath
By sightless lightning? — the intense atom glows
A moment, then is quenched in a most cold repose.

XXI

Alas! that all we loved of him should be,
But for our grief, as if it had not been,
And grief itself be mortal! Woe is me!
Whence are we, and why are we? of what scene
The actors or spectators? Great and mean
Meet massed in death, who lends what life must
borrow.
As long as skies are blue, and fields are green,
Evening must usher night, night urge the morrow,
Month follow month with woe, and year wake year
to sorrow.

XXII

He will awake no more, oh, never more!
"Wake thou," cried Misery, "childless Mother, rise
Out of thy sleep, and slake, in thy heart's core,
A wound more fierce than his, with tears and sighs."
And all the Dreams that watched Urania's eyes,
And all the Echoes whom their sister's song
Had held in holy silence, cried: "Arise!"
Swift as a Thought by the snake Memory stung,
From her ambrosial rest the fading Splendour sprung.

XXIII

She rose like an autumnal Night, that springs
Out of the East, and follows wild and drear
The golden Day, which, on eternal wings,
Even as a ghost abandoning a bier,
Had left the Earth a corpse. Sorrow and fear
So struck, so roused, so rapt Urania;
So saddened round her like an atmosphere
Of stormy mist; so swept her on her way
Even to the mournful place where Adonais lay.

XXIV

Out of her secret Paradise she sped,
Through camps and cities rough with stone, and steel,
And human hearts, which to her aery tread
Yielding not, wounded the invisible
Palms of her tender feet where'er they fell:

And barbèd tongues, and thoughts more sharp than they,
Rent the soft Form they never could repel,
Whose sacred blood, like the young tears of May,
Paved with eternal flowers that undeserving way.

XXV

In the death-chamber for a moment Death,
Shamed by the presence of that living Might,
Blushed to annihilation, and the breath
Revisited those lips, and Life's pale light
Flashed through those limbs, so late her dear delight.
"Leave me not wild and drear and comfortless,
As silent lightning leaves the starless night!
Leave me not!" cried Urania: her distress
Roused Death: Death rose and smiled, and met her vain caress.

XXVI

"Stay yet awhile! speak to me once again;
Kiss me, so long but as a kiss may live;
And in my heartless breast and burning brain
That word, that kiss, shall all thoughts else survive,
With food of saddest memory kept alive,
Now thou art dead, as if it were a part
Of thee, my Adonais! I would give
All that I am to be as thou now art!
But I am chained to Time, and cannot thence depart!

XXVII

"O gentle child, beautiful as thou wert,
Why didst thou leave the trodden paths of men
Too soon, and with weak hands though mighty
heart
Dare the unpastured dragon in his den?
Defenceless as thou wert, oh, where was then
Wisdom the mirrored shield, or scorn the spear?
Or hadst thou waited the full cycle, when
Thy spirit should have filled its crescent sphere,
The monsters of life's waste had fled from thee like
deer.

XXVIII

"The herded wolves, bold only to pursue;
The obscene ravens, clamorous o'er the dead;
The vultures to the conqueror's banner true
Who feed where Desolation first has fed,
And whose wings rain contagion; — how they
fled,
When, like Apollo, from his golden bow
The Pythian of the age one arrow sped
And smiled! — The spoilers tempt no second blow,
They fawn on the proud feet that spurn them lying
low.

XXIX

"The sun comes forth, and many reptiles spawn;
He sets, and each ephemeral insect then
Is gathered into death without a dawn,
And the immortal stars awake again;

So is it in the world of living men:
A godlike mind soars forth, in its delight
Making earth bare and veiling heaven, and when
It sinks, the swarms that dimmed or shared its light
Leave to its kindred lamps the spirit's awful night."

XXX

Thus ceased she: and the mountain shepherds came,
Their garlands sere, their magic mantles rent;
The Pilgrim of Eternity, whose fame
Over his living head like Heaven is bent,
An early but enduring monument,
Came, veiling all the lightnings of his song
In sorrow; from her wilds Ierne sent
The sweetest lyrist of her saddest wrong,
And Love taught Grief to fall like music from his tongue.

XXXI

Midst others of less note, came one frail Form,
A phantom among men; companionless
As the last cloud of an expiring storm
Whose thunder is its knell; he, as I guess,
Had gazed on Nature's naked loveliness,
Actaeon-like, and now he fled astray
With feeble steps o'er the world's wilderness,
And his own thoughts, along that rugged way,
Pursued, like raging hounds, their father and their prey.

XXXII

A pardlike Spirit beautiful and swift —
A Love in desolation masked; — a Power
Girt round with weakness; — it can scarce uplift
The weight of the superincumbent hour;
It is a dying lamp, a falling shower,
A breaking billow; even whilst we speak
Is it not broken? On the withering flower
The killing sun smiles brightly: on a cheek
The life can burn in blood, even while the heart
  may break.

XXXIII

His head was bound with pansies overblown,
And faded violets, white, and pied, and blue;
And a light spear topped with a cypress cone,
Round whose rude shaft dark ivy-tresses grew
Yet dripping with the forest's noonday dew,
Vibrated, as the ever-beating heart
Shook the weak hand that grasped it; of that
  crew
He came the last, neglected and apart;
A herd-abandoned deer struck by the hunter's dart.

XXXIV

All stood aloof, and at his partial moan
Smiled through their tears; well knew that gentle
  band
Who in another's fate now wept his own,
As in the accents of an unknown land

He sung new sorrow; sad Urania scanned
The Stranger's mien, and murmured: "Who art thou?"
He answered not, but with a sudden hand
Made bare his branded and ensanguined brow,
Which was like Cain's or Christ's — oh! that it should be so!

XXXV

What softer voice is hushed over the dead?
Athwart what brow is that dark mantle thrown?
What form leans sadly o'er the white deathbed,
In mockery of monumental stone,
The heavy heart heaving without a moan?
If it be He, who, gentlest of the wise,
Taught, soothed, loved, honoured the departed one,
Let me not vex, with inharmonious sighs,
The silence of that heart's accepted sacrifice.

XXXVI

Our Adonais has drunk poison — oh!
What deaf and viperous murderer could crown
Life's early cup with such a draught of woe?
The nameless worm would now itself disown:
It felt, yet could escape, the magic tone
Whose prelude held all envy, hate, and wrong,
But what was howling in one breast alone,
Silent with expectation of the song,
Whose master's hand is cold, whose silver lyre unstrung.

XXXVII

Live thou, whose infamy is not thy fame!
Live! fear no heavier chastisement from me,
Thou noteless blot on a remembered name!
But be thyself, and know thyself to be!
And ever at thy season be thou free
To spill the venom when thy fangs o'erflow:
Remorse and Self-contempt shall cling to thee;
Hot Shame shall burn upon thy secret brow,
And like a beaten hound tremble thou shalt — as now.

XXXVIII

Nor let us weep that our delight is fled
Far from these carrion kites that scream below;
He wakes or sleeps with the enduring dead;
Thou canst not soar where he is sitting now. —
Dust to the dust! but the pure spirit shall flow
Back to the burning fountain whence it came,
A portion of the Eternal, which must glow
Through time and change, unquenchably the same,
Whilst thy cold embers choke the sordid hearth of shame.

XXXIX

Peace, peace! he is not dead, he doth not sleep —
He hath awakened from the dream of life —
'Tis we, who, lost in stormy visions, keep
With phantoms an unprofitable strife,
And in mad trance, strike with our spirit's knife
Invulnerable nothings. — *We* decay

Like corpses in a charnel; fear and grief
Convulse us and consume us day by day,
And cold hopes swarm like worms within our living
clay.

XL

He has outsoared the shadow of our night;
Envy and calumny and hate and pain,
And that unrest which men miscall delight,
Can touch him not and torture not again;
From the contagion of the world's slow stain
He is secure, and now can never mourn
A heart grown cold, a head grown gray in vain;
Nor, when the spirit's self has ceased to burn,
With sparkless ashes load an unlamented urn.

XLI

He lives, he wakes — 'tis Death is dead, not he;
Mourn not for Adonais. — Thou young Dawn,
Turn all thy dew to splendour, for from thee
The spirit thou lamentest is not gone;
Ye caverns and ye forests, cease to moan!
Cease, ye faint flowers and fountains, and thou
Air,
Which like a mourning veil thy scarf hadst
thrown
O'er the abandoned Earth, now leave it bare
Even to the joyous stars which smile on its despair!

XLII

He is made one with Nature: there is heard
His voice in all her music, from the moan

Of thunder, to the song of night's sweet bird;
He is a presence to be felt and known
In darkness and in light, from herb and stone,
Spreading itself where'er that Power may move
Which has withdrawn his being to its own;
Which wields the world with never-wearied love,
Sustains it from beneath, and kindles it above.

XLIII

He is a portion of the loveliness
Which once he made more lovely: he doth bear
His part, while the one Spirit's plastic stress
Sweeps through the dull dense world, compelling there
All new successions to the forms they wear;
Torturing th' unwilling dross that checks its flight
To its own likeness, as each mass may bear;
And bursting in its beauty and its might
From trees and beasts and men into the Heaven's light.

XLIV

The splendours of the firmament of time
May be eclipsed, but are extinguished not;
Like stars to their appointed height they climb,
And death is a low mist which cannot blot
The brightness it may veil. When lofty thought
Lifts a young heart above its mortal lair,
And love and life contend in it, for what
Shall be its earthly doom, the dead live there
And move like winds of light on dark and stormy air.

XLV

The inheritors of unfulfilled renown
Rose from their thrones, built beyond mortal thought,
Far in the Unapparent. Chatterton
Rose pale,— his solemn agony had not
Yet faded from him; Sidney, as he fought
And as he fell and as he lived and loved
Sublimely mild, a Spirit without spot,
Arose; and Lucan, by his death approved:
Oblivion as they rose shrank like a thing reproved.

XLVI

And many more, whose names on Earth are dark,
But whose transmitted effluence cannot die
So long as fire outlives the parent spark,
Rose, robed in dazzling immortality.
"Thou art become as one of us," they cry,
"It was for thee yon kingless sphere has long
Swung blind in unascended majesty,
Silent alone amid an Heaven of Song.
Assume thy wingèd throne, thou Vesper of our throng!"

XLVII

Who mourns for Adonais? Oh, come forth,
Fond wretch! and know thyself and him aright.
Clasp with thy panting soul the pendulous Earth;
As from a centre, dart thy spirit's light
Beyond all worlds, until its spacious might
Satiate the void circumference: then shrink

Even to a point within our day and night;
And keep thy heart light lest it make thee sink
'hen hope has kindled hope, and lured thee to
the brink.

XLVIII

Or go to Rome, which is the sepulchre,
Oh, not of him, but of our joy: 'tis nought
That ages, empires, and religions there
Lie buried in the ravage they have wrought;
For such as he can lend,— they borrow not
Glory from those who made the world their prey;
And he is gathered to the kings of thought
Who waged contention with their time's decay,
nd of the past are all that cannot pass away.

XLIX

Go thou to Rome,— at once the Paradise,
The grave, the city, and the wilderness;
And where its wrecks like shattered mountains
rise,
And flowering weeds, and fragrant copses dress
The bones of Desolation's nakedness
Pass, till the spirit of the spot shall lead
Thy footsteps to a slope of green access
Where, like an infant's smile, over the dead
light of laughing flowers along the grass is spread;

L

And gray walls moulder round, on which dull Time
Feeds, like slow fire upon a hoary brand;

And one keen pyramid with wedge sublime,
Pavilioning the dust of him who planned
This refuge for his memory, doth stand
Like flame transformed to marble; and beneath,
A field is spread, on which a newer band
Have pitched in Heaven's smile their camp o
death,
Welcoming him we lose with scarce extinguishe
breath.

LI

Here pause: these graves are all too young as ye
To have outgrown the sorrow which consigned
Its charge to each; and if the seal is set,
Here, on one fountain of a mourning mind,
Break it not thou! too surely shalt thou find
Thine own well full, if thou returnest home,
Of tears and gall. From the world's bitter wind
Seek shelter in the shadow of the tomb.
What Adonais is, why fear we to become?

LII

The One remains, the many change and pass;
Heaven's light for ever shines, Earth's shadow
fly;
Life, like a dome of many-coloured glass,
Stains the white radiance of Eternity,
Until Death tramples it to fragments. — Die,
If thou wouldst be with that which thou dost seek
Follow where all is fled! — Rome's azure sky,
Flowers, ruins, statues, music, words, are weak
The glory they transfuse with fitting truth to speak

LIII

Why linger, why turn back, why shrink, my Heart?
Thy hopes are gone before: from all things here
They have departed; thou shouldst now depart!
A light is passed from the revolving year,
And man, and woman; and what still is dear
Attracts to crush, repels to make thee wither.
The soft sky smiles, — the low wind whispers
near:
'Tis Adonais calls! oh, hasten thither,
No more let Life divide what Death can join together.

LIV

That Light whose smile kindles the Universe,
That Beauty in which all things work and move,
That Benediction which the eclipsing Curse
Of birth can quench not, that sustaining Love
Which through the web of being blindly wove
By man and beast and earth and air and sea,
Burns bright or dim, as each are mirrors of
The fire for which all thirst; now beams on
me,
Consuming the last clouds of cold mortality.

LV

The breath whose might I have invoked in song
Descends on me; my spirit's bark is driven,
Far from the shore, far from the trembling throng
Whose sails were never to the tempest given;
The massy earth and spherèd skies are riven!
I am borne darkly, fearfully, afar;

Whilst, burning through the inmost veil of
Heaven,
The soul of Adonais, like a star,
Beacons from the abode where the Eternal are.

PERCY BYSSHE SHELLEY.

THE EVE OF ST. AGNES

I

ST. AGNES' EVE — Ah, bitter chill it was!
The owl, for all his feathers, was a-cold;
The hare limp'd trembling through the froze
grass,
And silent was the flock in woolly fold:
Numb were the Beadsman's fingers while he to
His rosary, and while his frosted breath,
Like pious incense from a censer old,
Seem'd taking flight for heaven, without a deat
Past the sweet Virgin's picture, while his prayer
saith.

II

His prayer he saith, this patient, holy man;
Then takes his lamp, and riseth from his knees,
And back returneth, meagre, barefoot, wan,
Along the chapel aisle by slow degrees:
The sculptur'd dead, on each side, seem to freez
Emprison'd in black, purgatorial rails:
Knights, ladies, praying in dumb orat'ries,
He passeth by; and his weak spirit fails
To think how they may ache in icy hoods a
mails.

III

Northward he turneth through a little door,
And scarce three steps, ere Music's golden tongue
Flatter'd to tears this aged man and poor;
But no — already had his death bell rung:
The joys of all his life were said and sung:
His was harsh penance on St. Agnes' Eve:
Another way he went, and soon among
Rough ashes sat he for his soul's reprieve,
And all night kept awake, for sinners' sake to grieve.

IV

That ancient Beadsman heard the prelude soft;
And so it chanc'd, for many a door was wide,
From hurry to and fro. Soon, up aloft,
The silver, snarling trumpets 'gan to chide:
The level-chambers, ready with their pride,
Were glowing to receive a thousand guests:
The carved angels, ever eager-eyed,
Star'd, where upon their heads the cornice rests,
With hair blown back, and wings put cross-wise on
their breasts.

V

At length burst in the argent revelry,
With plume, tiara, and all rich array,
Numerous as shadows haunting fairily
The brain, new stuff'd, in youth, with triumphs
gay
Of old romance. These let us wish away,
And turn, sole-thoughted, to one Lady there,

Whose heart had brooded, all that wintry day,
On love, and wing'd St. Agnes' saintly care,
As she had heard old dames full many times declare.

VI

They told her how, upon St. Agnes' Eve,
Young virgins might have visions of delight,
And soft adorings from their loves receive
Upon the honey'd middle of the night,
If ceremonies due they did aright;
As, supperless to bed they must retire,
And couch supine their beauties, lily white;
Nor look behind, nor sideways, but require
Of Heaven with upward eyes for all that they desire.

VII

Full of this whim was thoughtful Madeline:
The music, yearning like a God in pain,
She scarcely heard: her maiden eyes divine,
Fix'd on the floor, saw many a sweeping train
Pass by — she heeded not at all: in vain
Came many a tiptoe, amorous cavalier,
And back retir'd; not cool'd by high disdain,
But she saw not: her heart was otherwhere:
She sigh'd for Agnes' dreams, the sweetest of the year.

VIII

She danc'd along with vague, regardless eyes,
Anxious her lips, her breathing quick and short:

The hallow'd hour was near at hand: she sighs
Amid the timbrels, and the throng'd resort
Of whisperers in anger, or in sport;
'Mid looks of love, defiance, hate, and scorn,
Hoodwink'd with faery fancy; all amort,
Save to St. Agnes and her lambs unshorn,
And all the bliss to be before to-morrow morn.

IX

So, purposing each moment to retire,
She linger'd still. Meantime, across the moors,
Had come young Porphyro, with heart on fire
For Madeline. Beside the portal doors,
Buttress'd from moonlight, stands he, and implores
All saints to give him sight of Madeline,
But for one moment in the tedious hours,
That he might gaze and worship all unseen;
Perchance speak, kneel, touch, kiss — in sooth such things have been.

X

He ventures in: let no buzz'd whisper tell:
All eyes be muffled, or a hundred swords
Will storm his heart, Love's fev'rous citadel:
For him, those chambers held barbarian hordes,
Hyena foemen, and hot-blooded lords,
Whose very dogs would execrations howl
Against his lineage: not one breast affords
Him any mercy, in that mansion foul,
Save one old beldame, weak in body and in soul.

XI

Ah, happy chance! the aged creature came,
Shuffling along with ivory-headed wand,
To where he stood, hid from the torch's flame,
Behind a broad hall-pillar, far beyond
The sound of merriment and chorus bland:
He startled her; but soon she knew his face,
And grasp'd his fingers in her palsied hand,
Saying, "Mercy, Porphyro! hie thee from thi
place;
They are all here to-night, the whole blood-thirst
race!

XII

"Get hence! get hence! there's dwarfish Hilde
brand;
He had a fever late, and in the fit
He cursed thee and thine, both house and land:
Then there's that old Lord Maurice, not a whit
More tame for his gray hairs — Alas me! flit!
Flit like a ghost away." — "Ah, Gossip dear,
We're safe enough; here in this arm-chair sit,
And tell me how" — "Good saints! not here, no
here;
Follow me, child, or else these stones will be thy bier."

XIII

He follow'd through a lowly arched way,
Brushing the cobwebs with his lofty plume,
And as she mutter'd "Well-a — well-a-day!"
He found him in a little moonlight room,

Pale, lattic'd, chill, and silent as a tomb.
"Now tell me where is Madeline," said he,
"O tell me, Angela, by the holy loom
Which none but secret sisterhood may see,
When they St. Agnes' wool are weaving piously."

XIV

"St. Agnes! Ah! it is St. Agnes' Eve —
Yet men will murder upon holy days:
Thou must hold water in a witch's sieve,
And be liege-lord of all the Elves and Fays
To venture so: it fills me with amaze
To see thee, Porphyro! — St. Agnes' Eve!
God's help! my lady fair the conjuror plays
This very night: good angels her deceive!
But let me laugh awhile, I've mickle time to grieve."

XV

Feebly she laugheth in the languid moon,
While Porphyro upon her face doth look,
Like puzzled urchin on an aged crone
Who keepeth clos'd a wond'rous riddle-book,
As spectacled she sits in chimney nook.
But soon his eyes grew brilliant, when she told
His lady's purpose; and he scarce could brook
Tears at the thought of those enchantments cold
And Madeline asleep in lap of legends old.

XVI

Sudden a thought came like a full-blown rose,
Flushing his brow, and in his pained heart

Made purple riot: then doth he propose
A stratagem, that makes the beldame start:
"A cruel man and impious thou art:
Sweet lady! let her pray, and sleep and dream
Alone with her good angels, far apart
From wicked men like thee. Go, go! — I deem
Thou canst not surely be the same that thou didst seem."

XVII

"I will not harm her, by all saints I swear,"
Quoth Porphyro: "O may I ne'er find grace
When my weak voice shall whisper its last prayer,
If one of her soft ringlets I displace,
Or look with ruffian passion in her face:
Good Angela, believe me by these tears;
Or I will, even in a moment's space,
Awake, with horrid shout, my foemen's ears,
And beard them, though they be more fang'd than wolves and bears."

XVIII

"Ah! why wilt thou affright a feeble soul?
A poor, weak, palsy-stricken, churchyard thing,
Whose passing-bell may ere the midnight toll;
Whose prayers for thee, each morn and evening,
Were never miss'd." — Thus plaining, doth she bring
A gentler speech from burning Porphyro;
So woeful, and of such deep sorrowing,
That Angela gives promise she will do
Whatever he shall wish, betide her weal or woe.

XIX

Which was, to lead him, in close secrecy,
Even to Madeline's chamber, and there hide
Him in a closet, of such privacy
That he might see her beauty unespied,
And win perhaps that night a peerless bride,
While legion'd fairies pac'd the coverlet,
And pale enchantment held her sleepy-eyed.
Never on such a night have lovers met,
Since Merlin paid his Demon all the monstrous debt.

XX

"It shall be as thou wishest," said the Dame:
"All cates and dainties shall be stored there
Quickly on this feast-night: by the tambour frame
Her own lute thou wilt see: no time to spare,
For I am slow and feeble, and scarce dare
On such a catering trust my dizzy head.
Wait here, my child, with patience; kneel in prayer
The while. Ah! thou must needs the lady wed,
Or may I never leave my grave among the dead."

XXI

So saying, she hobbled off with busy fear.
The lover's endless minutes slowly pass'd;
The dame return'd, and whisper'd in his ear
To follow her; with aged eyes aghast
From fright of dim espial. Safe at last,
Through many a dusky gallery, they gain

The maiden's chamber, silken, hush'd and chaste;
Where Porphyro took covert, pleas'd amain.
His poor guide hurried back with agues in her brain.

XXII

Her faltering hand upon the balustrade,
Old Angela was feeling for the stair,
When Madeline, St. Agnes' charmed maid,
Rose, like a mission'd spirit, unaware:
With silver taper's light, and pious care,
She turn'd, and down the aged gossip led
To a safe level matting. Now prepare,
Young Porphyro, for gazing on that bed;
She comes, she comes again, like ring-dove fray'd
and fled.

XXIII

Out went the taper as she hurried in;
Its little smoke, in pallid moonshine, died:
She closed the door, she panted, all akin
To spirits of the air, and visions wide:
No uttered syllable, or, woe betide!
But to her heart, her heart was voluble,
Paining with eloquence her balmy side;
As though a tongueless nightingale should swell
Her throat in vain, and die, heart-stifled, in her
dell.

XXIV

A casement high and triple-arch'd there was,
All garlanded with carven imag'ries,

Of fruits, and flowers, and bunches of knot-grass,
And diamonded with panes of quaint device,
Innumerable of stains and splendid dyes,
As are the tiger-moth's deep-damask'd wings;
And in the midst, 'mong thousand heraldries,
And twilight saints, and dim emblazonings,
A shielded scutcheon blush'd with blood of queens
and kings.

XXV

Full on this casement shone the wintry moon,
And threw warm gules on Madeline's fair breast,
As down she knelt for heaven's grace and boon;
Rose-bloom fell on her hands, together prest,
And on her silver cross soft amethyst,
And on her hair a glory, like a saint:
She seem'd a splendid angel, newly drest,
Save wings, for heaven: — Porphyro grew faint:
She knelt, so pure a thing, so free from mortal taint.

XXVI

Anon his heart revives: her vespers done,
Of all its wreathed pearls her hair she frees;
Unclasps her warmed jewels one by one;
Loosens her fragrant bodice; by degrees
Her rich attire creeps rustling to her knees:
Half-hidden, like a mermaid in sea-weed,
Pensive awhile she dreams awake, and sees,
In fancy, fair St. Agnes in her bed,
But dares not look behind, or all the charm is
fled.

XXVII

Soon, trembling in her soft and chilly nest,
In sort of wakeful swoon, perplex'd she lay,
Until the poppied warmth of sleep oppress'd
Her soothed limbs, and soul fatigued away;
Flown, like a thought, until the morrow-day;
Blissfully haven'd both from joy and pain;
Clasp'd like a missal where swart Paynims pray;
Blinded alike from sunshine and from rain,
As though a rose should shut, and be a bud again.

XXVIII

Stol'n to this paradise, and so entranced,
Porphyro gazed upon her empty dress,
And listen'd to her breathing, if it chanced
To wake into a slumberous tenderness;
Which when he heard, that minute did he bless,
And breath'd himself: then from the closet crept,
Noiseless as fear in a wide wilderness,
And over the hush'd carpet, silent, stept,
And 'tween the curtains peep'd, where, lo! — how fast she slept.

XXIX

Then by the bed-side, where the faded moon
Made a dim, silver twilight, soft he set
A table, and, half anguish'd, threw thereon
A cloth of woven crimson, gold, and jet: —
O for some drowsy Morphean amulet!
The boisterous, midnight, festive clarion,
The kettle-drum, and far-heard clarinet,

Affray his ears, though but in dying tone:—
'he hall-door shuts again, and all the noise is gone.

XXX

And still she slept an azure-lidded sleep,
In blanched linen, smooth, and lavender'd,
While he from forth the closet brought a heap
Of candied apple, quince, and plum, and gourd;
With jellies soother than the creamy curd,
And lucent syrops, tinct with cinnamon;
Manna and dates, in argosy transferr'd
From Fez; and spicèd dainties, every one,
'rom silken Samarcand to cedar'd Lebanon.

XXXI

These delicates he heap'd with glowing hand
On golden dishes and in baskets bright
Of wreathed silver: sumptuous they stand
In the retired quiet of the night,
Filling the chilly room with perfume light.—
"And now, my love, my seraph fair, awake!
Thou art my heaven, and I thine eremite:
Open thine eyes, for meek St. Agnes' sake,
)r I shall drowse beside thee, so my soul doth ache."

XXXII

Thus whispering, his warm, unnerved arm
Sank in her pillow. Shaded was her dream
By the dusk curtains:—'twas a midnight charm
Impossible to melt as iced stream:
The lustrous salvers in the moonlight gleam;

Broad golden fringe upon the carpet lies:
It seem'd he never, never could redeem
From such a stedfast spell his lady's eyes;
So mused awhile, entoil'd in woofed phantasies.

XXXIII

Awakening up, he took her hollow lute,—
Tumultuous,—and, in chords that tenderest be,
He play'd an ancient ditty, long since mute,
In Provence call'd "La belle dame sans mercy."
Close to her ear touching the melody;—
Wherewith disturb'd, she utter'd a soft moan:
He ceased — she panted quick — and suddenly
Her blue affrayed eyes wide open shone:
Upon his knees he sank, pale as smooth-sculptured
stone.

XXXIV

Her eyes were open, but she still beheld,
Now wide awake, the vision of her sleep:
There was a painful change, that nigh expell'd
The blisses of her dream so pure and deep
At which fair Madeline began to weep,
And moan forth witless words with many a sigh
While still her gaze on Porphyro would keep;
Who knelt, with joined hands and piteous eye,
Fearing to move or speak, she look'd so dreamingly

XXXV

"Ah, Porphyro!" said she, "but even now
Thy voice was at sweet tremble in mine ear,

Made tuneable with every sweetest vow;
And those sad eyes were spiritual and clear:
How chang'd thou art! how pallid, chill, and
drear!
Give me that voice again, my Porphyro,
Those looks immortal, those complainings, dear!
Oh leave me not in this eternal woe,
For if thou diest, my Love, I know not where to go."

XXXVI

Beyond a mortal man impassion'd far
At these voluptuous accents, he arose,
Ethereal, flush'd, and like a throbbing star
Seen 'mid the sapphire heaven's deep repose;
Into her dream he melted, as the rose
Blendeth its odour with the violet,—
Solution sweet: meantime the frost-wind blows
Like Love's alarum, pattering the sharp sleet
Against the window-panes; St. Agnes' moon hath
set.

XXXVII

'Tis dark: quick pattereth the flaw-blown sleet:
"This is no dream, my bride, my Madeline!"
'Tis dark: the iced gusts still rave and beat:
"No dream, alas! alas! and woe is mine!
Porphyro will leave me here to fade and pine.—
Cruel! what traitor could thee hither bring?
I curse not, for my heart is lost in thine,
Though thou forsakest a deceived thing;—
A dove forlorn and lost with sick unpruned wing."

XXXVIII

"My Madeline! sweet dreamer! lovely bride!
Say, may I be for aye thy vassal blest?
Thy beauty's shield, heart-shap'd and vermeil dyed?
Ah, silver shrine, here will I take my rest
After so many hours of toil and quest,
A famish'd pilgrim,—saved by miracle.
Though I have found, I will not rob thy nest
Saving of thy sweet self; if thou think'st well
To trust, fair Madeline, to no rude infidel.

XXXIX

"Hark! 'tis an elfin-storm from faery land,
Of haggard seeming, but a boon indeed:
Arise — arise! the morning is at hand;—
The bloated wassailers will never heed:—
Let us away, my love, with happy speed;
There are no ears to hear, or eyes to see,—
Drown'd all in Rhenish and the sleepy mead:
Awake! arise! my love, and fearless be,
For o'er the southern moors I have a home for thee."

XL

She hurried at his words, beset with fears,
For there were sleeping dragons all around,
At glaring watch, perhaps, with ready spears —
Down the wide stairs a darkling way they found.—
In all the house was heard no human sound.
A chain-droop'd lamp was flickering by each door;

The arras, rich with horseman, hawk, and hound,
Flutter'd in the besieging wind's uproar;
And the long carpets rose along the gusty floor.

XLI

They glide, like phantoms, into the wide hall;
Like phantoms, to the iron porch they glide;
Where lay the Porter, in uneasy sprawl,
With a huge empty flagon by his side:
The wakeful bloodhound rose, and shook his hide,
But his sagacious eye an inmate owns:
By one, and one, the bolts full easy slide:—
The chains lie silent on the footworn stones;—
The key turns, and the door upon its hinges groans.

XLII

And they are gone: ay, ages long ago
These lovers fled away into the storm.
That night the Baron dreamt of many a woe,
And all his warrior-guests with shade and form
Of witch, and demon, and large coffin-worm,
Were long be-nightmar'd. Angela the old
Died palsy-twitch'd, with meagre face deform;
The Beadsman, after thousand aves told,
For aye unsought for slept among his ashes cold.

JOHN KEATS.

THE SCHOLAR GIPSY

Go, for they call you, Shepherd, from the hill;
Go, Shepherd, and untie the wattled cotes:
No longer leave thy wistful flock unfed,
Nor let thy bawling fellows rack their throats,
Nor the cropp'd grasses shoot another head.
But when the fields are still,
And the tired men and dogs all gone to rest,
And only the white sheep are sometimes seen
Cross and recross the strips of moon-blanch'd green,
Come, Shepherd, and again renew the quest.

Here, where the reaper was at work of late,
In this high field's dark corner, where he leaves
His coat, his basket, and his earthen cruse,
And in the sun all morning binds the sheaves,
Then here, at noon, comes back his stores to use;
Here will I sit and wait,
While to my ear from uplands far away
The bleating of the folded flocks is borne;
With distant cries of reapers in the corn—
All the live murmur of a summer's day.

Screen'd is this nook o'er the high, half-reap'd field,
And here till sun-down, Shepherd, will I be.
Through the thick corn the scarlet poppies peep,
And round green roots and yellowing stalks I see
Pale blue convolvulus in tendrils creep:
And air-swept lindens yield

Their scent, and rustle down their perfum'd showers
Of bloom on the bent grass where I am laid,
And bower me from the August sun with shade;
And the eye travels down to Oxford's towers:

And near me on the grass lies Glanvil's book —
Come, let me read the oft-read tale again,
The story of that Oxford scholar poor
Of pregnant parts and quick inventive brain,
Who, tir'd of knocking at Preferment's door,
One summer morn forsook
His friends, and went to learn the Gipsy lore,
And roam'd the world with that wild brother-
hood,
And came, as most men deem'd, to little good,
But came to Oxford and his friends no more.

But once, years after, in the country lanes,
Two scholars whom at college erst he knew
Met him, and of his way of life enquir'd.
Whereat he answer'd, that the Gipsy crew,
His mates, had arts to rule as they desir'd
The workings of men's brains;
And they can bind them to what thoughts they
will:
"And I," he said, "the secret of their art,
When fully learn'd, will to the world impart:
But it needs happy moments for this skill."

This said, he left them, and return'd no more,
But rumours hung about the country side
That the lost Scholar long was seen to stray,
Seen by rare glimpses, pensive and tongue-tied,

In hat of antique shape, and cloak of grey,
The same the Gipsies wore.
Shepherds had met him on the Hurst in spring:
At some lone alehouse in the Berkshire moors,
On the warm ingle bench, the smock-frock'd boors
Had found him seated at their entering,

But, mid their drink and clatter, he would fly:
And I myself seem half to know thy looks,
And put the shepherds, Wanderer, on thy trace;
And boys who in lone wheatfields scare the rooks
I ask if thou hast pass'd their quiet place;
Or in my boat I lie
Moor'd to the cool bank in the summer heats,
Mid wide grass meadows which the sunshine fills,
And watch the warm green-muffled Cumner hills,
And wonder if thou haunt'st their shy retreats.

For most, I know, thou lov'st retired ground.
Thee, at the ferry, Oxford riders blithe,
Returning home on summer nights, have met
Crossing the stripling Thames at Bab-lock-hithe,
Trailing in the cool stream thy fingers wet,
As the slow punt swings round:
And leaning backwards in a pensive dream,
And fostering in thy lap a heap of flowers
Pluck'd in shy fields and distant woodland bowers,
And thine eyes resting on the moonlit stream.

And then they land, and thou art seen no more.
Maidens who from the distant hamlets come
To dance around the Fyfield elm in May,
Oft through the darkening fields have seen thee roam,
Or cross a stile into the public way.
Oft thou hast given them store
Of flowers — the frail-leaf'd, white anemone —
Dark blue bells drench'd with dews of summer eves —
And purple orchises with spotted leaves —
But none has words she can report of thee.

And, above Godstow Bridge, when hay-time's here
In June, and many a scythe in sunshine flames,
Men who through those wide fields of breezy grass
Where black-wing'd swallows haunt the glittering Thames,
To bathe in the abandon'd lasher pass,
Have often pass'd thee near
Sitting upon the river bank o'ergrown:
Mark'd thy outlandish garb, thy figure spare,
Thy dark vague eyes, and soft abstracted air;
But, when they came from bathing, thou wert gone.

At some lone homestead in the Cumner hills,
Where at her open door the housewife darns,
Thou hast been seen, or hanging on a gate
To watch the threshers in the mossy barns.
Children, who early range these slopes and late
For cresses from the rills,

Have known thee watching, all an April day,
The springing pastures and the feeding kine;
And mark'd thee when the stars come out and shine,
Through the long dewy grass move slow away.

In Autumn, on the skirts of Bagley wood,
Where most the Gipsies by the turf-edg'd way
Pitch their smok'd tents, and every bush you see
With scarlet patches tagg'd and shreds of grey,
Above the forest ground call'd Thessaly —
The blackbird picking food
Sees thee, nor stops his meal, nor fears at all;
So often has he known thee past him stray
Rapt, twirling in thy hand a wither'd spray,
And waiting for the spark from Heaven to fall.

And once, in winter, on the causeway chill
Where home through flooded fields foot-travellers go,
Have I not pass'd thee on the wooden bridge
Wrapt in thy cloak and battling with the snow,
Thy face towards Hinksey and its wintry ridge?
And thou hast climb'd the hill
And gain'd the white brow of the Cumner range,
Turn'd once to watch, while thick the snow-flakes fall,
The line of festal light in Christ-Church hall —
Then sought thy straw in some sequester'd grange.

But what — I dream! Two hundred years are
 flown
 Since first thy story ran through Oxford halls,
 And the grave Glanvil did the tale inscribe
 That thou wert wander'd from the studious walls
 To learn strange arts, and join a Gipsy tribe:
 And thou from earth art gone
 Long since, and in some quiet churchyard laid;
 Some country nook, where o'er thy unknown
 grave
 Tall grasses and white flowering nettles wave —
 Under a dark red-fruited yew-tree's shade.

— No, no, thou hast not felt the lapse of hours.
 For what wears out the life of mortal men?
 'Tis that from change to change their being
 rolls:
 'Tis that repeated shocks, again, again,
 Exhaust the energy of strongest souls,
 And numb the elastic powers.
 Till having us'd our nerves with bliss and teen,
 And tired upon a thousand schemes our wit,
 To the just-pausing Genius we remit
 Our worn-out life, and are — what we have been.

Thou hast not liv'd, why should'st thou perish, so?
 Thou hadst *one* aim, *one* business, *one* desire:
 Else wert thou long since number'd with the
 dead —
 Else hadst thou spent, like other men, thy fire.
 The generations of thy peers are fled,
 And we ourselves shall go;

But thou possessest an immortal lot,
And we imagine thee exempt from age
And living as thou liv'st on Glanvil's page,
Because thou hadst — what we, alas, have not!

For early didst thou leave the world, with powers
Fresh, undiverted to the world without,
Firm to their mark, not spent on other things;
Free from the sick fatigue, the languid doubt,
Which much to have tried, in much been baffled brings.
O Life unlike to ours!
Who fluctuate idly without term or scope,
Of whom each strives, nor knows for what he strives,
And each half lives a hundred different lives,
Who wait like thee, but not, like thee, in hope.

Thou waitest for the spark from Heaven: and we,
Light half-believers of our casual creeds,
Who never deeply felt, nor clearly will'd,
Whose insight never has borne fruit in deeds,
Whose vague resolves never have been fulfilled;
For whom each year we see
Breeds new beginnings, disappointments new;
Who hesitate and falter life away,
And lose to-morrow the ground won to-day —
Ah, do not we, Wanderer, await it too?

Yes, we await it, but it still delays,
And then we suffer; and amongst us One,
Who most has suffer'd, takes dejectedly
His seat upon the intellectual throne;

And all his store of sad experience he
Lays bare of wretched days;
Tells us his misery's birth and growth and signs,
And how the dying spark of hope was fed,
And how the breast was sooth'd, and how the head,
And all his hourly varied anodynes.

This for our wisest: and we others pine,
And wish the long unhappy dream would end,
And waive all claim to bliss, and try to bear
With close-lipp'd patience for our only friend,
Sad Patience, too near neighbour to Despair:
But none has hope like thine.
Thou through the fields and through the woods dost stray,
Roaming the countryside, a truant boy,
Nursing thy project in unclouded joy,
And every doubt long blown by time away.

O born in days when wits were fresh and clear,
And life ran gaily as the sparkling Thames;
Before this strange disease of modern life,
With its sick hurry, its divided aims,
Its heads o'ertax'd, its palsied hearts, was rife —
Fly hence, our contact fear!
Still fly, plunge deeper in the bowering wood!
Averse, as Dido did with gesture stern
From her false friend's approach in Hades turn,
Wave us away, and keep thy solitude.

Still nursing the unconquerable hope,
Still clutching the inviolable shade,

With a free onward impulse brushing through,
By night, the silver'd branches of the glade —
Far on the forest skirts, where none pursue,
On some mild pastoral slope
Emerge, and resting on the moonlit pales,
Freshen thy flowers, as in former years,
With dew, or listen with enchanted ears,
From the dark dingles, to the nightingales.

But fly our paths, our feverish contact fly!
For strong the infection of our mental strife,
Which, though it gives no bliss, yet spoils for rest;
And we should win thee from thy own fair life,
Like us distracted, and like us unblest.
Soon, soon thy cheer would die,
Thy hopes grow timorous, and unfix'd thy powers,
And thy clear aims be cross and shifting made:
And then thy glad perennial youth would fade,
Fade, and grow old at last, and die like ours.

Then fly our greetings, fly our speech and smiles!
— As some grave Tyrian trader, from the sea,
Descried at sunrise an emerging prow
Lifting the cool-hair'd creepers stealthily,
The fringes of a southward-facing brow
Among the Aegean isles:
And saw the merry Grecian coaster come,
Freighted with amber grapes, and Chian wine,
Green bursting figs, and tunnies steep'd in brine;
And knew the intruders on his ancient home,

The young light-hearted Masters of the waves;
And snatch'd his rudder, and shook out more sail,
And day and night held on indignantly
O'er the blue Midland waters with the gale,
Betwixt the Syrtes and soft Sicily
To where the Atlantic raves
Outside the Western Straits, and unbent sails
There, where down cloudy cliffs, through sheets of foam,
Shy traffickers, the dark Iberians come;
And on the beach undid his corded bales.

MATTHEW ARNOLD.

THE HAYSTACK IN THE FLOODS

HAD she come all the way for this,
To part at last without a kiss?
Yea, had she borne the dirt and rain
That her own eyes might see him slain
Beside the haystack in the floods?

Along the dripping leafless woods,
The stirrup touching either shoe,
She rode astride as troopers do;
With kirtle kilted to her knee,
To which the mud splash'd wretchedly;
And the wet dripp'd from every tree
Upon her head and heavy hair,
And on her eyelids broad and fair;
The tears and rain ran down her face.

By fits and starts they rode apace,
And very often was his place
Far off from her; he had to ride
Ahead, to see what might betide
When the roads cross'd; and sometimes, when
There rose a murmuring from his men,
Had to turn back with promises;
Ah me! she had but little ease;
And often for pure doubt and dread
She sobb'd, made giddy in the head
By the swift riding; while, for cold,
Her slender fingers scarce could hold
The wet reins; yea, and scarcely, too,
She felt the foot within her shoe
Against the stirrup: all for this,
To part at last without a kiss
Beside the haystack in the floods.

For when they near'd that old soak'd hay,
They saw across the only way
That Judas, Godmar, and the three
Red running lions dismally
Grinn'd from his pennon, under which,
In one straight line along the ditch,
They counted thirty heads.

So then,
While Robert turn'd round to his men,
She saw at once the wretched end,
And, stooping down, tried hard to rend
Her coif the wrong way from her head,
And hid her eyes; while Robert said:
"Nay, love, 'tis scarcely two to one,

At Poictiers where we made them run
So fast — why, sweet my love, good cheer,
The Gascon frontier is so near,
Nought after this."

But "O," she said,
"My God! my God! I have to tread
The long way back without you; then
The court at Paris; those six men;
The gratings of the Chatelet;
The swift Seine on some rainy day
Like this, and people standing by,
And laughing, while my weak hands try
To recollect how strong men swim.
All this, or else a life with him,
For which I should be damned at last,
Would God that this next hour were past!"

He answer'd not, but cried his cry,
"St. George for Marny!" cheerily;
And laid his hand upon her rein.
Alas! no man of all his train
Gave back that cheery cry again;
And, while for rage his thumb beat fast
Upon his sword-hilts, some one cast
About his neck a kerchief long,
And bound him.

Then they went along
To Godmar; who said: "Now, Jehane,
Your lover's life is on the wane
So fast, that, if this very hour
You yield not as my paramour,

He will not see the rain leave off —
Nay, keep your tongue from gibe and scoff,
Sir Robert, or I slay you now."

She laid her hand upon her brow,
Then gazed upon the palm, as though
She thought her forehead bled, and — "No,"
She said, and turn'd her head away,
As there were nothing else to say,
And everything were settled: red
Grew Godmar's face from chin to head:
"Jehane, on yonder hill there stands
My castle, guarding well my lands:
What hinders me from taking you,
And doing what I list to do
To your fair wilful body, while
Your knight lies dead?"

A wicked smile
Wrinkled her face, her lips grew thin,
A long way out she thrust her chin:
"You know that I should strangle you
While you were sleeping; or bite through
Your throat, by God's help — ah!" she said,
"Lord Jesus, pity your poor maid!
For in such wise they hem me in,
I cannot choose but sin and sin,
Whatever happens: yet I think
They could not make me eat or drink,
And so should I just reach my rest."
"Nay, if you do not my behest,
O Jehane! though I love you well,"
Said Godmar, "would I fail to tell

All that I know." "Foul lies," she said.
"Eh? lies my Jehane? by God's head,
At Paris folks would deem them true!
Do you know, Jehane, they cry for you,
'Jehane the brown! Jehane the brown!
Give us Jehane to burn or drown!'—
Eh—gag me, Robert!—sweet my friend,
This were indeed a piteous end
For those long fingers, and long feet,
And long neck, and smooth shoulders sweet;
An end that few men would forget
That saw it—So, an hour yet:
Consider, Jehane, which to take
Of life or death!"

So, scarce awake,
Dismounting, did she leave that place,
And totter some yards: with her face
Turn'd upward to the sky she lay,
Her head on a wet heap of hay,
And fell asleep: and while she slept,
And did not dream, the minutes crept
Round to the twelve again; but she,
Being waked at last, sigh'd quietly,
And strangely childlike came, and said:
"I will not." Straightway Godmar's head,
As though it hung on strong wires, turn'd
Most sharply round, and his face burn'd.

For Robert—both his eyes were dry,
He could not weep, but gloomily
He seem'd to watch the rain; yea, too,
His lips were firm; he tried once more

To touch her lips; she reach'd out, sore
And vain desire so tortured them,
The poor grey lips, and now the hem
Of his sleeve brush'd them.

With a start
Up Godmar rose, thrust them apart;
From Robert's throat he loosed the bands
Of silk and mail; with empty hands
Held out, she stood and gazed, and saw
The long bright blade without a flaw
Glide out from Godmar's sheath, his hand
In Robert's hair; she saw him bend
Back Robert's head; she saw him send
The thin steel down; the blow told well,
Right backward the knight Robert fell,
And moan'd as dogs do, being half dead,
Unwitting, as I deem: so then
Godmar turn'd grinning to his men,
Who ran, some five or six, and beat
His head to pieces at their feet.

Then Godmar turn'd again and said:
"So, Jehane, the first fitte is read!
Take note, my lady, that your way
Lies backward to the Chatelet!"
She shook her head and gazed awhile
At her cold hands with a rueful smile,
As though this thing had made her mad.

This was the parting that they had
Beside the haystack in the floods.

WILLIAM MORRIS.

INDEXES

INDEX OF AUTHORS

INDEX OF FIRST LINES

INDEX OF TITLES

CHAVCER